X

20,000 ALARMS

FIRE DEPARTMENT
CITY OF NEW YORK

UNIFORMED FORCE

DEPARTMENT ORDER NO. 82   May 1, 1974

Effective this date Lieutenant Badge No. 51 has been retired from the service of the Fire Department, City of New York. Badge No. 51 was worn by Lieutenant *Richard R. Hamilton,* Rescue Co. 2, who retired effective 0900 hrs., this date. Lieutenant *Hamilton* was formally presented with the badge by *Hon. Abraham D. Beame,* Mayor of the City of New York, in a ceremony at City Hall this date in recognition of his years of distinguished and courageous service on behalf of the people of the City of New York. This is the first time in the history of the department that a badge has been retired from service.

Lieutenant Richard R. Hamilton
with Charles N. Barnard

20,000
ALARMS

THE MEMOIRS OF NEW YORK'S MOST DECORATED FIREMAN

℞₽
A PLAYBOY PRESS BOOK

To Ginny,
whose devotion and love
I cherish.

Published simultaneously in the United States and Canada by Playboy Press, Chicago, Illinois. Printed in the United States of America. Library of Congress Catalog Card Number: 74–33553. ISBN 87223–427–4. First edition.

PLAYBOY and Rabbit Head design are trademarks of Playboy, 919 North Michigan Avenue, Chicago, Illinois 60611 (U.S.A.), Reg. U.S. Pat. Off., marca registrada, marque déposée.

Design by Bob Antler

CONTENTS

20,000
ALARMS

1

"PUT A BOWLINE ON THE BIGHT AND GET INTO IT"

The coil of tough new manila is 150 feet long, 13/16 of an inch thick. There is one or more of these on every fire truck. The department calls them "roof ropes" and they have many uses. I hadn't seen everything that could be done with a roof rope yet because I'd only been in for a couple of years and I was still what they call a "Johnny." That's the rookie of the outfit, the junior member, the one who gets all the disagreeable jobs to do but seldom gets to grab for any glory. At this moment, however, I had a roof rope tied neatly around my legs and shoulders and I was being lowered, a little like a mountain climber, into a narrow concrete shaft with a roaring fire on one side and what appeared to be a madman running around at the bottom.

I suppose I knew that I would have to do this sort of thing

3

when I decided to join the New York City Fire Department. You read about rope rescues in the papers every so often, and in my basic-training school they had demonstrated how it should be done. The mechanics of the thing are simple enough; the rope is strong and so are the two men who are lowering you down. But at this moment I could see that there were other factors to be considered. Would the fire explode through those windows below me and turn the shaft into a chimney that I'd never get out of? And would that guy at the bottom do what he was supposed to do when I got down to saving his life?

Now that more than 22 years have passed during which I saved a good many other lives, this first rescue of mine seems a long-ago and not-so-important affair. But at the time, young and eager to succeed, I regarded it as a heaven-sent opportunity. I was going to be the best fireman in the whole world —if only they'd give me the chance to show them what I could do! When Captain Klepper said, "Hamilton, go get a roof rope, put a bowline on the bight and get into it," it was as if MacArthur had asked me to come ashore with him at Luzon!

The fire was in a lawn-furniture factory that took up the whole block between River and Exterior Streets in the South Bronx. I was with my first company, 17 Truck, which had its firehouse at 143rd Street between Alexander and Willis Avenues. The alarm had come in a little after nine that morning, and even before we got to the scene in the ladder truck we could see heavy clouds of smoke rising in the distance. I could feel the excitement on the truck. When the men saw the black sky ahead they stopped their chatter and started buckling up their coats and pulling on gloves. It looked like a good one. When we came down the hill, headed for the Harlem River, I saw people running on the sidewalks.

We pulled up in front of the building as workers from the factory stumbled out onto the street, coughing and crying. The furniture this company made used a lot of plastic and the stuff was burning now like fuel oil. As soon as our rig stopped rolling, the captain started giving orders, sending a couple of men into the building, a couple more to the roof, and then he told me and a couple of others to come with him. Fire Department officers often take the Johnny along with them when working a fire. It gives the younger man a chance to learn and may also keep him out of dangerous spots where he could lose his life as a result of inexperience.

The factory was on a slope. The front, on River Street, was four or five stories high, but the back, on Exterior Street, had two floors cut into the slope. The captain and I ran up the hill at the side of the building and then around the back. When we got there we found a steel grating in the sidewalk, and when we looked down we were actually looking down two stories to the building's street floor. There were windows in the back wall of the building down the shaft, and through them smoke was rising up the shaft, while the fire inside illuminated its depths.

At the bottom of the well, running back and forth like a caged animal in a zoo pit, was a man. He was screaming and his voice echoed against the walls as if it were coming out of a tomb. We couldn't understand what he was saying, but he seemed to be speaking Spanish. The words didn't matter, the meaning was clear: Get me out of here; I don't want to die! He had apparently been at the back of the factory when the fire exploded and he had escaped through one of the rear windows —only to find himself trapped. He couldn't go back where he came from, but he was 24 feet below street level and looking up at the bars above.

The first thing we tried to do was lift the grating out of the sidewalk, but it was cemented in. While two of the firemen went to work on this problem with the Halligan tools and axes, the captain sent me back to the truck for the roof rope. At the front of the building the street was now full of fire apparatus, the police were holding people back, and firemen were stretching hoselines in every direction. Somebody said they'd already taken two dead bodies out.

When I got back to the captain with the rope, he ordered me to hitch up with the kind of knot that forms a sort of bos'n's chair, and I knew then that I was the one chosen to go down into the hole. I wasn't a big man by fire-department standards

—five-foot-ten and about 165 pounds—a good size for lowering into tight places.

I remember how hard the rope felt where it was tied around me and how the two men who were going to lower me checked the hitch and the knots with quick professional tugs. How I admired those guys at that moment. They knew what they were doing. They were pros. No excitement, just deliberate, businesslike moves. It sure made me feel better about dangling on the other end of the rope.

The captain said, "When you get down there, get out of the rope, put the man into it in the same way you were, and we'll haul him out. Then we'll pull you out."

It seemed a simple enough plan. I stepped to the edge of the opening where the grating had been removed, braced my feet against the inner wall, took a good grip on the rope and nodded that I was ready. The firemen started paying out the rope as the captain watched.

It wasn't a very quick descent because they were being very careful in letting out rope. For the first few feet there didn't seem to be any hurry anyway; some smoke was coming up, but not too much heat. The windows still hadn't burst, and as long as they held, I'd probably be all right. Hell, I thought, the captain wouldn't send me down here if it was *too* dangerous. But the man below must have thought he was going to get roasted alive any minute the way he was tearing back and forth. The sight of me coming down didn't seem to calm him at all.

When I got level with the first window and looked in, I could see why. Inside the factory the fire was burning furiously and the heat came through the glass like a radiant oven. I thought I could see safety wires in the glass, which would explain why it hadn't popped already, but I couldn't remember how much heat that sort of glass could stand. If it ever let go, a flue of fire was going to come out at us for sure. The heat was worse now, but I was breathing okay because there was still oxygen down here. If the fire broke through, it would consume that oxygen, and that would be another problem.

I looked up at the slit of sky above me and the silhouettes

of the firemen leaning over the edge, holding my life in their hands. My boots scuffed against the wall. I was nearly down now and I was beginning to think of what to do next. Then, just as my feet touched, the man at the bottom lunged at me, screaming and cursing. He knocked me down, tangling me in the rope, and before I could get to my feet, he was on his way up, hand over hand, clawing his way to freedom. I could see him swaying above me and I could see the men from 17 Truck above that. For a minute I was afraid they might start pulling the man up with me still tangled in the end of the rope. I got out of the hitch as quickly as I could, then just stood there, no longer connected to the outside world, not even by 13/16 of an inch of manila rope. It was a lonely feeling, 24 feet down and everything around me a molten orange, the heat throbbing through the glass. I only hoped that if that lunatic fell off the rope, he'd only kill himself and not me, too.

Somehow, out of sheer panic I guess, he got to the top and disappeared over the edge. Then the rope came spilling down to me again and I was hauled up in one long, beautiful motion, leaving the fiery windows and the dirty concrete tomb behind. When I got to the surface I didn't care if the fire was still burning or not, I was so relieved to have completed my part of the job. The March morning felt cold again, but the backslaps from my buddies felt better than warmth. They were approval and congratulation. I'd done a great job, they said. I'd probably saved a life.

Where was the man I saved, I wanted to know. He took off like a shot, they told me. Just came out of the hole, dropped the rope and ran up the street and never looked back. Well, I thought, he's a citizen of the city of New York and I suppose he's got a right to expect his life to be saved, but I thought he could have waited until he knew whether I was going to make it too!

The captain asked me if I had been scared when I went down, and I said that I had been, a little, but had finally decided that he and the other firemen knew what they were doing up there and then I'd put the fear out of my mind. The captain seemed pleased by that and said he was going to write me up for a service commendation for what I did. I thought that was fine, of course, but what meant more to me was the approval of those veteran firemen. They seemed like gods to me. I thanked them for what they did and I think I even shook their hands, I was so excited. They just laughed at me. One of them said, "Yeah, okay, we got you out, but what if one of us had let go of the rope to scratch our butt? Where would you be then?"

I came back to the firehouse full of pride. The company Johnny had done a good job. Although six people died in the fire, mine was the only rescue that was made; everyone else got out under his own power. Captain Klepper kept his word and recommended me for an honor, which turned out to be what we call a Class A. It's no big deal, but it was my first. It was a beginning.

Many more awards were to come over the next two decades, so many that some people seemed to believe that Dick Hamilton was some kind of a superman who could walk on water, scale the highest buildings and pull people from certain death by a combination of ESP and superhuman ability.

Of course, none of that's true. Nobody knows better than I how hot a fire can be, how painful and slow-healing the burns are, how blinding the smoke when you're trying to see through it, how gagging and bitter the taste in your throat. I was as human and as mortal as the next guy in a fireman's helmet. But I was lucky—and I did the job well. And after 24 years I'm everlastingly grateful that I was given the chance to do what I did.

When I retired they told me I was the most honored, most highly decorated fireman in the history of the New York Fire Department. That may be. I can count the heavy gold medals, seven of them, and I can remember some of the many Class A and Class B awards which came my way as the years rolled by. I remember the words of the mayor of New York and the fire commissioner on the day I retired. I know that for the first time in the history of the department, no one will ever wear badge number 51 again. It is retired with me, forever. All of that makes me grateful, too. But what means a great deal more to me is the thought that there are some people alive today who might not be walking around and enjoying life if it were not for what firemen are trained to do. Not just the ones rescued by me, but by all firemen, including those heroes who did some of the same kinds of things I did, but didn't happen to be noticed when they were doing them.

When I look back on my 24 years in the department, it adds up to one of the greatest human experiences that anyone could ever have in any line of work. A lot of it was present in that very first rescue—danger, fear, ingratitude, honor, satisfaction. Before I was through, those ingredients would be multiplied thousands of times until I knew life in a way that only a fireman can. I knew it as heartbeats, as screams, as flashes of humor in the face of tragedy. Sometimes it was terrible and frightful. But it always left me with the feeling that it was worthwhile.

"MY BABY'S INSIDE!"

When we rolled up to the fire the woman was standing in the street in front of the apartment building screaming and pulling her hair and saying that her baby was inside. "My baby's inside, my baby's inside!" she kept saying, and you could almost feel the fear and terror in her voice. It's the kind of thing that makes firemen move fast.

The first problem was the door of the apartment. When the woman came out she must have locked it behind her. Smoke was pushing out into the public hall, heavy stuff with a funny smell. Pete Carino was with us, good old six-foot-one, 220-pound Pete. When he hit the door with his shoulder, it fell in like paperboard. Now the smoke was really bad, black and rich. We could see it was coming from a huge stack of old 78-rpm records in the living room. They were burning like a torch. All we had with us was a two-gallon hand extinguisher, and I wasn't going to waste it on old records if there was a kid to be saved.

The fire seemed to have started at the back of the apartment, so we crawled down the hall, me first, with Pete and Ronnie Foote following. I felt each door with my hand as we moved along. The first one wasn't hot, so we opened it and found a man sitting on a bed. We told him to stay put, he wasn't in any danger yet, somebody would come get him with a ladder. Then we moved on through the sickening smoke.

When we finally got to the last bedroom door, I knew it was the one where the fire was because it was scorching hot to the touch. Just then pressure in the room blew the door and it flew over our heads like a hurricane had lifted it. Inside, the room was an inferno. I knew if there was a baby in there, it was dead long ago. I also knew it would do no good to squirt two gallons of water on a fire like this, so I yelled, "Back out!" to the other two firemen. When I turned to see them, though, they were gone, and I could hear somebody moaning. It sounded like Ronnie. He was down somewhere in the smoke.

I crawled back. When I got to the living room again, the smoke was so thick that there didn't seem to be any door where we had come in. I finally found it by feeling up the walls until I located a chain lock. When I got into the hall again, I found Ronnie and Pete passed out on the floor. Louis deFina was also lying on the floor. Then I knew there must be something poisonous about the smoke from those records. Whatever it was, it hadn't hit me yet. I found my way back to the street and reported to the chief. I told him we tried but we couldn't get to the baby. "If there's a kid in there, it's gone for sure," I said. He just nodded.

They took us all to the hospital after that, and as soon as I was there I started vomiting and couldn't stop. They finally gave me some kind of shots to control it and I came around, but I didn't feel right for a long time, and neither did the other men.

The next day when I came on duty I asked about what happened at the fire. "Did they find the woman's baby?"

"She didn't have no baby, Loo," the men said.

"No baby? You mean we did all that for nothing?"

"Oh, she had a kid, all right," they said, "but he went out on the roof when the fire started and we found him later."

"A baby went out on the roof?" I couldn't seem to follow the story.

"Nah, he was no baby. He was about twenty-one. She just always called him baby. 'My baby.' That's what she always called him."

2

THE JOY AND PAIN
OF GROWING UP

People are surprised when I tell them that I'm not a native New Yorker. Twenty-five years or so of living in and around the great city must have given me a touch of its speech and perhaps its outlook on life. Like a lot of other people who came to New York looking for fame and fortune, I arrived from one of those rustic corners of the U.S. where kids don't always wear shoes and life is nothing like in the Bronx.

To begin this story properly, I was born on January 26, 1924, in the little town of Barracksville, West Virginia. It was near Fairmont and not far from Morgantown. Coal-mining country. My father worked for the Baltimore and Ohio Railroad as a flagman and a brakeman. He wanted to be an engineer. He worked on trains that went right past our farm. Our house, which had been my grandfather's, too, was on a hill looking down on Buffalo Creek, a tributary of the Monongahela River. The railroad tracks ran parallel to the creek.

When you get to the midcentury mark like I have and your life's work has ended as far as what they call "career" is concerned, you look back on your youth with a new interest. At least I do. I find myself thinking about those days in West Virginia as if they weren't so long ago. I search the early years looking for a connection between what I did then and what I did later in life. The question interests me.

My great-grandfather fought for the Union in the Civil War. (I still have his Civil War medals.) My grandfather was a streetcar conductor on a little line that went from Fairmont to Manington and around that area. His wife was from Virginia. My father was sort of a renegade. He was in the navy in World War I, and when his ship stopped in New York, he met my mother, a college girl from the big city. When they married after the war, he brought her down to West Virginia to live, but it seemed to be the wrong move. New York and West Virginia were two different worlds, and my mother wasn't happy. Further, her Virginia-born mother-in-law made it pretty clear that she wished her son had married a southern girl. It was the beginning of a stormy, on-again-off-again marriage which produced seven sons and a lot of unhappiness. I was the third-born. My mother left my father and returned to New York City when I was between three and four.

I went to school in Barracksville in a small, colonial-style schoolhouse which was grade school, junior high and high school under one roof. My schoolmates were mostly kids from coal-mining or glass-making families. Many of them were pretty poor, not nearly as well off as the Hamiltons, and *we* certainly weren't rich. My grandfather's farm had been a big one, and my father operated it like a country gentleman. We had orchards and cows and horses and vegetable gardens and hay from our own meadows. For a while my parents raised purebred chow dogs and German shepherds. We also raised our own hogs which grandfather would butcher himself. We even had a small coal mine of our own—a sort of deep cave in a bank where we would go with a horse and wagon and shovel out as much soft coal as we needed for ourselves. Sometimes we sold a little of it to friends and neighbors.

It wasn't such a bad life for a young boy, even without a mother most of the time. I had my two older brothers to play with. One day they decided it was time that I learned to swim —although they didn't know how themselves. They'd heard it said that if a nonswimmer is thrown into water over his head, he learns to swim instantly. So they picked me up and took me down to the edge of Buffalo Creek and tossed me in! I was only about six or seven, but I proved the theory right: I swam, somehow, back to the bank. Of course I was sputtering and angry at first, but I got over it and I became a good swimmer much sooner than my older brothers.

The things we did almost always had some element of daring or adventure. And I was usually the ringleader in these games. Like the time I decided a bunch of us should build a raft like Huckleberry Finn and float down Buffalo Creek until it joined the Monongahela. Where we were going from there I don't know. Pittsburgh, maybe! We made the raft out of railroad ties that still had a lot of fresh creosote on them, and since we seldom wore anything but our birthday suits when we were on the river, we ended up looking like we'd been tarred from head to foot. I can still remember how that kerosene stung when my father made me wash in it.

When passenger trains went by our swimming hole we usually hid our nude bodies neck-deep, but occasionally we'd time a dive into the river just as a train was passing. This was known as "mooning" and was considered a great joke.

We had a lot of fun when there were some massive spring floods and Buffalo Creek was swollen to a quarter-mile wide. When big trees came floating down in the current, we would time our strokes and catch hold of them, hitching a ride that was pretty sporty at times. If a barn or an outhouse came floating by with a chicken perched on the roof, we became expert at "rescuing" these birds for supper. No one ever missed a chance for a free meal during the Depression.

There was a covered bridge that crossed the river not far from our house, and all of us learned to dive from its railings into the river, being careful to pick a spot where the water was deep enough. Most of the kids learned to do it okay, so after a while it was no big deal. Of course, then *I* had to do something that would top everybody else. I was that kind of kid. I figured if I jumped off the *roof* of the covered bridge, that would be something that would be hard to top.

I remember the day I first climbed up there and looked down. I'll admit it now: I was scared. But I didn't admit it to myself then. I jumped, and proved to my friends and myself that I was still the top daredevil.

All our fun wasn't in the water, though. There were also cliffs to climb nearby, and sometimes I would go just by myself and see how far up I could make it. It was just me and the cliff, I thought. Was the cliff better than I? Not if I could get to the top.

Another thing we used to do was ride cows in the pasture. Not our own cows, other people's, because riding a cow is almost guaranteed to upset her milk production for a few days. I think we were all a little scared of this game, but each of us kept his fear to himself.

Much as we may have imagined that the cows were wild western horses just waiting to be roped and ridden, it was impossible to just come up to one in the pasture and hop on its back; cows literally don't stand still for that sort of game. So we would climb up into the low branches of trees and then lure the cows into position below by tossing apples to the ground. When a nice old Bossy was right underneath, down we'd drop —and our "wild mustang" would usually take off at quite a clip.

The bull in the next pasture was the ultimate test of courage in my crowd. Taunting him into a charge was considered an act of supreme bravery. And it did take a lot of nerve to do it. It was a little like the feeling you'd get when you took a long lead off first and the enemy pitcher would look over at you, meanlike, his eyes shaded by his cap. The bull had eyes, too, but all I ever saw were his horns, big ones.

There was a split instant when that pitcher's muscles first tensed to throw to the first baseman—or when the bull's head lowered just a fraction before his hooves started pounding. *That* was the moment! You could feel the fear and tension all through your body and you could control it, like you could control pain when you didn't want an opponent to know he'd hurt you in a fight.

The bull never caught me, but sometimes one of my stunts didn't work just right and I would wind up with a few bruises. Once I decided to hop a passing freight train, but even though I was a railroadman's son, I didn't know the technique for running along by the car and reaching up to grab the handrail. I swung up in the wrong way, slipped between the cars and got tossed pretty violently to the roadbed. When my father saw my bruises, I told him I'd been in a fight with some Italian kids who worked in a mine down the road.

"You look like you fell off a freight train to me," he said, straight-faced. He must have felt I'd learned my lesson, though, because there was no punishment.

My grandfather spent a good deal of time with us boys, too. He showed us how to set deadfall traps for rabbits by propping up a heavy boulder with a stick baited with an apple. We also shot squirrels with him, and during the cherry season, when the fruit was ripening on the branches, we were assigned the fun job of shooting the catbirds out of the trees with our BB rifles.

When summers ended and we all went back to school, I always looked forward to sports in the afternoon. I wasn't a great student. Although I had a fondness for history and did well in it, book learning couldn't match physical accomplishments. They were the real measure of our stature as kids. What could you *do?* What did you *dare* do? Somewhere along the way, I learned that many things weren't as risky as they seemed and that the bruises of failure went away and were soon forgotten.

I guess that's why I was willing to go through the overflow pipe at the carbide-factory dam.

The water behind the dam was deep and crystal clear, but we weren't supposed to swim there, and guards for the carbide company would chase us. But they weren't always around, so we often took our chances, especially on hot summer days when the water looked especially inviting. The dam was made of concrete, about 15 feet high and maybe 30 feet across from bank to bank. To get to the side where the water backed up, you had to climb over, through or under a wire fence that surrounded the property. Despite this obstacle, the dam was a favorite place and large crowds of kids would go there, both boys and girls. There was always a certain amount of showing off and horsing around.

No water ever flowed over the lip of the dam because on the back side there was a large iron pipe set into the concrete a few feet below the top edge. This carried water from the storage lake down into a pool in front of the dam. The pipe was about 30 inches in diameter and water flowed into it and through it with a powerful suction. Once or twice swimmers were pulled across the mouth of this pipe and it always took help from somebody else to pull them away. This is why swimming was forbidden here. The pipe was considered a deathtrap.

I was fascinated by that pipe. I would swim near it and feel the strong pull of the water. Then I'd study it from the other side. After it passed through the thickness of the dam, the pipe aimed its flow of water at the pool about ten feet below. It seemed a perfectly natural curiosity: why couldn't I just hold my breath and go through the pipe? How long would it take to traverse its length? A few seconds only, I thought. What would the inside be like? Well, it would probably be black as night, full of rushing water, and the sides might be rough—but none of these hazards seemed serious. I was making up my mind to be the first in my crowd to go through the pipe and shoot out into the pool on the other side when something happened to make up my mind for me. The company guards.

They showed up unexpectedly one summer afternoon and hollered at us to get out of the water. "All you kids scram," they yelled. "Don't you know it's dangerous around here?"

Well, everybody started to scram in all directions, meaning there would be a lot of ripped pants as they climbed over the fence. At just that moment it occurred to me that the overflow pipe provided the quickest, neatest and most original way to escape the guards and come out on the other side where they had no jurisdiction. I took a deep breath, ducked my head under the surface and headed for the mouth of the pipe.

I loved being daring. Doing what others were afraid to do. Being a little different.

There was no need to swim; the water pulled me forward into the pipe like a giant magnet that would pick up anything in its way. The pipe wasn't big enough to get into sideways, so straight ahead I went. As I had suspected, there was nothing to be seen. Water was everywhere and solid. It didn't seem like the same gentle stuff we had just been swimming in before the guards came. Now it seemed to have muscles.

It felt like a long time before I could see light ahead, then the light turned to pure sunlight and I was falling the last ten feet into the pool below. I'd made it! I'd made it through the carbide company's overflow pipe! The dreaded challenge held no more dread. I felt now as if I could go through the pipe repeatedly all afternoon. It was a nice trip.

Up top there was a commotion. One of the guards had seen a kid (me) go into the pipe and he was shouting for help. I guess they expected to see a body come out the other side. Instead, there I was laughing and waving at my friends. It was a great feeling.

Later, much later, I was telling someone about the pipe and he said, "Wasn't there any kind of a gate in there?"

"Gate?" I asked, puzzled.

"Yes, you know, something to cut down or shut off the

flow of water through the pipe. There's usually something of
that sort in those overflows. . . ."

"Oh," I said, "I knew there wasn't anything like that." But
in my heart I suddenly realized it was one thing I hadn't cal-
culated. What if there *had* been something halfway through the
pipe that I couldn't pass? Then there would have been no way
out—and no way to swim back against that water. I would have
been trapped, and in a few minutes—dead.

Well, anyway, there wasn't anything in the pipe. . . .

My growing up was divided into two parts. There were the
early years in West Virginia with my grandfather, father and
brothers; and then, when I was 11, my father decided I should
go to live with my mother in New York City. For me, it was
an unhappy decision. I still don't know why it was made.
Suddenly, I was to be uprooted from the only world that had
ever been familiar to me: Buffalo Creek, the meadows and
orchards of grandpa's farm, the friends I knew—and especially
my older brother, Junior. It made me hate my parents' separa-
tion. Why did this have to happen to us? The thought of moving
to the big city up North filled me with dread.

My mother lived at 125th Street and Lenox Avenue, a
dreary, Depression-poor neighborhood in Harlem. I arrived
there in the spring of 1935, shortly after I finished fifth grade
in West Virginia. My mother's uncle was the superintendent of
the apartment building where we lived, and her father lived up
on Webster Avenue in the Bronx. My two youngest brothers,
Billy and Tommy, were also living with my mother. I suppose
you could call it a sort of family, but it didn't seem so to me.
After West Virginia, Manhattan seemed just what somebody
had called it: a concrete jungle.

I got through that first summer somehow, but the joy had
been drained from my young life. There seemed to be no relief
from the heat and the dirt. There was no more Buffalo Creek
where you could moon passing trains; there wasn't even the
carbide-factory dam to get chased from. Harlem kids, black and

white, played street games that were all new to me. They looked different and they talked different, too. Or perhaps I should say it was I who looked and sounded different to them. I know I wasn't much for wearing shoes, especially in the summer, and my speech had the unmistakable accent of the coal fields. I was a natural to poke fun at—and almost everybody did.

When fall came I entered sixth grade at the local public school, at Lenox and 111th. I found that my education in West Virginia had been up to standard; I wasn't behind in any academic way. Socially, however, I felt even more of an outcast than I had during the summer. The torments of being different became more acute. My unhappiness led to a general misery. I felt as if I were the butt of every joke. Worse, I felt as if I didn't have a friend left in the world. If only I could just talk with my brother Junior. He was about two and a half years older than I, and we were the closest two in the family. I missed him terribly.

I guess my mother realized that things weren't working out too well for me in school. Within a month she arranged for me to be transferred to another school, this one in the Bronx, near where my grandfather lived. The results were the same, however; the shoeless kid from the South was doomed to have a rough time with city kids no matter where he went. I was having at least one serious fight a week.

After a month or more of school in the Bronx, another attempt was made to find me a home and a school where I could fit in. This time I would be sent back to the country, to the small town of Greenville, New York, in the Catskills where my mother had found friends of friends who would take me in. One weekend in November I was taken to meet the Hubie family. They were German-Americans and I was told they would look after me while I went to school in their town. It was apparently agreed between the grownups that I would do certain chores on the Hubies' chicken farm to help earn my room and board. I don't remember being a party to any such agreement, but I soon found that Mr. Hubie had a clear and unforgiving recollection of the deal: Young Hamilton was there to work. I still wasn't

12 years old, but I was strong and able, and maybe Mr. Hubie mistook this for maturity. At any rate, he was a hard taskmaster.

At first I didn't mind the work. Winter was coming and the farm chores weren't too bad. Mrs. Hubie seemed nice, and the farmhouse was a warm and friendly place compared to the apartment in New York City. I liked school in Greenville, too. The teachers were kind and the kids were more like the ones I had known in Barracksville. I can even say now that I wasn't homesick after my mother left me with the Hubies. The person I missed most was my brother Junior. I would go to sleep at night thinking of him and wondering what he was doing down there at home with dad.

When spring came, work picked up on the farm, at least it did for me. Mr. Hubie didn't seem to do much himself except listen to the news on the radio. He was a great fan of Adolf Hitler and he followed the rise of the Nazis in Germany like some people followed baseball. Sometimes, when Hitler would be making a speech, Hubie would stand and face the radio and give a Nazi salute right in the middle of the living room while he muttered things in German. Mrs. Hubie didn't pay much attention to him, but he scared me a little. I later found out that he was a member of the German-American Bund, but at age 12 none of this had any meaning for me.

What did have meaning were those 100-pound sacks of chicken feed Hubie had me lifting and hauling and the 55-gallon drums I had to roll to the well empty and roll back to the chicken houses full of water each night. This meant a lot of work early in the morning before school, and more work as soon as school let out in the afternoon. I wanted to play baseball, but Hubie didn't believe in athletics for kids. "You come home here right after school," he'd say. "There's no time for games around here!"

The athletic coach at school became a good friend of mine. He'd seen me perform in gym class and some intramurals and he wanted me to go out for junior-varsity baseball. I told him I couldn't; Mr. Hubie wouldn't let me. So, one day the coach took it upon himself to come over to the farm to talk with

Hubie. My hopes were high that this would do the trick and I'd get to join the school baseball team, but no such luck. Hubie, the old Dutchman, ran the coach away. "Get off my property!" he hollered at him, and that was the end of that.

I had written to my mother several times about how hard the work was on the farm, but she gave me no sympathy. I suppose she thought I was like any other kid, too lazy to work. I also wrote to my brother Junior, who had left West Virginia by now and had joined a CCC camp in Texas. I used to tell him I wanted to run away and join the "CCs" with him, but he'd write back and warn me not to do anything foolish. Pretty soon he left the CCC and joined the navy. I finally realized that the only way I was going to change things for the better for myself was to run away somewhere. But where?

A family named Mathias lived not far down the road from the Hubie farm. Jerry Mathias and his sister Melba and two younger brothers were in school with me and we were friends. Jerry was a good athlete. Melba was my age and pretty. I used to sneak off from Hubie more and more often that spring and run through the fields to the Mathias dairy farm to play softball with the three brothers. Mr. and Mrs. Mathias always welcomed me and had even said I could come and live with them anytime. I guess I had that offer in mind when Dutchman Hubie made the big scene about the dead chicken.

"You killed it!" he hollered. "You're not taking good care of these chickens!" He was shaking and muttering just the way he did in front of the radio. I made up my mind I'd had enough. I was only twelve, but that evening I just packed my clothes and walked out. The only place I had to go was the Mathias farm.

It was my fourth home in two years and in some ways it was the best. The Mathiases treated me like one of their own kids. They had two hired hands on the farm, so there wasn't as much heavy work for the youngsters, and there was always some time left for fun. I didn't really have to work for my board as far as they were concerned, but I pitched in anyway.

I telephoned my mother in the city and told her that I'd

quit the Hubies and was living with the Mathiases. She said she guessed that was all right—not that there was anything she could do about it by then. As for me, I knew right away that first summer that I'd found a real home. I even called Mr. and Mrs. Mathias "mom" and "pop" and whenever they were introducing members of their family to others, they'd always include me as if I were one of their own. "This is Richard" is all they'd say without any explanations.

Now I was free to go out for sports at school and I took advantage of the opportunity. I made every team. I was pretty well coordinated and very competitive. My coach wanted me to try for an athletic scholarship at a state teacher's school. Thanks to sports, I began to feel like I was somebody around school, not just an unknown kid from a German chicken farm. I was captain of the basketball team and the baseball team. I also went out for track and soccer. I enjoyed the feeling. I *wanted* to be somebody. Ever since my mother and father had separated, I had been afraid I might end up being nobody. Now that was all changed. I had a family of my own.

On birthdays and holidays and at Christmastime, we all exchanged gifts on the Mathias farm and the bond grew between us. Then came that wonderful day in 1940 when Mrs. Mathias wrote my brother Junior and invited him to spend his first 30-day leave from the navy on the farm with me! It seemed too good to be true. I think my greatest fear had always been that my favorite brother would drift away and I'd never see him again. Other people had drifted away in my life already and I saw how it could happen. I didn't want it to happen to my brother.

When the great day came for our reunion, the Mathiases drove me down to the bus depot in Coxsackie and we picked up Junior and brought him back to the farm. All the way home in the car we were talking about the patrol duty he was assigned to in the North Atlantic. The United States wasn't at war yet, but our navy was convoying plenty of supplies to the Russians via Murmansk, and that's what Junior was doing. He seemed a lot more worldly to me now.

The first day of Junior's leave, Mrs. Mathias said, "Go on, boys, take a walk together in the fields. You must have a lot to talk about." Well, of course, we did, but we didn't want to separate ourselves from the family. Soon Junior was playing softball with the rest of us after supper as if he'd lived on the Mathias farm all his life.

The month we were together was one of the happiest I can remember. Mr. Mathias took us to Albany to see the Albany Senators play baseball. They were a farm team of the Pittsburgh Pirates. And Mrs. Mathias fixed all her best dishes to eat.

The time went quickly, and when Junior left I cried.

I was visiting my mother in New York City on December 7, 1941. We were in a movie house on Amsterdam Avenue when the film stopped and the lights came on and a man came out on the stage and announced that the Japanese had bombed Pearl Harbor and that Hawaii was under attack. I went back to the Mathias farm wondering what would happen to my brother now.

In the following spring, 1942, Junior paid us a second visit in Greenville. His ship had come into New York and he had gotten a few days' leave. He brought me a baseball glove. After he was gone again, I slept with that glove under my pillow. I knew Junior was doing rough and dangerous duty. I worried for him. I dreamed about joining the navy and getting assigned to the same ship my brother was on. I was 18 now and in my senior year of high school. And I was about to be uprooted again.

I remember it was a beautiful fall day and Greenville was playing Windham in soccer and I was enjoying the feeling of performing well in front of the crowd. Suddenly, on the sidelines, I saw my mother. She had some other people with her. The coach substituted for me and called me over while the game continued.

"You're coming home with me right now," my mother said. I asked why and she said, "You've got younger brothers at home and you're going to help support them." I was stunned.

I appealed to the coach to let me finish the game, but my mother insisted. "Go get your clothes changed right now," she said. "These people I'm with can't wait around for you."

I could see some of my friends in the stands looking at me, wondering, I suppose, why I had suddenly been pulled out of the game. If I was going to have to leave, I at least wanted time to say goodbye to my friends. But my mother said no. "You're coming now," she said. Of course I thought they would take me back to the Mathias farm so I could pack my belongings, but I soon discovered that what my mother meant by now was *now!* After I got out of my soccer uniform, I was hustled from the locker room to the waiting car and off we went for New York City.

After five and a half years, not saying goodbye to the Mathiases seemed more cruel than anything I'd ever known. On the way to the city I just sat in the back seat, not able to believe what was happening to me. It was like being kidnapped. Anger and fear built up inside me. The only thing I could think of was that I'd join the navy and find my brother just as soon as I could. But first, my mother said I had to find a job and earn some money for her.

I found a job with an oil-burner company in Brooklyn and they taught me how to operate a machinist's lathe. Then they tried to get me classified as an essential war worker so I couldn't be drafted. When I became aware of this plan, I decided I'd had enough. Instead of going to work one day, I just took the subway down to navy headquarters on Church Street in Manhattan and signed up for six years.

"Where do you want to be assigned to duty?" the recruiting officer asked me.

"I want to go where my brother is," I said.

"Where's he?"

"He's on a ship in the North Atlantic."

The officer laughed. "Well, I hope you find him," he said. We've got a lot of ships in the Atlantic!"

RITE OF SPRING

The old pier was right under the Brooklyn Bridge and it was rotten clear through and unsafe, but in the early spring kids always went fishing there anyway. There were three of them this day, only about seven or eight years old. They were doing what kids have always done when winter's over and the waters warm up and sparkle in the sunlight.

Nobody could ever tell us how it happened, but two of the kids must have stepped on a rotten plank together and fallen through into the East River. The river flows swiftly under the bridge and it would take a strong swimmer to survive. The two little boys never had a chance.

Their friend didn't know that, of course, so he ran for help; and although there are any number of fire-alarm boxes in that area which he might have spotted and pulled, he headed instead for the only fire-alarm box he knew about for sure. It was 15 blocks away, near where he and his friends lived in the Farragut Houses.

Fifteen blocks is a long run for a little boy, but he made it and reached up and pulled the handle and stood right there as he had been taught to do until the big red truck with the word "Rescue" on the side pulled up.

"It's my friends!" he said. "They fell in the river!"

We took him into the truck and went where he told us, to the old pier. There was no crowd, no sign that anything had happened. Who was to know, after all, that a couple of lads had just left this world for good? I thought that the little guy who had turned in the alarm was probably the only one who even knew what had happened.

It was hopeless, I knew, but even if they were dead, we should try to recover their bodies. The chances for that weren't very good either because of the current, but I decided to give it a try.

I pulled on a Scott airpac, took off my coat and boots and jumped into the river. I swam along on the surface until I came to the encrusted old wooden pilings that held the pier up, and then I submerged. There was often a tangle of timbers and debris under the old piers and there was a chance that the two boys were caught in this. I tried to calculate where they had fallen from and where they might be now. I guess my geometry was pretty good, because I found them both in only a few minutes. When I brought their little brown bodies to the surface, they were still warm.

We laid them side by side on the pier and covered them and picked up the stuff they had left behind. Their fishing poles were two sticks with string and an open safety pin on the end. Their uneaten lunch was still in a brown bag: two peanut-butter sandwiches.

A crowd began to gather now. They milled around the truck and asked the firemen questions and some came out on the pier a ways to get a closer look. I told the little boy who had turned in the alarm to stay close by me. I explained that the police would be along soon to ask him some questions, but that he shouldn't be afraid.

Then a young man came sauntering along, hands in his pockets, looking like he wanted to talk. He looked at my helmet and came over to me.

"I saw those kids out here on the pier," he said. "I saw 'em fall in."

"Yeah?" I said. "Well what did you do then?"

"I didn't do anything," he said, keeping his hands in his pockets.

"Why didn't you?" I asked, thinking of the little fellow who had run 15 blocks to save his friends.

"Hell, man," he said, "why should I? They ain't *my* kids."

3

SEVENTEEN BATTLE STARS
AND A GREAT ADVENTURE

Before I saw anything of the ocean, the navy put me through boot camp, and then, because I'd done well on my mechanical aptitude tests, they sent me on to a Ford Motor Company school for motor mechanics in Detroit. I learned all about gas and steam turbines, diesel engines, electric motors, etc. I made good enough marks in all of this to have gone on to other service schools, but I was more anxious to get into action. I'd been exchanging letters with Junior, and he advised me against trying to get a duty assignment where he was. The North Atlantic was a cold, miserable place, he said, so if they give you a choice, take the Pacific.

They gave me a choice and I took the beautiful warm Pacific—and ended up in the cold fogs of the Aleutian Islands

on the cruiser *Wichita*. The Japanese had been on Sitka and
Attu but were gone by the time we got there. The cruiser shelled
some empty islands, mostly for gunnery practice, I think. I
couldn't see why anybody would want to occupy these places,
much less waste ammunition on them.

I wasn't aboard the *Wichita* long before a rumor spread
that she was a jinxed ship. Some people said she'd been hit by
a Japanese torpedo which didn't go off. What did this mean?
Was the torpedo still imbedded in the hull? The jinx rumor
seemed ridiculous, of course, but along with a lot of other swabs
I decided to ask for other duty the next chance I got. When the
Wichita returned to Pearl Harbor after a few more weeks of
cruising, I asked for a transfer. In the summer of '43 the navy
was looking for men to join the amphibious forces, and that
sounded good to me. It meant being in on invasions and seeing
some real action. I signed up and was assigned to an LCI
(Landing Craft Infantry) for a period of training in Hawaii.

I wasn't much impressed with wartime Honolulu, and
Waikiki Beach was a big disappointment even for a kid from
West Virginia. I don't know whether I expected to see girls in
grass skirts behind every tree, but they certainly were not.
Instead of hanging around the gin mills and fleshpots of King
Street and Alakea, I struck up a friendship with a Hawaiian boy
who was also in the navy and whose family farmed in the
beautiful green hills of rural Oahu. Whenever we had liberty,
Tippy and I would go visit his parents—and his pretty sister
who was just my age. I loved the farm life these people lived,
although their crops were sugar cane and pineapple, both unfamiliar to me. I can remember cutting cane a few times, using
a special curved knife to slash at the thick, sweet stalks. I
thought, It isn't so much different from cutting corn in West
Virginia or the Catskills. This was a happy interlude for me—
another kindly farm family that took me in with love and
affection.

Tippy and I were soon separated and went our different
ways to war. By the end of summer of 1943 my amphib training
was finished and we sailed for what soon began to seem like an

endless series of island invasions. I guess there were some I missed, but I made most of the big ones: Kwajalein, Tarawa, Bougainville, Saipan and the Marianas, then the Carolines and Bloody Nose Ridge on Palau. I seldom left the LCI to go ashore in these actions, but I won 14 battle stars for being under enemy fire. Although I had yearned for combat, when I saw what the marines were facing on the beaches I was glad I didn't have to be *that* close to the enemy. I was a motor machinist, eventually made first class, and my duty was keeping our LCI operating no matter what the Japs did to it. I spent a lot of my time in the engine room, which was my real pride. I *knew* we had the sharpest, best-maintained LCI in the fleet, one that always had just a little more speed and a little better maneuverability than the others. I was more interested in keeping my ship Number One than I was in killing Japanese. Sometimes when it was my job to help pull bodies from the water, I would look at our dead marines and at the dead Japs and feel equally sorry for them all. I just couldn't build up any hatred for the "enemy."

Once, just before one of the major invasions, I think it was Tarawa, our LCI was disabled by a great tangle of debris which stopped the propellers. The whole fleet was gathering, getting ready to move out together in a day or so, but my ship was so badly hung up with this mess of cables, netting and other underwater junk that it didn't look as if we'd be able to stay with the task force. It would be dangerous for a relatively defenseless ship to be left alone in the Pacific, and I asked the skipper's permission to go over the side and see what I could do about unsnarling the tangle. I don't think he believed I had any chance at all—it was a job for navy salvage experts—but until they arrived, he said, "Okay, see what you can do, Hamilton."

The ship was down by the stern several degrees because of the great weight of this stuff we were caught in. The engine room was shut down, and sailors were lining the decks in a gloomy mood. There was nothing worse for morale than sitting dead in the water. I decided that if I could just devise a way to breathe underwater, I might be able to cut us out of this trap.

The LCI didn't have any diving equipment aboard, but I rigged up a gas mask with an oxygen bottle and I went over the side to see how it would work. I found I could breathe okay and I could see fairly well, so I told the guys to lower some tools down to me and I went to work.

It was a real mess, worse than I had imagined. Not only was there heavy cable, both steel and manila, but all kinds of other flotsam had joined the web of ropes. I used a knife to saw away at the lines and a bolt cutter to sever the steel stuff. Both propellers were seized up tight. It looked almost hopeless, but I kept at it. Every half-hour or so I'd have to come up for more air. When I did, the pharmacist's mate would give me a shot of brandy. But what was even more stimulating was the reaction of my shipmates. "Come on, Ham," they were saying, "you can do it! You're going to get us out of here!" and that sort of spirit.

Finally, after four or five hours' work and no help from anybody, I cut through the last steel cable and the whole huge nest of stuff that had gripped the ship dropped off and started slowly to sink. The LCI, relieved of the burden, gave a lurch, and with that telltale movement there was a tremendous cheer on deck. We were free! When I climbed back onto the ship, sailors were all over me with back-slaps and congratulations.

When the celebrating died down a bit, one old chief came over and told me I'd done a great job. Then he added some words I'll remember all my life. "Hamilton," he said, "you're the type of guy that young boys *hope* to be and the old men wish they *had* been."

After we'd been away from Hawaii about a year and had been involved in several invasions, we got orders to return to Pearl. They said we'd get two or three weeks of R & R and might even be quartered in the Royal Hawaiian Hotel on Waikiki. That sounded all right to most of us. I looked forward to visiting Tippy's family again.

The morning we entered the narrow mouth of the famous old naval base that the Japanese had made such a mess of only a couple of years before, I was on deck looking at all the great ships and bustle of activity that had replaced the wreckage of December 7, 1941. Suddenly, my eye caught the numbers on a big gray hull that looked like a reefer ship, one that was refrigerated for carrying meat and other foodstuffs. I couldn't believe my eyes, but there it was—my brother Junior's ship!

What was he doing in the Pacific?

I bounded up to the bridge without paying any attention to proper protocol and asked the skipper if he could find out if my brother was aboard the big supply ship. The skipper told a signalman to blink out the message as our LCI passed. Within a minute a message blinked back: "Is your brother Herbert Hamilton, Jr?" Answer: "Yes!" Message: "He can't get to the deck right now, but you're invited over to have dinner with him tonight!"

Our ship moored in a far corner of the huge harbor, a long way from my brother's ship, but I borrowed a little dinghy we had on board and rowed the whole distance as soon as I was off duty for the day. I felt like a water bug struggling along in a pool full of hippos. When I came aboard the supply ship my brother was waiting for me—in a chief's uniform! We had a wonderful joyous reunion right there on deck and a great meal in the chiefs' mess. We talked so fast our words stumbled over each other. It seemed like a million miles and a million years to Barracksville, West Virginia. We traded war stories through most of the night. When it was time for me to go back to my LCI, my brother warned me about the dangers of rowing across Pearl Harbor in blackout conditions in an eight-foot boat. A small landing craft was pressed into duty, my dinghy was lifted into its empty interior, and I was taken home in style.

We only had a few more days to socialize before Junior's ship sailed off to Australia to pick up a load of beef. Once again I felt that empty fear inside. Someone very dear to me was going away and I might never see him again.

The pain was made even sharper when I discovered that my friend Tippy had been killed in action. After his family told me the news, I wasn't anxious to hang around Hawaii any longer; the war zones seemed almost preferable. I went back to the island invasions, and 1944 seemed like a very long year.

We were doing maneuvers in preparation for the invasion of Japan itself when the war came to an end. Since our LCI was one of the oldest in its class, it was scheduled to go home to San Diego to be cut up for scrap. The skipper said he needed only 21 men as crew to get the ship home. A lot of the draftees were getting out on points now, their service over, but I had about three years of my enlistment to go, so I volunteered to return to the States with the ship. We arrived in San Diego just a few hundred yards ahead of the battleship *New York*. As long as we didn't look behind us, it was possible to imagine that all those ships' horns tooting and moaning were for a beat-up old LCI and a war-weary crew of 21.

Once again the navy gave me a choice of oceans: Atlantic or Pacific. This time I chose the Atlantic. Junior was somewhere on the East Coast. Maybe now that the war was over we could get together again. Along with five buddies, I bought a 1942 Oldsmobile and we drove cross-country, dropping sailors off at their hometowns as we went.

That's a trip I'll always remember. We got as far as Texas when the tires began to give out. Now, in 1945, this was a serious problem because automobile tires were still strictly rationed, and the six of us, not being civilians, didn't have a ration coupon among us. We were driving through El Paso, wondering what to do, when a state cop pulled us over. "You can't carry six seabags on top of a car," he told us. We said something like, Gee, officer, we're sorry, we didn't know that, and he said okay, on your way sailors, and we were about to take off when I decided to ask him if he knew where we might buy some tires.

The cop turned out to be all right. He was a big guy with a big Texas hat. He said he thought he knew a place where we might get some rubber. "But I'll have to go with you," he drawled, "because we've put these people in jail once already for selling black-market tires."

So we followed the state police car down the highway, off

onto a county road, then onto a dirt road that led back into the hills. Finally we came to a cluster of old buildings and barns buried deep in a mesquite grove. The cop swung his car in a wide U-turn and touched the siren for a quick, short wail as he came to a stop.

Soon enough, an old woman and an old man came to the door of one of the shacks. They looked like the dirtiest hillbillies we'd ever seen. If the cop hadn't been with us, I think we would have been worried.

"These boys need tires," the cop said to the pair.

"Oh, we don't have tires anymore!" said the woman, holding her apron.

"You don't seem to understand what I said," drawled the trooper. "These sailor boys need five new tires."

"We're out of that business, honest we are, officer!"

"Okay then," the cop said, getting out of his car and putting his big hat on his head and hitching up his gun belt. "Guess I'll just have to search the place."

"All right! All right! We don't want no trouble!" the pair said. "We jes might find what the boys need."

And they did. In one of the barns there was a mountain of brand new U.S. Royals hidden under hay. They rolled out five and we all stood looking at those beauties lying in the dust and we knew they'd get us home.

Then, like a dope, I asked the woman what we owed her.

"Well," she said, "we usually get—"

The trooper interrupted her. "You know what you can get if you *sell* those tires, don't you?" he said. "These young men are going to get 'em the same way you did. For nothing."

We knew it wasn't exactly right, but when you've just been through a war, you don't worry much about civilians' troubles.

The tires served us well, and finally I reached my mother's new house in Bellrose, Long Island, where I spent the rest of my leave.

My next ship was the largest in the world, the aircraft carrier *Midway*. I reported aboard at Newport News, Virginia.

I'd never seen anything so big, like a giant hotel with 5000 guests and its own airport. It was very exciting, my first exposure to airplanes. If you played your cards right and got to know some of the pilots, it was even possible to be taken up on a flight every few weeks. The navy Hellcats and torpedo bombers weren't the screaming jets of today, but to me the experience of flight was like sprouting my own wings.

I went into the Arctic Ocean on the *Midway* when she took part in an exercise called Operation Frostbite. I went to Scotland to a submarine base. We did bombing runs on a target island off Cuba. As long as we were at sea and doing things, I loved it, but when the *Midway* was returned to port for what were going to be long repairs, I decided to move on again to where the action was.

My next, and last, ship was an auxiliary rescue ship based in Key West, Florida. It was a beautiful, fast craft with a long, graceful prow and a three-inch gun mount forward. Life aboard was pretty crowded, but it was an interesting change from the *Midway*. Now, however, a couple of things began to trouble me. For one, Junior was stationed more or less permanently in Italy where he was training Italian sailors about refrigeration ships and I didn't see any hope of my ARS getting all the way to the Mediterranean. Also, an old injury to my leg was beginning to cause me pain. Ligaments had been torn when I tried to tie down some fuel drums on the deck of the LCI in a storm a year earlier. Now, the navy doctors said, something called cellulitis had set in. Since there was no specific cure for this, and since they said the condition might disable me for duty, I was offered a chance to leave the navy before my six years were up—"for the convenience of the government."

I gave it some thought and decided that my military days were over. I was discharged in January 1947, and began a new kind of life.

COLD RUNNING WATER

The Verrazano Bridge is the longest suspension span in the world, longer than the Golden Gate. It connects Brooklyn with Staten Island across a narrow part of New York harbor. In February the waters beneath it are black, swift and numbing cold. On the night the automobile went off the bridge and into the harbor, the temperature was 14 degrees, there was a stiff breeze, and the water was only six degrees above freezing. It was a hell of a time to have to go for a swim, but if you know there's a human being who might still be gasping for breath down there in the air pocket of a submerged car, the chill of ice water seems a small discomfort.

Rescue 2 was venting a roof at a bowling-alley fire in Brooklyn when the dispatcher said we were needed at the bridge right away. Woman trapped in a car, he said. It was about 15 minutes before we could get there, and when we did, it looked like a hopeless situation. Police Emergency had already set up searchlights along the water's edge and we could see a big hole in the bridge railing above us. The car had shot out and fallen about 50 feet from shore and was now under 25 feet of water. There were a lot of small craft milling around over the spot, including one from the coast guard and a fireboat. But nobody could do anything because nobody had any scuba gear.

The Scott airpac that firemen use to go into heavy smoke conditions was not specifically designed for underwater work, but it can be used that way, and this looked like one time I was going to have to demonstrate. I pulled off my boots, helmet, coat and gloves and rigged a Scott up with a long extension hose to a big bottle of air. The winter wind was cutting through my blue work shirt and pants, and my feet, only in thin socks, were already turning numb.

A division chief told me the car had been in the water about 25 minutes already, that two men had escaped from it when it plunged, leaving a grandmother and a child in the back seat. The odds didn't sound good.

Just as I was about to get into a small rowboat with another fireman at the oars, a police captain came over and said to hold it, hold everything. "You going underwater?" he asked.

"Yeah," I said.

"But you're no skin diver," he said. "We can't let you do that."

"Look," I said, "I'm just going down to see if the keys are still in the car. If they are, I'll drive it up here on the beach and you cops can give it a ticket!" Then I took off in the small boat. I knew every second counted now and I didn't have any patience with delays.

When we got to the spot where I could just barely see the light-colored roof of the car in the beam of a light, I pulled the Scott mask over my face and let myself over the side of the rowboat on a rope. The water was so cold I couldn't feel it, but my arms and legs seemed to turn to stone. There were chunks of ice on the surface of the water when I submerged.

I just sank until I could feel my feet on the roof of the car. I couldn't see much now except for a dirty, greenish light coming down from the surface. I could feel that the two front doors of the sedan were open and the rears closed. I slipped inside and felt around. There were still about eight inches of air under the roof and there was a body floating up there; I thought it was probably the grandmother. She was pretty stiff. I hauled her out and then up the rope to the boat. While the other fireman hauled her in, I went down to search some more for the child. I found nothing.

When I got back to shore, they wrapped me in blankets and put me in the same ambulance with the body of the dead woman. But before we pulled away for the hospital, the same police captain came over and said, "Hold it, hold everything!

"You sure there wasn't any little girl still in that car, lieutenant?" he asked.

"I'm sure," I said, not feeling like giving this stupid cop more than two words. But I could see that wasn't going to be enough. He just stood there shaking his head, and then he got one last idea.

"Did you look in the trunk?" he said.

POSTWAR BLUES—
COULD I FIND A CURE?

It's something you read about now. Twenty-five years later, people understand how GIs felt when they came home from the war. But I'm not sure they did in 1947. We'd all been through the greatest adventure of our lives, and then we came home— to what? Oh, sure, there was the GI Bill waiting for us and some kind of a job. But how could anything match the excitement of being on the aircraft carrier *Midway,* the biggest ship in the world? There was no way to find the silent beauty of the Arctic Ocean in the Bronx. Or the romantic mysteries of the South Pacific on Long Island. Everything seemed drab. If you were like me and didn't hang around the bars at night and drink, where was the companionship we'd known with our buddies in the service?

Something very big in my life had ended, a four-year chapter in which I had found out a lot about myself. I had learned my own competence in a lot of fields. I knew what I could do. Now I wanted to go on doing it. Not firing rockets at a beachhead—there was no joy in killing—but anything would be better than fighting a traffic jam every day on the way to and from work. Like a lot of other guys who came home in '47, I was looking for adventure. It wasn't something you wrote down on a job application, and you might not even admit it to yourself because, after all, when you grew up you were supposed to stop being a kid, right? But in my heart it was there. Dick Hamilton wasn't going to be a desk jockey.

The navy had told me that because of my injuries and the cellulitis in my leg, it would be better if I didn't do any strenuous work for at least a year. I couldn't buy that verdict, however, so every chance I had I'd work myself hard. Somehow I knew that my body was the key to my ambitions. It had to be sound or I was sunk. I tested myself by going skiing right away that first winter. I went roller skating. I went swimming and diving when the spring of '47 came. Everything seemed okay. I felt as fit as I ever had. If there was an occasional twinge of pain, I didn't say anything about it. Twenty-three is too young to worry.

One of the things I did enjoy that first year out of the service was getting together with my brothers. I had moved in with my mother in Bellrose, Long Island, and that first summer my brothers and I made several trips up into the Catskills to see a two-acre piece of land that my mother and brothers had all chipped in to buy. It was a beautiful spot on a lake, and we thought it would be a great place to build a house. A family my mother had known for years lived on one side of the property, and a Mrs. Morrell and her two sons lived on the other side.

The Morrells' outhouse happened to be about 25 feet over the boundary line on our land, and a year earlier my mother had gone over to ask Mrs. Morrell if they could move it, but she just walked away in a huff. So this summer we got hold of the two Morrell boys and suggested that they move their toilet.

Now one of these guys was supposed to be a boxing champion in the army and he thought he was pretty tough. He said that the outhouse had been there before we bought our two acres and therefore it was going to stay there.

Okay, we said, we'll give you until next spring to move the outhouse because we're going to build on the land. If they hadn't moved it by then, we would.

The Morrell brothers just stomped off. It was like one of those scenes from a Harlan County, Kentucky, feud—the Hamiltons versus the Morrells. And neither side was going to give an inch.

When spring came we went up to the property, and sure enough the old outhouse was still right there, 25 feet over the line. Now my brothers and I had to decide what to do about it. It was fun, hanging together like this. It reminded me of our days as boys along the banks of Buffalo Creek. As a matter of fact, our solution to the problem was right out of the West Virginia coal fields: dynamite.

I didn't know how much dynamite was needed to produce the right result, but you can't buy less than one stick of the stuff so that's what we bought for the outhouse. We packed it underneath with a big crowbar, attached a three-foot fuse and then we touched her off and ran.

There was a terrific blast and it was instantly apparent that you don't need a whole stick of dynamite to blow up an outhouse. People came from all around the lake to see what had happened, the noise was so big. All they saw was a huge hole in the ground and some splintered boards and pieces of toilet paper everywhere up in the trees.

Pretty soon the state police arrived. They looked around and wanted to know what the hell happened. There was a big crowd by now.

"That was my outhouse!" one of the Morrell brothers said, pointing to the hole in the ground.

"Yeah," says the cop, "then what did you have stored in it?"

"Nothing," says Morrell, looking across at us. We smiled back.

"Is this your land?" says the cop.

"No," says Morrell, "but it was my outhouse!" We kept smiling.

The cop shook his head and turned to us. "Can you imagine that?" he said with that funny look people get on their faces when they discuss outhouses. "Their outhouse blew up!"

"Gee," we said, "that's too bad."

After that, the Hamilton brothers were known throughout the mountains as people you shouldn't mess with.

Besides having my brothers around, I also had two uncles who lived in the city. Uncle Harry lived in Jackson Heights and worked for the Department of Public Works. Uncle Bill was a fireman with 29 Truck up in the Bronx. Both of them were anxious to help me when I came home. Uncle Harry had no kids of his own and he looked upon me as a son. He wanted me to come to work for the DPW; he told me not to be a fireman, that a career in the DPW would be better. I went along with him. It wasn't exactly high adventure, but it did enable me to use some of my skills as a motor mechanic that I'd learned in the navy. I liked working with tools and machinery; I liked the kind of big projects that the DPW was involved with: giant sewers, earth-moving projects, that sort of thing.

I started out as a temporary employee at DPW, worked my way up to be permanent and learned a lot about municipal sewer plants and heavy equipment, but after a couple of years of this I still yearned for the kind of life I had enjoyed in the navy.

One morning in 1950, Uncle Harry and I were driving along the Jericho Turnpike on our way out to work on a house he was building in Northport. I was driving and we were talking away in the car when all of a sudden, out of the corner of my eye, I saw an airplane coming down low over a potato field. Just as I turned to look at it directly, it hit the dirt with a big whoomp and a cloud of dust. Then it bounced up about 30 feet and flew straight into a thicket of trees not far off the road.

I hit the brakes, swerved off the highway and pulled the car to a stop. "Uncle Harry," I said, "I think we might be able to help that guy if he's still alive." I jumped out of the car, hollered back to my uncle to bring a couple of tire irons that were in the trunk, and headed up a dirt path that led in the general direction of the trees where I'd last seen the plane. There was no smoke or fire from the crash to mark the spot, but I ran ahead as if I'd suddenly been given some kind of new strength. I felt like the old Dick Hamilton of navy days. Here was something I knew something about.

When we got to the plane I could see that it was some kind of a military fighter, the same general type I'd become familiar with on the *Midway*. I knew Republic Aviation had a test field nearby; it was probably one of theirs. It was flipped over, upside down, and pretty badly bent. There was still no fire, but I could smell fuel and oil all over the place. It could blow any minute. The Plexiglas canopy of the plane was almost touching the ground, and inside the canopy I could see the pilot hanging upside down in his safety harness.

On the *Midway* we used to be around the planes all the time. Sometimes I'd climb up on them and sit in the cockpit and think about what it must be like to be a pilot. I knew how tight a cockpit was, I knew where the straps were attached. I also knew how quickly one of these things can turn into a flaming bomb when it crashes. I'd seen some of those on the *Midway*, too.

First I tried to slide the canopy back, but it was jammed, so I grabbed a tire iron and smashed the Plexiglas until I had a hole big enough to pull the pilot out. Inside, he was conscious but groggy. I tried to release the buckle of his harness, but I couldn't find it, so I felt along the leg of his flight suit until I found the knife I figured would be there. I cut the straps that were holding him and lowered him gently toward the opening.

By now, the pilot was aware of what was going on. He may have had a broken collar bone, because when I moved him he hollered. I said, "I'm sorry buddy, but this airplane could go up like a Roman candle any minute and I'd rather not be here when it does." My uncle and I pulled him away from the wreck.

The whole thing had taken only a few minutes. By now there were other people running through the fields in our direction, and pretty soon an ambulance came and took the pilot away and a volunteer fire department arrived to stand guard over the plane—which never did catch fire. That was it, as far as I was concerned. When I saw the ambulance drive off, I was ready to leave. But my uncle seemed to be enjoying the attention I was getting. He was proud, and he wanted me to hang around and talk with the reporters. But I said no, let's just get out of here and get to work on your house. "It was nothing," I remember saying. "We were just lucky to be able to do it for the guy."

"It didn't seem like nothing to me," my uncle said.

I wanted to tell him that he hadn't been through World War II. He hadn't been on the *Midway.*

Later, Republic Aviation sent a representative to my home and wanted to do something for me, even offered me a job. I said thank you but I didn't want a job, I had a job. It was okay. I just thank God I happened to be passing by; somebody else might not have known what to do.

When I went back to work at the DPW in the coming week, however, I couldn't get the incident out of my mind— how it had made me feel to go into action that way again. There was some danger, yes, but that isn't what I remembered. It was the feeling of being in command of a situation and being in command of myself. Was it wrong to feel this kind of pride? Was it ego? I didn't know, but I was sure of one thing: the DPW didn't make me feel that way.

Shortly after the plane crash, my uncle Harry died very unexpectedly. It was a tremendous shock to me. Somehow, his death seemed to fit into my own mood. Now that he was gone, there seemed no good reason for staying on in his Department of Public Works. It was time to move on.

But where?

My uncle Bill in the Fire Department talked with me. I told him how much I missed Uncle Harry, how I'd just as soon leave the DPW now and look for something else. Naturally, Uncle Bill suggested the Fire Department.

Before the war I'd had no interest in the Fire Department. Even though Uncle Bill's company was not far from where we used to live in Manhattan, I never remember even going to the firehouse. It just never interested me, probably because I didn't know much about what a fireman really does. Squirting water on fires didn't seem so heroic to me. Later I came to realize that a fireman's life is a pretty rugged affair and often demands a good deal of personal courage. When Uncle Bill suggested the FD as a career in 1950, I was ready to listen. I promised I'd put in an application.

But I also put one in with the state police. There was adventure there, too.

CINDER

Somebody pulled an alarm near one of the housing projects in Brooklyn, and when we got there in the Rescue truck, a woman standing near the box said somebody in the building had just thrown a newborn baby down the incinerator chute.

I wanted to ask her how she knew, but this was no time to play cop. If it was true, every second might count. We piled off the truck, grabbed some dry chemical extinguishers and raced down into the incinerator room in the basement. The super was there and he was saying there was nothing to get excited about. We weren't excited, we were just doing our job. We took one look into the firebox of the incinerator and could see there was no fire. Thank God for that. Now, if there was a kid in there, we might have a chance.

A couple of the men tried getting into the firebox through the iron door, but it was too small, so we went to work on the cinder-block wall with axes. The stuff came flying apart while the super hollered that all this was unnecessary.

"Look," I said, "it may seem unnecessary to you, but what if you were in there or one of your kids? Wouldn't you want us to get you out as quick as possible?" Secretly, I wasn't at all sure the woman had been telling the truth.

The super was still mumbling about the damage as two of us went into the firebox, which is like a small room, about eight by eight feet and full of all the filth and junk that a whole apartment building doesn't want anymore. Stuff was coming down even as we were in there, and we could see that, if there was a baby down there, it had already been covered with bags of garbage. There wasn't room to stand up straight, but we started digging.

After about five minutes of pawing through this stuff, one of the guys found the little brown baby. When he picked it up out of all the rubbish, it started to cry. The cord was still dangling from its stomach.

Some of the other men were outside the incinerator, waiting with the sheets we wrap burned people in, and also blankets. We passed the infant, not more than an hour old, out from hand to hand until she was wrapped up, and then we put her in the Rescue and took her to the hospital.

When the cops arrived at the scene to investigate, they learned that the baby's mother was 14, unmarried and lived on one of the top floors. She had had the baby alone and just decided she didn't want it. So she threw it down the chute.

The nurses at the hospital called the baby girl Cinder, and guys from the Rescue would stop by once in a while for the next few months to find out how she was doing. Finally we heard that Cinder had been put up for adoption, and then we learned that she was taken by a family who really wanted a child.

Cinder is old enough to be in school now. Of course, she's got a real name today and she probably doesn't know about those first hours of her life. Chances are that Cinder and the fireman who found her will never meet each other again.

Their paths in life only crossed for a few very important minutes.

5

"HEY! THE PROBIE'S HERE!"

The Fire Department called my application before the state police did. It was as simple as that. If it had been the other way, I might have been a trooper all my life instead of a smoke eater.

I joined the NYFD on November 1, 1950. I was almost 27 years old, still single and still living with my mother in Bellrose. I was older than many of the 37 other probationary firemen who were in my "probie" school class, although there were other veterans there, too. I was determined to be the best fireman I could, just as I had always wanted to be the best at anything I tried. Also, I wanted to *belong* to something—a family of sorts. I hoped the Fire Department would give me that sort of companionship, that sense of belonging.

Probie school, on 68th Street in Manhattan, took nine

weeks and consisted of a lot of classroom work on such topics as physics, hydraulics, first aid, plus plenty of practical training with the hoselines, ladders and assorted equipment that are a fireman's everyday tools. I liked the physical training, but the classroom stuff bored me. I also soon learned that, just as in the navy, not every man who came into the Fire Department was as dedicated as I was. There was a lot of showing off among the probies, a lot of big talk and bragging. Some of the guys in my group were always trying to impress each other.

Like one day we were training with portable ladders and one of the bigger men in the class picked up a 35-foot wooden ladder, which weighs over 200 pounds, and he pressed it over his head with a pair of arms that looked like locomotive pistons. It was a stunt, nothing he'd ever have to do as a fireman. To me, it didn't prove anything, but nobody said anything, so I kept quiet.

Our commanding officer in probie school was a Captain George McGinty. He seemed a wise and kind man to me. He'd been seriously injured in a big Manhattan fire some years before, so now he was teaching others what he used to do himself. It didn't take long for me to become aware that McGinty had taken a liking to me. Not only that, but he sometimes seemed to be using me to make a point. So when the big probie put the ladder down from over his head, McGinty strolled over in front of the class and said, "That's quite a trick, lifting a big ladder like that. But remember, size isn't everything in this Fire Department of ours." Then he beckoned me to step closer. "Think you can lift that ladder, too, Hamilton?" he said.

I didn't know how to answer at first. I wasn't sure I could do it, but I could see that McGinty wanted me to try. Thirty-six other probies were watching to see what I would do. I thought, Well, it's heavier than Mr. Hubie's bags of chicken feed, but that was 15 years ago and I was just a kid. I reached down, grabbed the varnished rungs of the big ladder, lifted it waist-high, braced my feet a little wider and gave a big shove upward. The ladder was over my head, turning a little in the sun. I held it there for a minute, then put it down. My fellow probies were enjoying the competition. So was Captain McGinty.

"You see," he said, "size and muscles aren't everything in this business. Hamilton may be smaller and lighter than most of you, but he's got something else that's going to make him a good fireman. It's determination."

I didn't know whether to be proud or embarrassed. I wasn't trying to show off by lifting the ladder, but it was a challenge I had to answer.

Another time we had some firemen from Argentina visiting our school and they were interested in the techniques we used for jumping out of buildings into nets. McGinty was in charge of the demonstration that day and several of the probies jumped out of a second-story window of an old school building. The visitors from abroad were impressed. Was it possible, they wanted to know, for a fireman to survive even higher jumps in an emergency? "Oh, yes," says McGinty, "we've got men who can do better," and his eye skimmed along our ranks until it came to me. "Go on up there, Hamilton, and show them," he said.

I hustled up to the third floor of the school, leaned out one of the front windows and hollered that I was ready.

"No, not there!" McGinty hollered up. "Go up to the fourth!"

The thought sobered me. I figured I could make a three-story jump because two didn't seem so bad, but I'd never considered four. I went up one more flight of stairs, went to the front window again and looked down. It seemed a long way, but then, I thought, McGinty wouldn't be telling me to do it if it weren't all right. I believed in him that much. I could hear him calling up to me with his pleasant Irish brogue. "Son, are you ready?"

"Don't worry about me," I said. "Just be sure those probies holding the net are ready!" And out I went. Before I was halfway down, I knew it was going to be fine. I was enjoying the applause even before I hit. Afterward, some of the probies asked me how it was and I told them it wasn't bad, it was easy. I wouldn't have said anything else unless I'd broken my neck.

McGinty used to set up competitions between teams of probies to see how fast we could stretch a hoseline from the street to the top floor of an old building. We did this with a 2 1/2-inch-diameter hose that had no water in it, but it was good training in running up stairs while pulling the length of heavy hose behind us. Later, of course, we did the same thing with hose lines under pressure, but in the beginning McGinty just wanted to see how quick we could move and who had hustle and who didn't. Of course, the fact that he made a stopwatch contest out of it challenged me—and almost got me in trouble. I had an idea.

"Look," I said to the guys on my team, "as soon as we get inside the building with the hose, I'll unscrew this nozzle and run up the stairs ahead of you. Then I'll stick the nozzle out the fourth-floor window and holler, 'Time.' You come up after me with the hose, but McGinty will never know we weren't connected all the way."

The first time we did it, we were something like 30 seconds faster than anyone else and McGinty is all excited and he's saying, "See? See? See what can be done?" His favorite probie was Number One again and the captain was enjoying every minute of it. "Do it again," he said. "Show these other men what real leadership can accomplish!" So we did it again, although by now I was beginning to feel that the joke was going too far. I loosened the nozzle, rushed up the stairs, hit the top-floor window, stuck the nozzle out and hollered "Time!" Then I put the nozzle on the floor and sat down to catch my wind.

But before the rest of my team got into the room with the hose, there stood McGinty in the doorway! He was glowering at me, looking very much like John L. Lewis with big bushy eyebrows. "Hamilton," he bellowed, "how do you explain the fact that you don't have any hose up here with you?" I couldn't tell whether he was truly angry, or disappointed in me, or whether he saw the mischief in what we had done. At any rate, he told me to stay after school that afternoon. I was ashamed. I dreaded what was coming.

When the rest of the probies had all gone, McGinty asked me, "Well, Hamilton, what do you think of what you did today?"

"I knew I shouldn't have done it," I said.

Then he just put his arm around me and he said, "You know, that trick of yours made me feel forty years younger! I would have done the same damn thing when I was a probie!"

We also did a lot of training with ladders in probie school. I liked working with the scaling ladders. These are short, 10- or 12-foot sections of ladder with a hook at one end and "rungs" that are just stuck through a central shaft, so they aren't really whole ladders at all. They're a device for climbing up the outside of buildings, window to window, from one floor to the next. When you looked down to the street from your perch on a scaling ladder, it really stirred your blood up a little. We were told that if we ever rescued somebody in a fire by means of a scaling ladder, we were a cinch to win a Fire Department medal. I thought about that and made up my mind that I'd be as good as any man in scaling buildings.

The big aerial ladders required practice, too. We had to learn how to help people down the 85-footers even when they were frozen with fear of the height. (Later, the Fire Department had some 144-foot aerials; they narrowed down to only a foot wide at the top, and not even firemen liked being up there.) In my class of 37 probies, only one man flunked out at the end of nine weeks, and that was because he froze at the top of an aerial ladder and wouldn't let anyone help him down. It was too bad; he might have made a great fireman in every other way, but if you can't stand the heights, you don't get past probie school.

To get practical experience in fighting fires while we were still in school, we spent every Saturday night of our nine weeks assigned to duty with a fire company. I was assigned to 17 Truck in the Bronx (which I had requested) and I remember the first night I went up there. I was full of curiosity. Probie school couldn't prepare anyone for what the real thing would be like, but now I was about to find out. Would there be a big fire? Would I know enough to do anything right in the eyes of professionals? I walked through big firehouse doors for the first time in my life and told the man on house watch who I was. He hollered back into the firehouse, "Hey! The probie's here!"

The fact was that 17 Truck hadn't had a probie assigned to them in eight years. Nobody had left the 28-man company in all that time. It was an outfit composed of veterans, and they covered one of the toughest sections in the whole city. I might have expected them to be a surly bunch who wouldn't welcome a rookie with anything but contempt, but within five minutes I knew they weren't that way at all.

The group or "tour" that was on duty the night I arrived was the usual six firemen and one lieutenant. The firemen invited me into their "sitting room" at the rear of the firehouse where they started kidding me in a good-natured way, feeling my muscles and that sort of thing and saying, "Well, what have we got here? Is this kid going to be any good or isn't he?" I told them I had an uncle, Bill Rath, on 29 Truck, which was nearby in the Bronx, and they said, "Well, we'll have to have a talk to him about you." Then they showed me all over the firehouse, told me where things were, and then they said I'd better go upstairs and introduce myself to the "Loo," which is what firemen call their lieutenant. I went up to the second floor to meet a man who would have an influence on me for the rest of my days as a fireman.

Lieutenant Radican was called Packy. He was a man in his forties, a little gray in his hair already, with a warm and friendly manner. He told me to sit down and started telling me what to expect. There'd be a lot of needling, he told me, and if I couldn't take it, life would be rough. I said I was sure I could manage. Then he asked me why I had chosen 17 Truck in the South Bronx for my first duty. I told him it was because I wanted to be in a busy fire company so I could learn faster. He looked at me for a minute and then he said, "Yeah, sure, but not everybody wants to do that so I thought I'd ask."

I must have seemed like a pretty naïve kid, despite my 26

years. I remember telling Radican that I wanted to be the best fireman I could, or something like that, and he said, "Okay, I'll help you. When we go into fires tonight or any other time, wherever I go, you go with me. I'm responsible for you and I'll try to teach you all I know." Then he asked me if I smoked and I said no. Drink? No. "Fine. Go downstairs then and join the men. They'll show you how to slide down the pole and a few other things you might as well learn right away."

It would be interesting to report that there was a big blaze somewhere that night, but there wasn't. All I saw were a couple of rubbish fires in empty lots, and that certainly wasn't very dramatic. But the firemen let me handle the small extinguishers, and when my tour was up at 9 A.M. the next morning I felt like I was a real fireman.

Monday morning in school, Captain McGinty asked all the probies how they had liked their first night in a firehouse. I heard some mutterings and complaints. Apparently, some of the new men had been asked to wash the dishes, and they didn't like it. McGinty explained that there wasn't anything unusual about that; when you're a probie you get all the dirt, he said. Washing dishes didn't sound so bad to me. I washed them at home for my mother.

My second Saturday night with 17 Truck was more interesting. We had a two-alarm fire in a mattress factory and it generated the worst kind of smoke. When we rolled into the block, 17's firemen were saying, "We got something!" and you could see they were excited. So was I! I'd seen some big fires at a distance during the war, but I'd never been *in* one. This factory was big; it filled an entire city block. The fire seemed to be on the second floor, and our company's job was to locate the exact origin of the fire so we could direct the engine company in with the hoselines. To do this we had to go right into the blackest wall of smoke I'd ever seen. We didn't have the Scott airpacs that firemen use today, either. We just had to stay low and breathe whatever air we could find.

Lieutenant Radican told me to hang onto the back of his coat as we worked our way to the second floor. "I don't want to lose you," he said, and I had to agree; I certainly didn't want to get lost in this place. I couldn't see anything more than three feet away. I had an axe in one hand and I grabbed the back of the lieutenant's coat with the other. I realized I wasn't making much of a contribution. I wasn't even sure how long I could stand these conditions without rushing back to the fresh air in the street again. I was coughing and the tears were running out of my eyes and at one point I thought I was going to be sick. My determination to be a superfireman was being put to a tough test, and I wasn't at all sure I was going to pass it.

Then, as we pressed forward on the second floor, groping with our hands, stumbling with our feet, I noticed Radican was coughing and spitting and so were the other guys around us. I could hear them cursing the stuff as they retched in the darkness. That made me feel a little better. At least the conditions affected all of us the same. Years of experience as a fireman didn't make smoke any less poisonous, apparently.

Pretty soon the fire was located and the engine came in and started soaking the mess. Venting the roof lifted the smoke and cleared the air. When I could see again, I let go of Radican's coat and pitched in with my axe and a hook, helping "overhaul" after the fire was out. Then we all went out in the street where the Red Cross had its coffee wagon set up. One of the guys from 17—I didn't even know his name yet—brought me my coffee and a sandwich. "Gee, thanks," I said. "You didn't need to do that for me." And this big guy in his battle-scarred fireman's clothes just shrugged and said, "So I did it for you, so what?" That made me feel good.

When we got back to quarters, everybody got washed up first and then I was told to clean up the tools on the truck— all the axes, hooks and other stuff that was dirty from use at the fire. While I was busy doing this, I saw Radican come down the stairs and go into the sitting room where the men were having more coffee. I heard him say, "How did the probie do?" and one of the men spoke up and said, "Hell, he's better than some of the guys we got here already!" That remark got a laugh from the others, of course, but I could tell he wasn't joking. Boy, how that sounded!

I had all the axes clean by then, but suddenly I felt so good that I decided to take them all over to a grinding wheel and put a good sharp edge on them, too.

THE CHIEF WHO MADE US LAUGH

Firemen have a phrase they use when they talk about a moment of emotional relief in the middle of hours of a tough job. We say "It took the edge off." A joke at the right moment, a laugh, a bit of bitter humor, even if it sometimes has to be at someone else's expense. One of the duties of leadership, it always seemed to me, was to know when the edge had to be taken off, when, in the middle of a long, rough fight against a fire, the men had had just about enough. It wasn't always easy to come up with a joke or a prank at precisely the right moment, but over a good number of years I could always count on one particular battalion chief to provide us with a chance for a laugh.

Everyone called him Waxey because he had a handlebar moustache which he kept handsomely groomed with some stuff called Canard Wax. It was such a long and imposing affair that it was probably a fire hazard, come to think of it. Waxey was in his sixties, nearing retirement age. He was the perfect throwback to the grand old firemen of the horse-and-steamer age. He wore his turnout coat very long, almost to his ankles, like they did in the old days, and on his helmet he had a great golden eagle mounted as a custom touch. He was a very dedicated man, very sincere, but he took everything so seriously that he was a setup for jokes. Why he stood for so much of this prankster fun, I'll never know, except perhaps he'd been around enough fires to understand the meaning of "taking the edge off." At any rate, he was the perfect fall guy.

One day we were just getting the upper hand on a smoky fire in the basement of a shoestore when Waxey joined us. "How's it going, lieutenant?" he said, looking around and seemingly satisfied that we had things under control. I knew my guys were dead beat by now, but there was no relief in sight and we still had some hard work ahead of us before we could return to quarters. I decided it might be time to take the edge off.

Hanging near where Waxey was standing in the basement were the melted remains of what had been a wall telephone. The receiver was still in its proper place, but the intense heat of the fire had stretched it out to about double its normal length. The wires were charred black and the phone was obviously dead. But it was such a funny-looking thing, I thought it might make a good prop for a gag.

Waxey was just about finished with his inspection when I picked up the receiver and pretended to talk. "Hello?" I said. "I can't hear you very well. . . . Who do you want? . . . Who? . . . The chief?"

"It's for you, chief," I hollered, holding up the ridiculous-looking phone. "For me?" he asked, as if there were nothing particularly unusual about getting a call in the burned-out basement of a shoestore. He came to the phone, took the thing out of my hand and pushed one end up under his helmet to his ear.

By now, my guys are all watching the scene and they are nearly doubled up. They don't know whether to pay attention to the fire or see what's going to happen with the telephone. "Hello? Hello?" he says. Of course, there was no sound in the phone. Only then did good old Waxey notice that when the phone was at his ear, the mouthpiece was a foot away. He looked around the room for a minute, searching for a guilty smile, but he didn't find any so he stomped off. When he was out of range, we broke down laughing. Several hours of miserable hard work were suddenly forgotten and we could all go on as if somebody had put fresh batteries in us.

Waxey forgave us, as always, thank God—even when he'd come to the firehouse and somebody would lift the phone from the wall and say, "It's for you, chief. . . ."

MY FIRST ROAST

After graduating from probie school I was assigned permanently to 17 Truck. I would remain on probation for six months as the Johnny of the company, the rookie. I'd wash dishes and sweep floors and run errands and do all the small chores that the veterans found distasteful. I didn't mind. I realized that this was an old tradition in the Fire Department and that the way you reacted to it was crucial to other people's opinion of you. "Remember," Captain McGinty had said, "no matter what they ask you to do, smile!"

As a full-time fireman now, I worked shifts—8 A.M. to 4 P.M. 4 P.M. to 12 P.M.; 12 P.M. to 8 A.M. I had a little trouble getting used to this in the beginning, but I worked it out. I drove to work from Long Island to the Bronx, and day by day, week by week, I learned my new trade. I was surprised to see how many of the things we learned in probie school were falling into place. Of course, there are some things they can never teach you in any school. There's just no way of telling a young fireman how hot his ears will feel in the middle of a fire. And there's no way to tell him what the screams of a dying person will sound like the first time he hears them in a burning building. I was in 17 Truck for several months before we had our first "roast." That's what firemen call a fire in which someone is burned to death. It may sound like a callous phrase, but it isn't meant that way. A roast is always a tragedy, and a young fireman's first roast is an unforgettable thing. At least it was for me.

The fire was at 501 Brook Avenue in one of those old tenement buildings that are the hallmark of the South Bronx. It was on the fifth floor of the building and was going pretty good when we rolled up. It looked like there may have been a few minutes' delay in turning in the alarm, because the smoke was really rolling out. We were the first company to arrive and we went right about our duties. A "truck company" is Fire Department shorthand for a "hook-and-ladder outfit." Our prime responsibility when we arrive at a fire is to get the doors open if they are locked, get into the building fast, find the fire, and vent—meanwhile making a quick search for any people who may be trapped. The engine company is never very far behind the truck company, of course. "Engine" means the pumper, the truck that takes water from the street hydrant and pumps it out through hoselines under great pressure.

Lieutenant Radican led the way up the stairs. I followed, carrying a 2 1/2-gallon water extinguisher. I was still the Johnny, of course, so I stuck to my officer and watched every move he made. I had absolute faith that no one knew more about fires than he did, and up to now, I'd never had any reason to question his judgment.

When we got to the fifth-floor hall, the door to the rear apartment was open and we could see that the fire had probably started back there, because the rooms at that end were really roaring.

Over the noise of the fire I could hear some hollering from the rear. Screaming was more like it. Radican and I were down on our knees now because the heat in the hall was building fast and there can be several hundred degrees' difference in temperature between two feet off the floor and six feet. Only by keeping low could we survive at all. It would be another minute or two, maybe more, before the engine would be up with water. The screams kept coming. I didn't have to ask what they meant. I just looked at Radican, and he nodded. Together, we started to move down the hall toward the rear. There was too much smoke to see clearly, but there seemed to be a door all the way back on the right and the screams were coming from there.

I'd never been in such a situation before. Another human being was only 20 or 30 feet away, unseen, but crying for my help. The sheer animal tone of those cries was frightening, but it also made me mad. I wanted to run through the flames, tear at the walls, do anything to pull that person out of danger. What was keeping us? We were firemen, weren't we? Was there something I hadn't learned to do?

We moved a few more feet down the hall, but the fire was coming over our heads now and the heat made my lungs feel like they were on fire. That was the answer to my question: We were human, too. That's what was holding us back. There was only so much we could take. But the screams continued. Whoever was in there was taking more than we were. The cries came in rhythmic sequence—one with each dying breath, I thought. They bellowed at us, accusingly. Now I was afraid to hear them stop.

The fire extinguisher I was carrying was probably useless. But if I could just get to the doorway and aim a stream at the man inside, couldn't I save him? The linoleum was beginning to melt under our boots and we slipped as we crawled. Radican signaled me to turn around, back out. He was shaking his head no. Back out, he said. Back out. At first I couldn't believe it. Weren't we going to do all we could to save the person in that room? Radican kept shaking his head and ordering me back.

Behind us on the stairs I could hear the Engine coming

now, the heavy sounds of the hose being humped along. As the men's heads came level with the fifth floor, they opened the nozzle and started playing a solid stream of water on the hall ceiling. The crashing sound was louder than the fire and they moved forward behind the water, blowing in the doors of the apartments with the power of the stream. Finally, they reached the end of the hall. Radican and I worked our way up behind the enginemen, but now the screams from within this last room had stopped. We pushed open the door, and the man with the nozzle quickly killed the last of the flames inside. When they died the room went totally black, a burned-out shell, full of steam and charred wood—and a body.

It was still hot as an oven when I crawled in. The humid heat that comes right after water goes on a fire is sometimes worse than the dry heat of the flames themselves. It slips into your clothes like scalding steam. I crawled for about ten feet, feeling in front of me with my gloved hands. Radican was behind me, searching in another direction. Then I felt what had to be a bed in front of me. I searched along the frame, then up over the edge of a mattress, and then I touched my first roast.

When the smoke cleared and they brought lights, we could see that he had been a young man, maybe in his twenties. He was a ghastly sight, all drawn up in a ball, all burst open, the bones of his knees coming through his skin. I knew that things like this were part of every fireman's experience sooner or later and I tried to keep cool about it. I helped the other men put the corpse into a body bag. Then, in a while, we all went back to quarters.

After we had washed up, the men were sitting around talking about the roast. Radican saw me sitting a little apart from the group. I was listening, but I didn't feel like talking. I think he knew my mind was full of confused thoughts. He motioned to me to come upstairs to his office. We went up without saying anything, and then he closed the door behind us and invited me to sit down. He went over to his desk and pulled a bottle of Irish whiskey out of the bottom drawer, poured himself a glass, gulped it down, then offered me one. I said no thanks, I didn't drink, not even after a roast.

Radican came right to the point then. "What are you thinking about what happened tonight?" he asked.

I said, "Well, I'm still wondering if we might not have saved that guy somehow, Loo. I mean, we had the extinguisher with us. Couldn't we have made a dash for him somehow? Those screams were terrible. I felt we had to do more than we did."

"Okay," said Radican, "let's talk about it." And he explained how advanced the fire was when we got to the floor, how there was no sign of the Engine coming soon with the water, how the linoleum was starting to melt, how quickly two and a half gallons of water would evaporate in the face of such furnacelike heat. I just listened. I knew he was right. The lieutenant was a veteran. He didn't like a roast any more than anyone else, but he'd seen enough fires so he could calculate odds better than I could. "The guy didn't have a chance," Radican explained. "Even if we'd been able to get to him, he probably would have been dead or dying." His analysis was like a baseball player knowing whether a runner on first can make third on a single to center. He puts all the variables together in the equation: the speed of the runner, the sharpness of the hit, the strength of the fielder's arm. . . .

Radican put the bottle back in the drawer then, stood up, shook some drops from his glass and said, "We're only expected to do so much, you know. We're not supposed to kill ourselves in hopeless causes. I don't want this thing to stay on your mind and bother you."

I said I wouldn't brood about it, and then I thanked him and went back downstairs. The others were finished talking about the roast by then, too. In a few minutes the bells came in again and we were all pulling on the boots and rolling out the big doors on the truck.

Some nights there wasn't even time to clean the tools between alarms.

DEAD OR ALIVE?

Firemen are in the business of saving lives. We aren't doctors, but we are supposed to know when somebody is dead or whether there is some sign of life to be supported. Sometimes in my experience it was a fine line, and maybe sometimes we played God. There were some people who surely looked dead, but on whom we never wanted to give up—and there were some people obviously still "alive" for whom death seemed the only merciful solution.

I remember the automobile packed with six adults which spun around one night at Bedford Avenue and Madison Street in Brooklyn. It had then careened across the street and struck a storefront backwards. The gas tank ruptured and the whole thing went up like a bomb. By the time we got there, there was nothing to do but douse the flames and remove the corpses. It was going to be a rough job. The fire had been so hot and had burned for so long that the bodies were welded together, three in the front seat, three in the back. It was such a complete roast that you couldn't really tell males from females. They were just six charred hulks, motionless, expressionless, their arms and bodies locked together like a piece of weird modern sculpture.

We pried the doors open and I leaned into the back seat to decide what would be the best way of removing these awful remains when I saw the figure in the center move slightly and make the sound of breathing. In an instant, red bubbles of blood appeared where the mouth had been. They rose and fell, popping and gurgling. This (I think) woman was still alive! Incredibly, deep inside her cooked body, life was struggling, lungs were moving, a heart was still beating. It was one of the most horrible sights I can remember in all my years as a fireman.

Now the problem. Should I take all the swift and routine measures I had taken so often to save the last visible flicker of life in a fellow human's body? Oxygen? Resuscitator? Mouth-to-mouth? I almost vom-

ited at the latter thought. I was faced with a decision. I made it by turning my attention to the occupants of the front seat who were, thank God, perfectly still and perfectly dead. I gave orders to the men about some cutting tools we needed, then I walked around the car, calculating the problem someone else was going to have in getting it off the sidewalk. After a minute or two of stalling, I looked into the back seat again. The bubbles had stopped.

On another day in another place, the little seven-year-old girl whose body lay on the sidewalk seemed as still as her dead mother who lay next to her. We had pulled them both out of a raging tenement fire, victims not of the flames but of deadly smoke poisoning. A doctor had checked their hearts, their pulses, their eyes, their vital signs and said they were dead. It was a scene firemen see too often. But this time something about the girl seemed different. Dead? Despite the doctor's verdict she didn't look quite *dead to me. Two firemen were huddled over her, operating the resuscitator.*

"We've got a real good cycle on her, Loo," one of the men said, meaning a good rhythm of induced breathing. Sometimes it worked if you were patient. At this point we could leave her there on the street with the doctor's Dead On Arrival tag, or we could take her in our truck to the hospital. "Let's take her with us, Loo," Jackie Farrell said, and we did.

They put the small body on one of the big tool shelves in the back of the Rescue truck and they never stopped the good cycle while we honked and sirened our way toward Cumberland Hospital. From the front seat I could see five firemen around the shelf, boots and coats still on, intent on only one thing.

Then came the cry: "She's breathing, Loo! She's breathing! On her own, no resuscitator!" There was a tumult of joy in the rear of the truck.

I looked ahead into the traffic, at all the people moving about and I was glad we hadn't left the little girl with her mother.

7

I CALLED HER GINNY

I wasn't much for romancing girls. That doesn't mean I didn't like girls, it just means that I had a certain independence that I couldn't seem to help. When I was a kid in West Virginia, it was always other boys I was most anxious to impress. Oh, sure, there were girls around the carbide-company dam who thought I was something, and I didn't mind girls cheering my home runs in baseball. But I just wasn't the romantic type. I guess I didn't know how to be. I had no sisters and I saw very little of my mother over the years, so females were something I didn't understand very well.

There were a few times when Melba Mathias and I had nice talks alone, and Tippy's sister in Hawaii liked me a lot, I think. But somehow there was always something that seemed

65

more important to me. It was still that way in the summer of 1950 when I was with the DPW. It was so much on my mind to do a good job that I wasn't looking around for much social life. Besides, I didn't like girls to try and tie me down. If one of them asked me when she was going to see me again after a date, I'd be likely to say, "Well, gee, I just saw you today. . . . Maybe in a week or so?"

About this time my younger brother, Tommy, was working for the Civil Aeronautics Authority at what was then called Idlewild Airport on Long Island and he was dating a girl named Virginia Prigge who also worked for the CAA. One night he came home after a date and told me he had volunteered me and my car to take Virginia and two of her girl friends up to a place called Williams Lake the next day. Since this Williams Lake was near the two-acre plot of property that my mother and brothers owned up near the Catskills, Tommy thought I wouldn't mind. He also knew I was looking for any excuse to drive and show off my new car!

The next morning Tommy and I arrived promptly at Virginia's house. I had never met this girl before, but a very funny thing happened when I saw her come out the front door. I can't explain it even today, but at that moment I suddenly *knew* that this girl was going to be my wife. Nothing like this had ever happened to me before, but they say when love strikes, you know it. I certainly did.

We had a nice ride up to the lake. I had all I could do to concentrate on my driving because Virginia seemed to be directing most of her conversation to me. I noticed this was having an irritating effect on my brother, by the way!

I didn't see Virginia again for several months. After all, she was Tommy's girl and I didn't want any family trouble. But I thought about her often. Then, in October, I found out that Tommy wasn't dating Virginia anymore, so I decided now was the time to call her. When I did, she said yes, she remembered who I was, and agreed to a date.

After our first date I knew that for the first time in my life I had found a girl who seemed to have real warmth—and a real concern for me. Love had always been a scarce commodity in my life. I had taught myself to do without it and found other things to take its place—my constant pursuit of excellence, for example. But when love came along, I at least knew enough to recognize it.

We didn't have too many dates that month of November because of my new hours at probie school. Besides, Ginny was still pretty well booked up with dates with other fellows. Her popularity made me jealous! But by December of 1950 we were a twosome, and on New Year's Eve I proposed and she accepted. We were married October 7, 1951. She was 19, I was 27.

In the beginning we lived with Ginny's parents, but because we were both working we didn't have much time with each other and we longed for a place of our own where we could be alone. Eventually we found a house in Wantagh, Long Island, that we thought we could afford and we managed to scrape together just enough cash for the down payment. A home of our own at last!

Life is never easy for a fireman's wife, but I suppose those early years were the most difficult for Ginny. She was aware of the risks in my work and whenever I was on duty she worried about my safety. She always listened to the radio news when I was at work and if she heard of a fire in my area she would say prayers. When I worked nights, a telephone call was enough to give my young wife a numbing stab of fear.

There were other firemen who lived in our area, but Ginny didn't like to get together with their wives. Firemen's wives are notorious gossips, always full of tales about hanky-panky around the firehouse, or drinking or gambling bouts. Ginny believed in me; she didn't want to hear this stuff. But that cut off some companionship.

Things changed somewhat for the better when our first child, Richard Junior, was born on October 9, 1953. Now Ginny had something important to occupy her. She worked very hard at being a good mother to this boy of ours.

I guess it goes without saying that we didn't have a lot of

money. A Third Grade fireman was making about $300 a month in those days, and what with mortgage payments and trying to furnish and fix up a new house, things were always tight. Like most firemen, of course, I was a pretty steady moon-lighter. I'd find jobs working on new houses or sometimes I did appliance-repair work, or anything I could find that would bring in a few extra bucks.

I was determined that I wasn't going to be uprooted again. I was digging in. I'd found love and affection for the first time in my life. I had a son, a home of my own, a job I liked, a boss I could respect. Packy Radican was the kind of boss everybody should be so lucky to have. I remember saying to myself, Why couldn't my father have been like this man? That's how I felt about him.

Everything was going so good, I should have known it wouldn't last.

GOODBYE TO A FRIEND

The fire was at Lincoln Place in a tenement. It started out like all the others, but it ended up in tragedy. I'd been with 17 Truck for a couple of years by now, and there was getting to be a routine feeling about responding to alarms like this one. The excitement I felt at my earliest fires, when I went in holding onto the back of Lieutenant Radican's coat, had passed. Technically, I was still the Johnny of the company, but nobody needed to feel responsible for me. I'd seen enough of death and danger so I knew this was no kid's game I was in. A fireman does a lot of growing up in two years. Radican knew this, too. He said to me once that I might still be his junior man but that I'd been weaned. I was glad he realized that.

When we got into the building at Lincoln Place the fire was

going strong on one of the top floors and the chief ordered our company to take a hoseline from Engine 83 and go after it. Truck companies are sometimes asked to take a line into a fire for a variety of reasons and we knew how to handle the job, yet it wasn't something we did every day. The satisfaction of aiming those powerful streams of water at the flames is usually reserved for the firemen in engine companies. Whenever somebody else gets his hands on the big brass nozzle and 240 gallons of water a minute, there's a certain extra thrill. Being "on the nob" is something every fireman loves because it's the point of the attack on the enemy.

This time, when Radican got the order to stretch the line, he gave the job to me. "Take it in, Hamilton," he said, which meant I was going to be on the nob for the first time. Two or three other firemen came along with me because handling a 2 1/2-inch line is never a one-man job. With Radican leading the way, we worked our way up the stairs of the old building, hauling the heavy line behind us, waiting for the moment when we could open 'er up. When we finally reached the floor where the fire was, Radican leaned close to my ear and said, "Okay, let's move right down this hall, room to room, and show 'em we know how to do the job." There was always something about the way this man said things that made me want to knock myself out for him.

We kicked in one door and hit the room hard and fast with the water, then moved to a second room down the hall and did the same. The heat was bad, and the steam made it worse, but because I was given this chance to show what I could do, I wasn't thinking of any discomforts, I was just trying to impress my boss. All we had to do now was hit that third room, then shut down and get out. Quick and neat, that's the way professionals do it, I was saying to myself. I could already feel the fresh air blowing on me at the back of the truck as we returned to quarters. Then I felt something else.

Someone seemed to be leaning on my back as I tried to move toward the last room. It was one of the other guys with me, but what was he doing falling on me like that? I turned my head to see who it was and all I could see was a lieutenant's frontpiece on a helmet which was hanging over my shoulder. Radican!

I said, "Are you all right, Loo?" which isn't the kind of question a Johnny usually has to ask his officer, in fact it would be an insult except I could see something was wrong. Radican wasn't leading us down the hall anymore, he wasn't even paying attention to the fire. He was just leaning on me. Then he said, "Dick, can you get me out of here?" The use of a first name in the middle of a fire was unusual in itself, and the tone of command had gone out of his voice. Something was seriously wrong, but we hadn't been exposed to enough heat or gas or anything else in this hall to explain it.

I handed the nozzle over to one of the other men, fireman "Footsie" Curry and started backing out, dragging the lieutenant behind me. He was almost dead weight. I knew they were kicking in the last door down the hall and heard the *whoomp* of the water as it hit the fire, but I was more interested in what was wrong with my officer. I knew I couldn't get him out of the building alone, so I waited for help at the top of the stairs. I took his helmet off and held his head in the bend of one arm. He was barely conscious but he knew who I was. "I don't feel good," was all he said, and then closed his eyes. When he opened them again he said I should be sure to remember all the things he'd taught me. I said, "Sure, sure, Loo, but first we've got to get you out into some fresh air."

Two other firemen came up the stairs just then, and the three of us picked Radican up and took him down the stairs as gently as we could.

When we reached the street-level vestibule of the building, there was the usual confusion of firemen and tools and hoselines and people hollering, and nobody paid any particular attention to our arrival with our sick comrade because there's nothing unusual about a fireman staggering out of a building after he's had a bit too much smoke. I hollered for someone to bring the oxygen, and while we waited, squatting down against the wall where all the mailboxes were, Radican made another effort to speak. He was dirty from the fire, his voice was weak and he smiled just a little.

"You're a good guy, Dick," he said. "Thanks for the help. And remember, don't get in with the wrong crowd." Then, just like in the movies, his head turned, his eyes closed, and he was gone. Packy had died right there in my arms.

We tried the oxygen, of course, and they took him to the hospital in an ambulance in the next few minutes, but his heart had failed. The guy I had learned to love like a father was gone.

What was the matter with me? Why was I always losing things? Is this the way life is supposed to be? I was sad and angry at the same time. This job killed people in more ways than one. Who would it take next? Not me, I had no fear of that. But Radican's death brought an end to a chapter. As long as I had him to look up to, I was still a rookie. Now I had something more to accomplish.

Later in the year we had a memorial service for Packy at the firehouse. It was the first one of these melancholy affairs I'd ever been to and it made quite an impression on me. We moved the apparatus out onto the street and hung black crepe over the door and made the place as spotless as it had ever been. The fire commissioner came, and Packy's widow, and there was a priest to say the invocation and the prayers. Everyone stood at attention in their dress uniforms and white gloves as they unveiled a bronze plaque on the wall which said what a good man the lieutenant had been and how much his company respected his leadership. It had been several months since he'd died, but this brought it all back to me. His widow told me how much her husband had thought of me, his Johnny, and how often he had talked about me at home. I didn't know what to say. I didn't know anybody ever talked about me.

When it was over they tolled the big chrome bell on the truck for Packy. It was the same clanging, shouting bell he had yanked on when we went to fires, but this morning it was wrapped with a towel and the sound it made was muffled and sad, as if it came from afar.

So now he was gone. All gone? Forever gone? I hoped not.

I hoped that something of my first Loo would remain in me so I could pass it on to my own probies someday. That was the only way his death made any sense.

Now I had the expectations of two fine people to live up to: Captain McGinty and Lieutenant Radican. I won't say that the responsibility weighed on me—I wasn't that egotistical—but I certainly wouldn't have wanted to let these men down. I started thinking about my career in the Fire Department and where it was leading me. I liked 17 Truck all right, it was a busy company; but I was looking for the next rung to climb.

My Uncle Bill kept talking about rescue companies, how they were the élite of the Fire Department. You couldn't get into a rescue outfit until you were a First-Grade fireman—that is, been in for three years—and even then there wasn't any more money in it, just prestige. People like my uncle, who knew what the rescue companies did and the challenges they faced in the line of duty, had a tremendous respect for them. Of course, I knew a few wise-apples who said Rescue was no better than anybody else, but on the basis of what I'd seen myself I didn't agree. In my eyes the men with Rescue 3 in the Bronx were superfiremen.

I knew there was only one rescue outfit in each of the main boroughs of New York City, four all together, about 100 men total. Out of a 12,000-man department, that sounded exclusive to me. I decided to find out more about it. When I went to fires where Rescue 3 was called on the same alarm, I'd watch everything their men did, and if I got the chance, I'd talk with some of them.

One thing I noticed: They were disciplined and thorough. Every move they made was smooth and professional, and they never walked away from any job leaving it half finished. They obviously knew what they were doing—and they had a range of skills far beyond those of the average fireman. They had fantastic tools on their truck and they knew how to use them all. They were also big guys, all of them looked well over six feet and strong. The more I watched them, the more I began to feel they must be the best firemen in the whole world. I wanted to be one of them.

What I didn't know was that all the while I was watching the Rescue guys, they were watching me. I don't know what to thank for this. Maybe it was the fact that I'm just geared to hustle, never to loaf on a job. Maybe I learned something about thoroughness and perfection from my father. Maybe it was this little extra drive I've always had to *be* somebody. Whatever it was, Captain McGinty had noticed it, Lieutenant Radican had noticed it and now, wonder of wonders, the men in Rescue saw it, too.

I found out about my good luck from Captain Klepper of 17 Truck who called me into the office one day in the fall of 1953 and said I might be transferred to Rescue 3 if I was interested. If I was interested! But how could this be happening? I wasn't even a First-Grade fireman yet; I had several months to go before I would have three years in the department. Phelan didn't know the reasons. Maybe my uncle had something to do with it. The mystery made me uneasy. There wasn't anything in the world I wanted more, but I didn't want to make the move as some kind of a privileged character. When the big doors of Rescue 3 swung wide for Richard Hamilton, I wanted it to be kosher, no special deals, nothing that might jeopardize my success with the company. I wanted this opportunity too much to louse it up. That's what I told the captain.

Maybe I was being overcautious. At any rate, I stayed with 17 Truck until my three years were up and I'd made First Grade. Then the call came again. I could go to Rescue 3 on a six-month trial basis. I found out later that every man in the Rescue had voted to get me, they'd been watching me that long. The captain told them that anybody who didn't want Hamilton in the company could just put a note in the box. In those days they used to have the power of blackballing any new man. There weren't any votes against me.

I was five-foot-ten and a half, 160 pounds, but I felt like a giant.

TYRONE

When someone runs up to the doors of the firehouse and hollers that there's a fire down the street, that's what we call a verbal alarm. You inform the dispatcher and you roll—quick. There's a special feeling about an alarm in your own neighborhood. These people are your friends; it's the guy you know next door who's going up in smoke; you can't help but hustle a little faster.

This time was back in '61. I hadn't been at Rescue 2 very long. The verbal came in and we rolled about four blocks up the street to an old tenement building already fully involved with fire at the rear. I ran in the front door and down the hall to the last room at the back because I guessed that's where the fire had started. I kicked in the door and found the room fully ablaze and two little kids in their underwear crawling around on the floor among a bunch of overturned paint cans. The cans were burning, the floor was slippery with paint and burning —and the kids were burning. They had apparently started their own fire.

The younger of the two was about four years old. He seemed to have gotten into a container of shellac, and flames were sputtering all over him. The other boy was about seven and he wasn't as bad off. But there was no time to help either of them, except to get them out of that room as quickly as possible. I made a swooping grab for the little fellow, slipped in the paint and almost went sprawling myself. As soon as I could get my legs under me again, I grabbed the bigger one, too, tucked each of them under an arm and got out of there quick.

As soon as we were out of the building, other firemen rushed up with extinguishers and blankets and the two kids were rolled and sprayed until the flames that were eating at them were put out. Then they went to the hospital.

The little one's name was Tyrone something-or-other. After a good deal of time, we saw him playing around the neighborhood again. He *was pretty badly disfigured. His mouth was twisted to one side, his hands were bad, and he walked with a funny gait. All of us at Rescue took an interest in the kid. If people asked me about him, how come he was so badly burned, I'd tell them that Tyrone was one of my souvenirs. Another 30 seconds in that fire and he might have been a statistic instead.*

As he grew up, Tyrone needed frequent operations on his knees to enable him to bend them freely and to walk. He told me once that his parents couldn't afford to have this done for him—not surprising in our neighborhood—so I called the Welfare people to investigate the case and see what could be done. Tyrone got his operations, but I don't think his parents cared whether he did or not.

As the boy grew up, a relationship grew between him and the firemen. We knew him; he knew us. He went by the firehouse a dozen times a day when he started school, and somebody always said "Hi, Tyrone" to him. We used to bring him clothes he could wear, sneakers, a baseball glove.

Then 1967 came, and the race riots, and, as I said, some days and nights things got pretty ugly in the Bedford-Stuyvesant section of Brooklyn. Fireman were stoned, shot at and cursed. Garbage cans were dumped in front of the firehouse doors. Fire trucks were attacked, and bricks were tossed from rooftops while we were trying to do our job at fires.

One day we heard rocks hitting the front of the firehouse and the crash of glass bottles breaking. Across the street, a gang of kids was taunting us, throwing anything handy, calling us pigs. Some of the gang were teen-agers, some were younger. They milled around, leaderless, and we watched them with a mixture of pity and contempt. Then we saw a familiar face among them. Tyrone. He hurled a bottle that ricocheted in the street and skidded in under the Rescue truck. The same truck that had taken him to the hospital.

9

I JOIN THE GIANTS

Up to now I'd been just a fireman. Not that that isn't something to be proud of—if you're a good one. But the day I walked into Rescue 3's firehouse in the South Bronx I had to learn to become a fireman-plus. A superfireman, if you will. A jack-of-all trades: high-wire artist, doctor, frogman, psychologist, engineer. The three years I'd put in in the Fire Department so far were merely basic training for what I had to learn now.

I knew that's the way it would be, but it all became real for me the moment a big man stuck out his hand and said, "I'm Howie Wanser, welcome to Rescue." Howie Wanser! So that was his name! I'd seen him at fires. He was one of the giants. So was Lieutenant Bill Beck, a former major in the Army Corps

of Engineers. Between them, they worked hard to make a rescueman out of me.

"When the bells come in for us," Wanser explained the
first day, "it could mean anything. Remember that. It's not just
smoke and flames anymore. It could be an ammonia leak, and
you have to know what to do about it. You have to know that
when carbon tet heats up, it makes phosgene gas, which is
deadly. You have to know which way the current may be
pulling a kid who's fallen through the ice. You have to know
the difference between the symptoms of heart attacks and
strokes. You have to know the smell of chlorine, methane,
propane. . . ."

As Wanser talked, my head was reeling, but I listened
hard.

The Rescue truck itself was all new to me, too, a big
enclosed affair that housed a bewildering array of specialized
tools: chain saws, circular saws, ring cutters; oxygen bottles,
inhalators, resuscitators, Scott airpacs; mechanical jacks, hy-
draulic jacks, wedges, blocks; ropes, safety belts, blocks and
tackle, harnesses; tools to pry with, to bend with, to open things
with, to close things with; canvas stretchers, wire Stokes bas-
kets, plastic body bags, blankets, sterile sheets; explosive me-
ters, Geiger counters, pressure gauges; rubber exposure suits,
first-aid kits, splints, tourniquets, burn sprays, compresses; electric generators, emergency searchlights, assortments of fuels,
lubricants, storage batteries; welding torches, cutting torches;
fittings for gas lines, steam lines, electric lines; extinguishers full
of foam, water, dry chemicals . . .

The first time I went out in the Rescue truck on an alarm
I felt an altogether new emotion. A siren on a hook and ladder
didn't mean anything to me anymore; it was just a big noise that
a lot of other people in the street didn't pay attention to either.
But inside the Rescue truck, the feeling of speed was much
greater and the siren had a new sound. To my ear it spelled out
the word R E S C U E—we're coming, we're coming! It wasn't
just a fire, it was an emergency if we were called. Six giants in

a big red box. Suicide? Building collapse? Fire bombing? We were on our way.

Of course, there were just plain fires, too. Each rescue company has a local area—call it the neighborhood—where it responds to ordinary alarms just like any other fire company. We also go to any big fire which is an all-hands situation, and to all multiple-alarms. Rescue is special.

I soon found out that there wasn't as much sitting around the firehouse for a rescue company as there can be for engine and truck companies. Because of the wide variety of problems we were called to face, training drills were important—and frequent. Almost every day, from after lunch until 2:30, if we weren't out on an alarm we were practicing something. We'd go out to the railroad yards and find an empty boxcar and pretend there was somebody stuck under it. Then Lieutenant Beck would say, "Okay, let's see how we'd lift this car off a person." We'd go to refrigeration plants and drill on gas leaks. Factories. Warehouses. Stables. Swimming pools. Breweries. We went to them all. We'd find an abandoned car in the street and we'd use it to practice on. "Let's see how fast we can cut the top off this one!" Howie Wanser would say.

At night, in the firehouse, we drilled some more. Charts. Lectures by the Loo. This is how this works. Here's how you take this tool apart.

Ever since I joined 17 Truck I had kept a notebook of my own. It was full of facts that were important to me. Things to remember. If some fireman told me a story with a lesson in it, I'd write it down. If I figured out the best way to dig the dirt out of a cave-in, I made a note of it. When I discovered how to shut down a runaway diesel engine by putting a blanket over the air intake, I wrote it down. Sometimes, when I was on house watch, I'd just take my book out and review it. I called it my bible. After I got to Rescue 3, the bible grew very rapidly.

I was used to being a Johnny, of course. That's all I'd ever been at 17 and I sure was a rookie at Rescue 3. I was very sensitive to the way the men were reacting to me and my work.

I knew I was on a six months' trial, knew I had a lot to live up to. I looked for clues as to how the others were accepting me, knowing they must be watching me now, just as they had been watching me when I was at 17 Truck. Did the fact that I was smaller than most rescuemen matter to them? Apparently not. In fact, sometimes they found me a handy size in tight quarters. Big Wanser would lift me up into scuttles and hatches overhead like I was his kid brother. We worked well together as a team —and, oh, what that meant to me!

I remember the first time we went up to vent a roof together. There was a good hot fire underneath that roof and the tar was beginning to turn liquid. I wasn't sure whether we should go out on it or not. Some truckies from another company seemed to have the same question because they were standing around on the adjoining roof when Wanser just climbed over into the running tar, took a huge belt at the roof with his axe and hollered to me, "Looks like it will hold us, Dick. Come on!"

Success meant so much to me that I spent a lot of my own time practicing. I wasn't sure I was skillful enough with the axe, so I used to go out behind the firehouse and chop for hours, toughening my hands, sharpening my eye. I quizzed myself, too. What would I do if this tool broke? What would I use as a substitute? How quickly can I change this blade? Would it be better to use a saw or acetylene?

If I was in awe of the rescue company, that didn't mean that I couldn't see good and bad around me. Lieutenant Beck, for example, seemed like an ideal man for rescue work. He was thorough and he knew a lot about construction and engineering. He might not have had the compassion of Radican, nor the humor of McGinty, but he was a sharp, tough leader. I thought about these men and I constructed a composite officer, the man I would like to be. A little of one, a little of another. It may seem surprising, but as things turned out, there were one or two men in the outfit that I didn't want any part of. In the case of one lieutenant, this got me into a tough spot.

Call him Wiggins, a nice, easygoing, fun-loving guy, devil-may-care, light on the discipline, maybe a little too heavy on the booze. Oh, yes, the Fire Department has its share of those problem guys like any other organization. He didn't overdo the drinking, but it doesn't take much alcohol to make a man worthless in an emergency.

I found out about Lieutenant Wiggins the hard way in a hot, vicious fire in a wholesale meat market in Mott Haven. We were called because it was a multiple and because manpower was what was needed more than anything else. We were told to stretch a line for another company and go on into the building. I took the nozzle and we worked our way in until we could see that the main body of fire was on a mezzanine level where there were a lot of offices. To get to this level you had to go up some short iron stairs. The fire was being contained temporarily because the doors to the mezzanine offices were still closed, but the glow of flames coming through the glass partitions looked pretty ominous. When we got up there with the line we made a plan to leave the first door, the one in front of us, shut until we had water, *then* kick it open and hit the fire inside hard and fast. To open the door before that would only be inviting real trouble.

It usually only takes about a minute for a good MPO—motor pump operator—on an engine to get water into a hose-line. You can feel it coming. The line stretches, the nozzle hisses air, and you brace yourself. We still didn't have any of these clues when Lieutenant Wiggins hollered at us, "What's keeping you guys? Let's go!" Go where? I thought, holding the dry hose, but I didn't say anything. Then Wiggins rushed the first door, kicked it in, and the fire came out with such force that it nearly blew us all off the mezzanine. I tumbled backward down the stairs, the hoseline and the other men on top of me. We picked ourselves up in time to see Wiggins rushing off in another direction. "Stay out of our sight, Loo!" one of the men shouted after him. It was such a dumb thing to do, the men were really upset. We went back up the stairs then and worked on the fire until it was out, but there was a good deal of muttering about the stupid Loo once we got back to quarters.

I didn't see what good it would do, though, to sit around the kitchen and talk about this behind the officer's back. We were all in this dangerous business together, and although I had every respect for a lieutenant's rank, I didn't think he should be above criticism. I decided to go talk with Wiggins myself. I might have been only the Johnny of the outfit, but when the fire came out that door at me, my life had been put in danger. I put my courage in my pocket and climbed the stairs to the office. I knocked on the door, opened it and walked in. He was sitting at the desk making out reports. When I entered, he turned. Before he could say a word, I spoke. "Lieutenant," I said, "don't you *ever* do that to me again."

"I didn't realize," he said.

"Yes you did. You should have."

"I thought you had the water."

"You knew damn well we didn't."

Then he went over and sat on the bed and started to cry. I walked out.

Wiggins went his way eventually. He didn't belong in Rescue. But along with Beck and Wanser and some of the others, he taught me something. He taught me that there are firemen who can get other firemen in trouble.

I thought I knew a lot about the Bronx when I was with 17 Truck, but in my first few months with Rescue I saw and learned even more. Fights, stabbings, fire bombings. The kind of things that need emergency help—and sooner than any ambulance can get there. I came to recognize the look on a little kid's face when we pulled up to an alarm box and he said his mom and dad were having a terrible fight upstairs. These people didn't always know where they could find a cop, but they knew where the fire alarm was, and they knew we would be there in a minute or two. If someone got knifed and the blood was pumping fast or the blue-gray of his intestines spilling out, they dragged the victim to the alarm box, pulled it and ran. Alarm boxes don't talk, and those guys in the big Rescue truck knew what to do. They had stretchers and bandages and a radio to call for help.

Fire bombings were bad, often the result of jealous rows between husbands and wives, lovers, mistresses, pimps and whores. Flaming anger followed by flaming revenge. Two gallons of gasoline dumped in the vestibule of a tenement, followed by a match. In an instant a five-story building all in flames. Not just in the intended apartment, but roaring up through the stairways so firemen can't make a foot of progress until we have hoselines and lots of water.

You always knew it was a touch-off before the Rescue truck stopped rolling. Glass all over the street from the initial explosion. Smell of gasoline in the air. And then, inevitably, somebody tells you there was a terrible argument earlier. Curses. Threats.

The full moon brought them out of the woodwork. Arsonists. Sick people with a grudge. It was always worse when the moon was full. You could look at the calendar and know when you would be busy. Also the day the welfare checks arrived. They brought trouble, fights, false alarms around the bars.

For the most part I was glad to see that the men I was working with stayed pretty cool about the ugly world they were paid to protect. We didn't sit around grumbling about it much. We were supposed to help them all, the winos, the rotten kids, the jumpers, the nice family from Ohio visiting relatives in New York. What difference did it make? There wasn't ever time to pick your customers even if you wanted to.

Sometimes I felt like a young doctor trying to learn a lot about life and medicine by working in a big emergency room. The people passed through in a long parade, but what I was most interested in was perfecting my own skills. I still knew I had to be Number One. I had to be as good as Howie Wanser some day. Why not? Kids from broken homes can do just as much as any other kid, maybe more. Why not? I had my own home now, didn't I? And I had a son now who was named for me. If I could just get enough at-bats, I'd start hitting those home runs.

10

MRS. GRAZIANO'S
ROSE GARDEN

Sometimes when I look back at all the experiences I had as a fireman, my life seems like one long tour of duty, a continuous rolling out of the big firehouse doors in response to the never-ending alarm bells. How many times did I pull on the canvas coat and the boots and climb on a truck to answer a cry for help? Maybe 20,000, maybe more. No wonder most of the fires and car accidents and suicides over the 24 years have become a blur in my memory.

But there are some particular events I will always be able to recall in every detail. They are as clear in my mind as a siren in the night, and every move I made comes back slowly, precisely, frame by frame, like a movie you've seen many times.

Even the names of the people involved in these well-remembered episodes have become a part of my life, though I often spent only a few minutes with them: holding them tight in my arms on a ladder, or breathing oxygen into their mouths, or tightening a tourniquet to stop the spilling of their blood. Their names were written into reports and appeared in captions under newspaper pictures and these went into scrapbooks, and sometimes their faces looked down from official photos on the firehouse wall for years afterward. While thousands of people we helped will be forever nameless as far as I am concerned, some few became almost as familiar as members of my family. Maybe that's what they are, after all: members of a human family which I somehow assembled at random: Mott, Patterson, Turner, McKeon, Geraghty, Graziano . . .

Mrs. Elizabeth Graziano of 342 Brook Avenue in the Bronx is a good example. Until the cold winter afternoon of February 21, 1954, I didn't know the lady and she didn't know me. But this was going to be a supremely important day to both of us: It was the day I would save Mrs. Graziano's life in a fire —the first time in my career that, acting alone, I would put my own life on the line to save someone else's.

Actually, it was a fire I might not have gone to except that one of my former officers at 17 Truck, Captain Joseph E. Contrastano, had requested my services for a day as his chauffeur. He was acting as chief of the 14th Battalion which is headquartered in the same firehouse with my old friends of 17 Truck. So, on this day, instead of going to work at Rescue 3, I went down to my first firehouse once again. It was the kind of temporary detail you enjoyed because it gave you a chance to get together with all the old gang. And being a chief's driver or aide wasn't such bad duty for a day. You wouldn't have to jump into any burning buildings or pick broken glass out of your skin, and no fireman ever complains about a day off from inhaling smoke from burning mattresses or garbage fires.

The log for the day says the alarm came in at 4:26 P.M. It was a cold, gray day, the sun had dropped behind the tenements and the chill of a winter evening was beginning to penetrate the South Bronx. By the time Captain Contrastano and I got to the fire there were other companies already there, including my uncle's outfit, 29 Truck. I looked around for Uncle Bill, but I didn't see him.

The fire was on the second floor of a three-story tenement building and it was pushing a lot of smoke already. I could see we had a good one on our hands as soon as we rolled into the block. Captain Contrastano headed for the action at once and told me to get on the radio in his car and tell the dispatcher where we were and that it looked like a "worker," a big fire. I hopped back into the front seat of the red sedan and relayed the message over the handset to the dispatcher. Then I took off after the captain.

This part of Brook Avenue was a sort of nondescript neighborhood of small apartment buildings, a whole block of them all alike, in fact. On the street level there were Chinese laundries, kosher delicatessens, hardware stores and fish markets, and every 25 feet or so there was a pair of doorways with vestibules and stairs leading up to the railroad flats above.

I headed for an entrance where I saw firemen milling around. One fireman had already tried to reach the second floor by climbing up on a meat-market sign, but the sign had snapped off and the fireman had fallen back into the street with a broken ankle.

"Serves you right, Levy!" the guys were kidding him. "That was no place for you, the sign said 'pork only'!"

You could already feel the heat at the front of the building. The truckies were pushing in now and the Engine was stretching a line, getting ready to hit the fire with water as soon as we could find a way in. I thought to myself, If there's anyone in that apartment, it looks like it might be tough getting to them. There was a smell of oil in the smoke and I guessed it might have been a kerosene-stove explosion. They're tough because they ignite everything at once.

Even though I wasn't dressed in fire clothes, I ran into the nearest vestibule to see what I could do. I didn't realize it at the moment, but there were two entrances next to each other and I had chosen the wrong one; the fire was in the building next door. In all the confusion it was an easy mistake to make—and, as it turned out, a fateful one.

Once inside I looked around, and at the top of the stairs I saw a little old lady hitting her hands together like a trapped bird beats its wings. She kept saying, "Fireman! Fireman!" as if she wanted me to come up. By now I knew I had come in the wrong door, but there was something about the fear in this woman's voice that made me stay. "There's someone pounding on my living-room wall!" she cried. Then I knew. Her apartment was back-to-back with the apartment where the fire was. Someone was in there, and whoever it was was still alive.

For the moment.

I ran up the stairs and the little old lady fluttered ahead of me down the hall to her apartment. As I followed, a plan was beginning to form in my mind. I knew there were no fire escapes on the front of the building. Maybe there would be one at the back. I went through the lady's apartment—neat as a pin, I remember, with a bright, shiny kitchen floor—and I found what I was hoping for: a party fire escape at the rear. It was a sort of rusty iron balcony that joined the two second-floor apartments in the adjacent buildings by their kitchen windows. It didn't go down to the ground or up to the floor above. I ducked out and looked to my left and saw the other kitchen window glowing dull orange and already soot-streaked on the inside.

As I leaned out, I heard the screams. Somewhere behind the orange window with the smoke pushing out around all four sides, there was a person trying to stay alive. The firemen who were in the yard below could hear the screams, too, but there was no way for them to get up to the fire escape where I was, and no way I could help them up; I had nothing with me. With no rope, no mask, no boots, helmet or fire coat, I was hardly prepared for the occasion. But there was only one thing to do anyway. With only minutes, possibly seconds, left, I had to go into the apartment and try to pull that person out of the inferno. I remembered Packy telling me that sometimes, no matter how much we try, we just can't save a life. But I hadn't yet given it a try.

I kicked in the window and went in.

It wasn't like anything I'd ever seen before—in fact, after I dropped over the sill, I couldn't see a thing. I knew I was in a kitchen, but the smoke was all the way to the floor and a deep orange light, almost red, was staining through the gray like a sunset up ahead.

Time is deceptive in a fire. Sometimes, if you're waiting for water to come through a dry hose, seconds seem to be long minutes. If you're working hard with the Scott mask on your face, a 20-minute bottle of air seems to go in seconds. This Brook Avenue fire was one of those quick, one-apartment blazes and they don't usually take long to control. I know that now, but when I remember going into the fire, all the separate and individual parts of the sequence seem to add up to a lot of time. I remember squatting for a moment while I watched the fire suck fresh air in through the window I'd just entered. The new supply of oxygen made everything burn more fiercely. The smoke lifted from the floor, maybe a foot or two, and it seemed as if that let the screams come through more clearly. I looked under the bottom edge of the curtain of smoke to see where they came from. On my right was a sink, on my left a gas stove, all above was smoke. But straight ahead was an archway leading to another room, and in that room, up against the wall, what looked like a bundle of old rags was propped up, moving a little, hitting the wall, screaming, then praying, then screaming again. It was Mrs. Graziano.

I wouldn't know it until later, but she was 83 years old and she weighed almost 200 pounds. She was about 25 feet ahead of me. I don't remember how I moved toward her. I might have crawled under the smoke, but I think I duckwalked because that's faster. It probably only took 15 seconds, but when I got to Mrs. Graziano she had started to burn.

In the old apartments, the heat of a fire melts the layers of paint on the walls and ceilings. This stuff may be as much as a quarter-inch thick, and when it gets soft it runs and drips and ignites as it falls, little balls of fire with orange tails raining down like hundreds of incendiary bombs. I felt one land on my neck and burn its way down under the collar of my shirt. It reminded me of how well designed that old leather fireman's helmet is. And made me wish I had one on. The flaming paint was falling on Mrs. Graziano, too, dropping in her hair and on the old black sweater she was huddled in. It ignited the kerosene she had been sprayed with when her two-burner heater exploded in the middle of this room. I could see its outline through the flames. It had probably blown not more than five or six minutes ago. Now it looked like we had about a minute left.

Mrs. Graziano's hair, silver gray, was burning down to her scalp. Her face was red and swollen, her eyes wet with tears and wide with fear. Strands of burned flesh were beginning to fall from her hands as she pounded on the wall and clawed at me. Whatever she was saying was incoherent, but the words sounded Italian and they were hoarse with terror. I tried to get my arms around her, under the shoulders, but she seemed to be fighting me.

In the hall outside the apartment, I could hear the men from Engine and Truck trying to force a door. There was no sound of water yet—the fire was all in here—but I could hear the heaving and cursing of the firemen and the splintering sounds of the Halligan tools tearing at a door frame. They were trying to break into the room where I was. I couldn't see the door itself, but somewhere near the sound I could see a jam of old furniture shoved against the wall like they stack it up in secondhand shops. There were dressers and beds and other stuff, all piled up. If the door is behind that barricade, I said to myself, the Engine isn't going to make it with the water, at least not in time to do me any good.

I tumbled Mrs. Graziano down from her position against the wall, rolled her on her back and started tugging her, one or two feet at a lurch, toward the kitchen. She had stopped screaming, and it may have been about then that she lost consciousness. She was certainly dead weight. I wondered if she might actually *be* dead. The skin was hanging off her ears now, and the smell of her burnt hair and smoldering clothes was ickening as I leaned over her. My God but she's heavy, I thought. I knew I should be careful where I pulled on her. Her clothes were smoldering everywhere now.

The fire was moving toward the kitchen with us, sweeping overhead, heading back for the open window. Fed by the paint and kerosene, but still not getting enough oxygen, the flames were turning a rich red and coming down the walls around us like rambling roses. Thinking about it later, it struck me that the scene looked like a beautiful arbor of red roses. But while I was worrying about getting out of there, it didn't look pretty at all.

The Engine was still trying to crash into the other room. I could hear furniture falling over, but still no water. By now I was back to the kitchen window and all I had to do was get Mrs. Graziano up to the sill and roll her out onto that fire escape. If I could somehow find the strength.

The heat of the fire had blown out the upper glass in the window frame by now and the flames were roaring out over my head. I knew I'd never be able to pull this woman up and over the windowsill because I'd have to stand up to do it. Instead, I stayed low, got behind her and jacked her legs up to the ledge, one at a time. She was wearing long underwear and what seemed like layer upon layer of clothing. She felt like she weighed a ton. If only another fireman would appear on that fire escape at this moment! I had been in the apartment for a long time, hadn't I? Wasn't it time for some kind of help to arrive? Of course it had only been two minutes since I'd broken the window, but it seemed an eternity. I finally got one shoulder under the heaviest part of Mrs. Graziano and heaved her up and out onto the steel grating of the fire escape. Then I tumbled out after her into the fresh air. Smoke and fire were still swirling around the window, but I could take five seconds now to fill my lungs with cold winter air. But I couldn't taste it or smell it, my nostrils were too seared.

At the other end of the fire escape, the little lady from next door was still leaning out her kitchen window, wringing her hands and calling on everybody's help, mostly God's. I've got

nothing against religion, but at that moment I felt that befor
God or anyone else could help this woman, a fireman name
Hamilton was going to have to haul her out of danger. I pulle
her along the fire escape, wondering if she was alive, and fearin
what the rough handling might be doing to the base of her spin
if she were. I knew I had to get her into that next apartmen
dead or alive. Somehow, I found just enough strength to hau
her in through the window, flop her on a bed and race down
stairs to get medical help.

There were burn holes in my shirt, my eyebrows wer
singed off, and soot was hanging from my nose, but Captai
Contrastano didn't seem to notice any of this when I found hir
at the front of the fire. Perhaps he wondered where I'd been fo
the last four or five minutes, but he didn't ask. He only said
"There's a woman still in the fire apartment, Dick, but we can
seem to push a hoseline in there!" Smoke and flames wer
pushing hard now.

"I got the woman, captain," I said, but I could see that h
didn't understand.

"Not this woman, you didn't," he said a little irritated
"Nobody's got in there yet!"

Then I told him how I had gone around back through th
adjoining building and taken Mrs. Graziano out through th
party fire escape.

"Show me what you mean," he said, still confused an
only half believing me.

I told one of the men to call an ambulance and bring firs
aid, and then I led them into the building and up to the littl
old lady's apartment.

When we got there, two cops had moved in on the scen
One was lying on the floor, moaning and gasping, the other wa
leaning up against the wall in the bedroom. Mrs. Graziano wa
still on the bed where I had put her. She was moaning—she wa
alive! The neighbor lady was still wringing her hands.

I asked the cops what they were doing there, and the on
who was standing said that he had just helped his partner pu
this woman out of the burning apartment next door. Chi

Contrastano looked first at me and then at the neighbor lady —who was looking contemptuously at the cops. "You didn't save nobody," she said. Then added, "There's the man who went into the fire," and she pointed at me. "He went in. He went in." She kept repeating the words and shaking her head as if the whole experience were more than she could bear.

Contrastano had apparently seen this sort of fake rescue before. "Get the hell out!" he said as the hero cop got quickly up off the apartment floor, mumbling something about give us a break, we were only trying to pick up a commendation.

Other firemen took Mrs. Graziano downstairs to the street on a stretcher, and by the time they had her in the ambulance, the fire was being knocked down. A lot of people were beginning to realize that a life had been saved and were asking me questions. The ambulance pulled away, siren wailing. The civilian onlookers buzzed.

Rescue 3 had responded to the all-hands alarm, so men from my own company were surrounding me now, slapping me on the back, asking if I was all right. I said I had a few burns here and there. "Don't even mention them," said Howie Wanser. "Rescuemen are supposed to be tough."

I started to say, "I went in the wrong building by mistake —" but Contrastano grabbed me by the arm and pulled me behind a truck. "Don't ever say a thing like that where the public can hear you," he said. "You're supposed to know what you're doing. Firemen don't make mistakes!"

But the truth didn't bother me. I knew that if I hadn't gone in the wrong door, Mrs. Graziano would probably be dead by now, wrapped in a body bag in her burned-out apartment instead of on the way to the hospital wrapped in sterile sheets. It was just the way things work out sometimes. I knew that.

My uncle with 29 Truck was at the fire after all. He was one of the men in the hall who were trying to break down the door. When the fire was out, he came along with a few of us when we went back into the apartment to look around. The truckies were overhauling now, pulling ceilings, ripping out baseboards, checking for hot spots.

"We couldn't get in here because she had that door barricaded," Uncle Bill said. "Poor old lady. She was probably afraid of being robbed." The powerful hose stream had knocked the pile of old furniture all over the room.

We found her parakeet dead in its cage, and her dog hidden under the couch, roasted out of its skin. It had been a hot fire.

I looked around the demolished apartment as if I had never been there before. I looked again at the place where I had found her, against the wall. With my eye I measured the distance from the spot to the kitchen archway and from there to the kitchen window. I wondered how I had done it.

"I still don't see how you did it so fast," the captain said.

"I was in a hurry," I said.

Now that the smoke was gone, the rooms seemed bigger, the distances longer. There was no more gas from burning paint, no more kerosene. The rich red color was gone.

I tried to gather my thoughts while the others were talking. I tried to understand what I had done, how I had done it—and why. This last question was important because it would tell me something about myself that I knew I could only learn in a real fire. Something I might as well know about myself for as long as I would be a fireman because there would almost certainly be a next time, another Mrs. Graziano. Now I thought I knew what my automatic, unthinking response would be. I would go in that window again if there was a chance to save a life. And once I was halfway in, I wouldn't turn back. I knew that now. But I wasn't sure I wanted Ginny to know it.

The next day I was back on duty with Rescue 3 and the guys were all coming around saying that I'd put them on the map. It made me feel good. The firemen I admired most, like Howie Wanser, were congratulating me. There was a story in the *Daily News* and I was getting calls from friends. They were saying that I'd probably win a medal for saving the woman's life. I'd never thought much about medals before. I knew the Fire Department had a day every June when a couple of dozen firemen were honored for acts of heroism during the past year, but out of 12,000 firemen, I figured it was luck if you won a medal. But now they said I would probably get one, and Captain Contrastano "wrote me up," recommending that my name be put before the Honorable Board of Merit for consideration.

Mrs. Graziano lived. Her family got in touch with me after a few days and said their grandmother would like to see the man who had saved her life. I didn't like the idea very much. As far as I was concerned, it was over now. I'd already been to other fires since the one at 342 Brook. The chorus of alarm bells had resumed. But Mrs. Graziano's relatives pleaded with me, so I agreed to make a trip to the hospital to see her.

When I went into her room there were a lot of other Grazianos around, people of all ages, people I didn't know, and they were all very kind and full of thanks. I was uncomfortable. I wanted to get out as fast as I could and get back to my firehouse.

"She won't know you," someone said, "but she wants to see you anyway."

I went up to the bed. She was all bandaged from the neck up, with just slits for her eyes. Her two hands, with bandages like boxing gloves, reached out to me, and she spoke. Her voice was muffled and weak now, and she seemed much smaller than the day of the fire. "She says you are a good boy," I was told.

I said something about only doing my job, and then I thanked everybody and started to back out. It was true that this was the first life I'd saved in my three years in the department, but these people didn't have to do this. I was a professional. I got paid the taxpayers' money to help people.

What did they think I was going to do? Leave their grandmother in there?

MR. BLACK RAINCOAT

Some firemen say they get numb to false alarms, that they are so much a part of the business that they don't notice them anymore. I never felt that way. To me, a false alarm was an insult. I resented it. Here we were, risking our lives to save others, yet there were people who enjoyed playing games with us, making our job tougher, decreasing the protection we could give the public. Of course, that's all an old story, but out of all the thousands of false alarms I went out on, there was one situation I'll never forget.

I'd just made lieutenant and I was especially conscious of doing my duty as an officer in every way. One night I was serving as a covering officer at Engine 234 in Brooklyn and we were called out for an alarm which turned out to be false. When we got to the box, I jumped down off the truck and looked around, but there was no fire. "Anybody see who pulled the box?" I asked the crowd on the street as a man from a truck company rewound the mechanism. Nobody answered. There's always a lot of smiles at a false alarm, it seems, but very little information. We got back on the truck, gave the dispatcher the 10-92 signal for a false alarm and returned to quarters.

Within a few minutes, the same box comes in again. We roll. The same crowd is on the sidewalk, some of them still smiling. I noticed one of the good citizens in a black raincoat who was hanging around the first time. I picked him out and went up to him and asked if he saw anything. Nothing, he said. Nothing at all. Okay. We rewind the box and leave. The 10-92 again. Back to quarters.

The third alarm was in the same neighborhood, another box. When we got there, Mr. Black Raincoat was moving quickly away from the box, going up the street into the darkness. I went after him before the truck stopped rolling. "You pull that box?" I asked. "Not me," he said. "Let's talk about it," I said. "I don't want to talk with you," and he started cursing firemen. The cops pulled up just in time, so I told them to hold this guy.

"You pull that box?" the cop asked him. "Yeah, sure, I pulled it," he said. He talked to the cop in a different way. "I pulled it because I saw a fire."

"Where's the fire?" I said.

"It's up the street in one of those buildings." He smiled.

We looked up the street, but of course there was no fire.

By now a chief had arrived at the scene and I told him about Black Raincoat. "Bag him," said the chief, meaning "have him arrested." That meant I'd have to go to night court with the cops and make the complaint on behalf of the Fire Department.

It was about 2 A.M. by the time we got before this lady judge, and it seemed as if I'd spent all night on just these three false alarms.

"What's the charge?" she asked.

"Turning in a false alarm."

"What do you have to say for yourself?"

"Well, Your Honor, I was on my way home from work when I saw this fire in this building, so I went down to the corner and I turned in the alarm."

"And they arrested you for that?" she said.

"Yes, ma'am."

When it was my turn to talk, the judge didn't seem to be listening. Finally she said, "You had this man arrested for doing his civic duty?"

"No I didn't," I said. "There was no fire, but there had been three false alarms and he was at all of them. He lied about pulling the box, then changed his story."

"Are you calling this citizen a liar?"

"Well, I don't think he's telling the truth."

"Do you have anything against black people?" the judge asked.

I said, "No, but this man was running away from the alarm box when he should have been standing by it to give us directions."

It seemed to go on forever, and I was beginning to wonder what I was doing there. The cop was bored, and the defendant kept smiling. Finally the judge said she didn't need any lectures from me about how the Fire Department operates, and she dismissed the case.

I went out into the dark and I felt ashamed. Black Raincoat had made a joke out of me and a joke out of the Fire Department. I wondered if he'd ever be trapped in a burning building someday, waiting for us to save him.

Or did I wish it?

11

REASONS FOR LIVING —REASONS FOR DYING

The recommendations for a medal worked their way through channels slowly. I tried not to think much about it, but other men in the Rescue wouldn't let me forget. Fantastic! they said. You're here only a few months and you win honors for the outfit. I said I hadn't won anything yet, but they said they were sure I would. Meanwhile, I still felt that I had plenty to learn. Maybe I had pulled one old lady out of a burning apartment, but that didn't mean I was a professional rescueman yet. My six months' probation in Rescue 3 wouldn't even be up until June.

One day in April, a couple of months after the Graziano thing, Rescue Captain Phelan called me to his office and asked me to sit down for a talk.

"How do you like it here?" he asked.

I said I liked it fine and hoped I was going to make it when my six months were up.

"There'll be no problem about that," he assured me. "You're as good as any man in the company right now." With that, he reached down into his desk drawer and took out a new helmet frontpiece that said Rescue 3 on it. "Here," he said. "Take that 17 Truck thing off your hat and put this on."

I couldn't believe it. Not only was he saying that I'd made it into the outfit early, but this officer had gone to the trouble of going downtown and buying a frontpiece for me. It gave me a great feeling of belonging, of being accepted, like having another family of people who cared for me.

The medals for heroic deeds done in 1954 were awarded on Medal Day, June 23, 1955. My Graziano rescue had begun to fade a little by then as far as I was concerned. True, I hadn't done anything like it in the last 16 months, but I'd seen a lot of other action and I'd seen firemen do some pretty courageous things. But when they told me that I was scheduled to receive the Chief J. J. McElligott medal as well as a department medal for what had happened on that long-ago day, I realized it must truly have been something unusual. It was classified as a Class Two honor, meaning one which involved "great personal risk." Other firemen agreed that that's what had done it for me—no fire clothes, no extinguisher or hoseline, just a bare-handed rescue. But on Medal Day I had on white gloves and my dress uniform and I'd have to say that it was the biggest moment of my life up to then.

It was a beautiful day, clear skies and a good breeze, when Ginny and my two-year-old son Richard Jr. and I left home in Wantagh to drive to the city. In those days, ceremonies were held in City Hall Plaza. There was a reviewing stand and a parade led by mounted police and flags whipping in the wind. The Power Memorial High School Band played as we marched. The men who were going to get medals walked right behind the flag, followed by platoons of firemen from each borough and from each man's own company. I was excited, nervous and emotional, all at once.

When a bugler played taps to honor the Fire Department's own dead, the mournful notes echoed off the faces of the apartment buildings and passed over lower Manhattan like a faint cry of goodbye. I thought of Packey then, of how proud he would be to see me standing here with just a handful of guys being honored. The sharp cracks of the rifle salute brought me back to the platform.

The acting mayor, Abe Stark, stood with Fire Commissioner Edward I. Cavanagh, Jr. Behind them were the medal boxes where all the glittering awards with their crimson ribbons were displayed. The medals are awarded in order of their antiquity in the Fire Department, starting with the oldest and grandest of them all, the James Gordon Bennett. For 27 years this award was the only one given by the department for valor. The men who won it in those days must truly have been heroes, I thought. It was still Number One.

The names of the other awards were called, one by one, each a golden prize, each a source of pride for life. The Brooklyn Citizen's medal. The Bonner medal. Trevor medal. Crimmins medal. The Dr. Harry M. Archer medal, so exclusive that it is given only every three years. I listened to the names of the winners—men from all kinds of outfits, from all parts of the great city: Curran, O'Hanlon, Gibbons, Campbell, Springer, Calfapietra . . . Hamilton.

Mine was the thirteenth award of the day, and when they called my name I took the prescribed two steps forward and stood at attention. Then someone read the words from the citation. They seemed to come right out of the past, like the words of a narrator on a stage.

" . . . The living room, part of the adjoining bedroom and the kitchen on the second floor were ablaze when the apparatus arrived. . . ." I looked straight ahead. " . . . It was learned that Mrs. Graziano was in the burning apartment . . ." Yeah, and I remembered how it was learned—by mistake! " . . . Access to the apartment through the public hall and front windows was cut off by heavy smoke and heat. . . ." Nothing unusual about that, I thought; heavy smoke and heat are the name of the game. " . . . Fireman Hamilton, acting quickly, gained entrance to the burning apartment by way of the rear party wall balcony. Despite the terrific heat and smoke he managed to find Mrs. Graziano, eighty-three years old, lying on the living-room floor. . . ." I wondered about her, poor old lady. She was out of the hospital by now, no doubt. Scarred, but alive. Of course, she could be dead by now, too. How many days of life had I saved for her? How many more candles on the cake because of me?

The words of the citation droned on, not very interesting, but official-sounding, like the things that always have to be read off before someone is shot—or decorated. Finally they pinned the Department medal and the McElligott medal on me, shook my hand as the photographers' flashbulbs went off, and that ended the formalities. Then the band played some more and there was an invocation and the police horses' hoofs clattered on the street and the crowd began to break up and it was all over. In a few minutes I went from being a small part of a big show to the center of attention of my own family—Ginny and Richie and the guys from Rescue 3. We went back to the firehouse in the Bronx and they had a party for us—sandwiches, cold cuts, drinks and a wonderful, wonderful feeling of celebration. You did it, Dick! You did it! You're going to be a legend before you're through. Bet you'll win another next year!

I suppose it was a natural reaction. This was the first medal that had been won in the company in some time. (As things turned out, it would be the only medal won at Rescue 3 in the three years I was there.) The guys felt I had made them all look good, although, honestly, it seemed to me that some firemen had won medals that day for what rescuemen do as routine. I'm sure I was wrong about that, but I still wasn't willing to look at myself as any legend. In fact, if anybody wanted to be technical about it, I was still the company Johnny and I'd continue to be for quite some time, probably, because rescue outfits didn't take in new members very often.

But this legend thing had gotten started, and later there would be no stopping it. One of my main reasons for rejecting any such idea was that I was beginning to develop a philosophy about my work. As my skills increased and I was able to do my job without concentrating a thousand percent on every move I made, I found I had time to think about what I was doing in another way. A larger way. *Why* was I doing this? Why does any fireman? I used to talk about it sometimes with Ginny. I don't know whether I ever explained it well enough.

Everybody who likes his job usually speaks about the personal satisfactions. Well, of course that was true. But I was becoming very aware of the fact that a fireman does something special for humanity. You couldn't go through a Medal Day without feeling this. You couldn't listen to the names of the dead without thinking of them as men who gave their lives for something more than their own satisfaction. These men didn't die by accident, any more than it was an accident that they were firemen. Such thoughts weren't the sort that guys would express when sitting around the firehouse kitchen, because you knew that people would only laugh. It's embarrassing to voice such sentiments in public. But I could speak them to myself. In my own mind, I worked it out this way.

First of all, I knew I loved life very much myself. I loved my family, yes, and I loved the beauty of life itself. I'd seen the oceans and the mountains and I knew how beautiful a day could be. I loved the *process* of living. It was precious to me. Well, I thought, if *I* feel this way, a lot of other people must, too. They love life, they don't want to lose their chance to live. Who wants to die? Really? I'd already discovered that a lot of would-be suicides didn't *really* want to die. I'd crawled up on bridges and buildings and talked to them. And they usually came down because they really wanted to live. So I made up my mind that anybody who wanted to live as much as I did would get a fair shake from me. I'd risk my life for theirs. I'd try as hard as I could. And if I lost my life in doing this, well, at least my family could hold up their heads and know that I had done something decent and worthwhile.

I didn't have this all worked out in my head that day I went after Mrs. Graziano, I know I didn't. I guess ideas like this just have to grow.

12

A PROBLEM OF MORALE

When an opportunity came in 1955 for me to transfer out of Rescue 3 to Rescue 4 in Queens, it was described as a step up, a new challenge. I tried to see it that way, but I also found it very hard to think of leaving all my old friends. Rough as it was, I also had a soft spot in my heart for the Bronx. Its people and their problems had become a part of my life. Of course, I knew the people in Queens needed help, too.

Ginny and I talked about the transfer in another way. It would mean a much shorter drive for me, plus saving a dollar a day in bridge tolls. For three years I'd made the two-hour drive from Wantagh to the Bronx and back each day. A lot of firemen who live that far away from their work will stay overnight at the firehouse a couple of nights a week when they're on the day shifts, but I had never done that. I'd taken my marriage vows seriously. If Ginny was going to be home alone, I couldn't feel right about being away from her. So, after much discussion, we decided it would be better to take the Queens post and see how it worked out.

I wasn't the only fireman who was recruited out of Rescue 3. I soon discovered that Tony Novello, who was a good, strong man, had also been asked to make the switch. We compared notes and came up with the theory that a new captain who had recently taken over at Rescue 4 must have been unhappy with the personnel he found there. They need a couple of hotshots like us, Tony said, half kidding. As it turned out, our theory was correct. When Tony and I got there, we found that Rescue 4 was a basket case as far as morale was concerned. Its captain, John Adams, didn't say as much, but he knew that a couple of new men from a sharp outfit like Rescue 3 might make a difference.

I remember the first big fire we went to in Queens. It was a jewelry shop in a row of taxpayer stores under the elevated. Tony and I jumped off the truck and without waiting for any particular instructions started right in to do what had to be done. This was a multiple-alarm so there were several truck and engine companies there already and they had their hands full. One of the things we could see right away was that the fire was going to extend into adjoining stores if we didn't pull down a lot of ductwork in the jewelry-store ceiling. Those ducts were acting like a bunch of chimneys in spreading the flames. I got a hook and went to work on the ducts.

When things quieted down and the fire was under control, several of our new firemen friends from Rescue 4 took Tony and me out into the street and started giving us a lecture. "You guys are new," they said, "so maybe you don't understand. You're showing up the rest of us when you jump into a fire without orders like that."

Tony and I just listened. We'd never heard talk like this before, and we certainly didn't expect to hear it from a Rescue outfit!

"In this company," the firehouse lawyers explained, *"we only do what we're told.* Remember that. Somebody gives you an order, you do it. No order, no work."

I don't think I said anything in particular in reply to this novel theory, but I suddenly had the feeling that this transfer had been a terrible mistake.

The next big fire we went to, Tony and I did the same thing. And this time I noticed that a couple of the fellows from 4 joined us and pitched in. They seemed to prefer to be doing something rather than standing around in the street doing nothing. They asked me whether this was the way we did things in 3, and I said, "Sure, how else?" I guess a little of my reputation had come with me from the Bronx because the younger guys in 4 seemed willing to listen. But there were a bunch of older men who seemed more interested in their moonlighting jobs than in their duties as firemen.

To make matters worse, there was a lieutenant—Douglass we'll call him—who sided with them. He was the next one who would give me a hard time. "If you're so anxious to work like they do in a truck company," Lieutenant Douglass asked, "then why didn't you transfer to a truck company instead of coming here? I give the orders in this outfit," he went on, "and I don't want you doing anything that I haven't told you!"

I said yessir, but I still had other thoughts. For one thing, I knew 4's captain didn't feel that way. I decided to go right on trying to boost the outfit's morale—or get out of it.

One problem in Queens was the nature of the area itself. Most of the fires and many of the emergencies were more residential, almost suburban, in nature. There just weren't as many alarms per day to respond to, and when they came, the situations often weren't as rough and demanding as they had been in Harlem and the South Bronx. There were more food-on-the-stove fires, fewer fire bombings. This produced a more easygoing attitude on the part of the men. Because they had more time on their hands, they thought more of other things. Being a fireman was part-time.

The truck at Rescue 4 carried the same equipment as we

had at 3, of course, but the tools were a mess. When we had drills, I'd tell the other guys that we should be taking better care of our equipment. "Just because we don't use all these things every day doesn't mean that they shouldn't be tip-top," I argued. Pretty soon I succeeded in motivating some of the men from 4 to take a little more pride in their outfit, their equipment and their work. Gradually, everything on the truck was put into perfect condition and our work at fires began to have a new spirit and hustle about it. Captain Adams noticed this. One day he said, "Hamilton, you're the best medicine that ever happened to this outfit." I felt like answering that that was no thanks to the Loo, but I kept my mouth shut.

I'd only been with 4 about six months when we were called out to an emergency that was strictly a Rescue operation, no fire. Four workmen had gone down into an unfinished sewer line in Long Island City and after an hour they hadn't come back. Two more men then went down to find the first four, and they didn't come back either. Six men were now lost somewhere in a huge sewer tunnel, a tunnel big enough to drive a jeep through. Although the tunnel wasn't yet completely hooked up to the rest of the sewer system, there was enough sewage flowing through it already to produce the deadly methane gas.

We didn't have all these details as we raced to the scene in the truck, of course, and I noticed that Lieutenant Douglass wasn't saying much from the front seat, either. At Rescue 3 the officers used to talk to us five men in back on our way to the alarms, telling us what they were getting on the radio, preparing us for what might be ahead. Either our Loo didn't know what we were getting into, or he was still operating on the idea that he'd be the one to give the orders when we got there and that would be sufficient.

At least I knew it was a sewer problem, and because of my three years with the Department of Public Works, I knew what that might mean. I'd been down in those big trunk lines before. I knew how deep they were, I knew how dark they could be— and I knew how quickly methane could kill if you didn't have a proper mask or airpac. I started to suit up with my Scott airpac while we were still on our way.

I remembered one more thing from my DPW experience: You can't get through a manhole with a Scott bottle on your back! I hooked up my air supply to the mask, but I held the bottle in my hands.

When we got to the scene there was a big crowd, lots of police, a couple of other fire companies, people from the DPW —all of them apparently waiting for us. I could see the open manhole in the street where the men had gone down. There was obviously only one thing to do: Go in after them. As soon as the truck stopped rolling, I jumped off the back, ran to the manhole, held the Scott bottle over my head like an African carrying a water jug and started down the iron rungs in the side of the deep concrete shaft. If there was anybody alive down there, every minute counted.

Some people on the surface were yelling, "It's going to blow! It's going to blow! " But I didn't think so. The concentration of gas was probably so rich by now that an explosion was impossible. Another fireman, Eddie Brennan, had the same idea. He grabbed a light and some rope and came down the ladder behind me.

The tube we were in was just wide enough for one man, and we had to descend about 50 feet before we hit the bottom. Rung by rung, my boots found their footing as we went down. I could smell the methane coming up now, so I started taking breaths of air through my mask. There was no light, only the bright circle of sky over our heads, and Brennan blocked most of that for me.

When we landed in the main sewer tunnel there was no sound except our feet splashing around in about a foot of water at the bottom. We didn't know whether to go left or right. We flashed our light around the area, but there were no clues. We knew we had only 20 minutes to make our search because that's all the air time there is in a Scott bottle. And without air, we were dead.

As my eyes became accustomed to the place, I could see that the big pipe ran straight in both directions with no bends. Looking one way, I thought I could see a light. It was faint and seemed to go on and off in the distance, but it was worth following. I beckoned to Eddie and we went in that direction. We walked down the middle, our boots sloshing, the beam of our light stabbing ahead. Once in a while I would switch it off to see if I could see that speck of light again. It was still there. We hollered through our masks, hoping the men would hear our muffled voices. There was no reply. If there was anyone up ahead, they were probably down and out. We kept moving.

When we came to them, the six bodies were all laid out in various positions along the canal. Some still had masks on, but theirs were the wrong kind for such concentrations of methane. Some had pulled the masks off in desperation. A couple of lanterns they had carried with them were still burning faintly, and these were the lights we had seen. I couldn't be sure, but the men looked dead. Their skin was scarlet, and they had started to swell up already. It was a sad, grim moment. We notified the surface and told them to lower a rope down the shaft.

One by one we got the bodies out. When our air supply ran short, we asked for replacement bottles and they were lowered. Finally, the last corpse went up on the rope and Brennan and I came back out into the sunlight of Queens. There was an even bigger crowd when we got to the surface and there were congratulations from everybody, including Chief Peter Loftus who was now at the scene. We hadn't saved anybody's life, but we'd given it a good try, and it was obvious that a lot of people appreciated what rescuemen can do.

In the midst of all this, however, I noticed that Lieutenant Douglass wasn't saying anything and I guessed that his nose was out of joint. I decided to ask him: "You got something on your mind, Loo?"

"Yeah," he said, "you disobeyed orders."

"With guys dying down there, did I have to wait for orders from you?"

"You know what I told you, fireman. I give the orders."

"You didn't give any orders on the ride over here," I reminded him. "You should have made some decisions before we got here."

By now I was getting ready to say it all. Maybe it was because I'd just come up out of that hole, but I was ready for Douglass and I told him all that was on my mind.

"If you don't like my work, Loo, don't have me in the company, but I'm not going to stand around and have some other guy pull my strings! I know what I can do and I don't want anybody holding me back!"

And I walked away.

That night at the firehouse Captain Adams said he was proud of what his company had been able to do at the sewer, and that made us all feel good. I decided not to say anything about Douglass.

The next day we were called back to the sewer, and this time they wanted me to take a chemical engineer down into the hole with me. He was going to analyze the gasses and make a report. This guy was a nervous wreck, but he went down with me, took his samples and climbed out as if he were leaving hell. I really didn't think it was that bad and I didn't feel that what I'd done was anything extraordinary, but Chief Loftus seemed impressed with Fireman Hamilton and the fact that I would go down into that hole two days in a row. He ordered Lieutenant Douglass to write me up for what I'd done. It meant another medal.

Douglass was sore. When Loftus left the scene he told me, "You're getting written up for disobeying orders as far as I'm concerned."

I told him to forget it, I wasn't looking for medals; I'd rather get along with him.

"You'll get your write-up," he said. There was no forgiveness in his tone.

Eventually, Douglass made captain and went on to other assignments. I wasn't sorry to see him go, although we managed a sort of truce in his final months with the group. There was a postscript to his story, however, which I heard about much later.

It seems that Douglass was assigning his men to duties at a tenement fire one night when his you-do-what-I-tell-you rule backfired on him. "You and you go to the roof," he ordered, "and you two get that rear door open, and two more come with me." It sounded like a routine disbursement of manpower— except that Douglass had neglected to tell the two men detailed to the roof to cut a hole in it and vent the fire. Normally, this would be taken for granted. It was really the only reason for sending men to the roof. But he hadn't *said* to vent the roof, had he? The two men shrugged, went to the roof and stood around. The result was a fire which mushroomed inside the building and then spread laterally to other structures. It went to a fourth alarm. In the chief's investigation that followed, it was discovered that Douglass's men had never vented the roof.

"Why not?" the chief asked.

"We got no order to vent, sir," the men replied.

"No order? Do you need an *order* to do such a fundamental thing?"

The two fireman looked from the chief to Douglass and back again. Then one of them said, "In this outfit you need an order to go to the bathroom, sir."

So much for Captain Douglass.

A MATTER OF FAITH

The Fire Department is heavily Catholic, which was all right with me even though I'm technically a Lutheran and didn't spend much time in prayer. In most of the fire companies I knew over the years, there would be about 24 Catholics and 4 of us left-footers. But firemen also have a sort of universal religion of their own, a practical faith, hard-headed and sometimes brusque. I'd like to think that there isn't a rabbi, minister or priest who wouldn't understand and approve of this nondenominational "church" of ours.

Sometimes, of course, people don't understand when a fireman has to do his job first and foremost and—pardon the expression—to hell with God until the emergency is over.

When I was in Rescue 4, there was a lieutenant who had been put on light duty because of a heart attack. (Heart trouble is not an unusual occupational hazard for firemen; it takes as many lives as the Red Devil himself.) We got a call from the dispatcher one morning telling us that this officer was at home and having trouble breathing. I grabbed a resuscitator and, with another fireman, hopped into my own VW and drove to the sick man's house in Woodside. When we got there we found the man in bed and in considerable distress. I straddled him, gave him some oxygen and respiration and helped him to breathe normally again. Then we sat back to wait for the doctor.

We knew this lieutenant was a devout Catholic and even had two daughters who were nuns, but this was even more apparent in his home. His wife was saying prayers, and candles burned everywhere. In fact, there was so much smoke from the candles that I finally asked, as respectfully as I could, if they might be extinguished in the bedroom at least. I figured this man needed all the clear air and oxygen he could get. But his wife refused. So the next time she went out of the room, I blew them out myself.

When the wife returned she screamed at me, called me a heathen.

I tried to explain that it was only for her husband's good. One of the nuns slipped into the room and quietly removed the candles.

At this point, as far as I was concerned the doctor couldn't come too soon to get me out of this dreadful family scene with its heavy overtones of religion. I felt like a Peeping Tom—and the show wasn't over yet. God himself was the next one to feel the wife's angry lash! God, she suddenly announced, was no damn good. Why should he be taking her husband away from her? The nun tried to comfort her mother. Still no doctor. The patient's breathing was uneven. I was ready to use the resuscitator again.

The next sound I heard was the whack of a string of rosary beads as they hit the wall and clattered to the floor. I looked up to see the wife standing in the doorway with a butcher knife in her hand. She said she wouldn't be needing the rosary anymore because she was going to see that justice was done herself. The knife was for the landlord who had had a big argument with her husband about the rent this morning. The argument was killing her husband, she said. It was murder, she said.

We all took the knife away from her and picked up the rosary beads just as the doctor arrived. The sick man didn't seem to be aware of any of the commotion. Maybe he had heard it all his life and was used to it. Now he was concentrating on his own survival, or his own death, which was it?

The nun brought a holy picture into the bedroom. I thought perhaps it was to make up for the lost candles. The doctor looked grave. I knew I should be getting back to the firehouse, but I paused.

Suddenly, the sick man sat straight up in his bed, uttered a terrible cry and fell back with a convulsive tremble that shook his whole body. The doctor gave him an injection straight to the heart, but there was no response. The man was dead. His wife fainted.

When we got back to the firehouse I told some of the men what we'd just been through, how a good man's final hour had been made a turmoil.

"You know what you should have done in a case like that?" one of the young Catholic firemen sitting in the kitchen said.

"What?" I asked.

"You should have called a priest. He could have been very helpful."

13

MY GOLD RUSH BEGINS

If the move to Rescue 4 hadn't turned out to be the happiest decision I ever made in some ways, it had turned out well in others. I could spend a lot more time at home now and I used it to good advantage in improving the house. Our daughter, Sherree, was born August 19, 1956, and after that Ginny needed all the help and convenience I could provide. The house was small and it sat on a quarter-acre plot which didn't leave much room for privacy or recreation. I knew that when the kids were older we would want a bigger place. As the old saying goes, you can take a boy out of the country, but you can never take the country out of the boy. In my case that's true. I always dreamed of a farm, a place where we could have chickens and a garden and a pony for the youngsters. But on a salary that

115

was running about $5500 in those years, I knew that dream would have to wait.

Like most firemen, I took as much outside work as I could reasonably accomplish without reducing my efficiency for my number-one job. In my case this meant helping on construction jobs, carpentry, bricklaying, iron work, pruning trees—anything that would bring in a few more dollars. I don't think it ever added up to more than $2000 extra per year, but that was a lot to us. Ginny used to call me a workaholic, but she realized that we were saving the money for a good purpose.

These were the Eisenhower years in America, and everything seemed to be going just fine. I was really happy. I had a son and a daughter now and we'd go places together as a family, and even if we didn't have enough money, we had fun. We'd go to the beach, or on trips up to New Hampshire. Richie Jr. was getting old enough to go fishing with his dad. We had more Fire Department friends now, too. Ginny didn't like to sit around and listen to the men "blowing smoke" (as we call shop talk), but our social life was a lot better than when I worked in the Bronx.

The sewer rescue earned me another Class Two award, the William H. Todd Memorial medal. We went to our second Medal Day together, and this time a lot of people were kidding me about being back so soon for another piece of gold to hang on my dress blouse. They didn't seem to be kidding when they brought up the legend business again. I just figured the Fire Department had a certain public-relations need to build up the heroic work of its members. After all, if they didn't call attention to it, who would know? But a legend? I wasn't ready to accept that term. True, I'd won a couple of major awards in only a few years, but that might have been just chance. Anyway, I didn't take it too seriously. All I wanted was to do every job as well as I possibly could, whether it was making a Formica top for someone's kitchen counters, or being a father or being a fireman.

By the end of my first year with Rescue 4, the outfit had

shaped up into something to be proud of. It might never be the tough, able company that 3 had been—there wasn't any Howie Wanser or Lieutenant Beck at 4—but a lot of the old hairbags, as we called them, transferred out or retired when they saw that a new and different kind of fireman had arrived.

I enjoyed the challenges of the work as they came along now. I had a sewer excavation cave in on me and it could have been serious if not fatal, but I got out of it and shrugged it off. I had a hairy experience with a leaking acid tank that could have been pretty dangerous, but we licked that problem. As they say: You see a mountain, you want to climb it. That was me. A lot was beginning to be expected of me, too. "Hey, Dick, what do you think?" the men would ask. "Can we do this, Dick?" My usual answer was "We'll never know until we try!"

I guess that's what I was thinking when I went in after the McKeon baby and won myself another award.

It was March 20, 1959, at 9:52 in the morning. A Lieutenant Kuveck had replaced Douglass in command of my group by now and I liked him a lot. On this day we had been up to Astoria Boulevard on a Saturday-morning drill and we were on our way back to quarters when we heard the alarm come in on the radio. The dispatcher said a house had blown up in Astoria and gave the address. "Hey," I hollered at the new Loo, "we can make that, we just passed the neighborhood!" So we made a U-turn over the divider in the road and raced back. When we got to the house an Engine and a Ladder were just arriving and there was a young woman standing out in the street with all her clothes on fire.

One of our guys bounded off the truck, wrapped a blanket around the woman and threw her down so he could roll her. Somebody else started wetting her with an extinguisher. She was in pretty bad shape, but she was still able to tell us that her baby was upstairs in the house.

The place was a two-story private residence and it seemed to be burning everywhere at once. It looked and smelled like a gas explosion. In fact, a Brooklyn Union Gas Company crew was down at the corner of the block and they came back to tell us that they'd just fixed a gas leak in this Mrs. McKeon's kitchen.

Gas leak or not, there was a kid in that house and we knew what we had to do. Bill Malew, Nick Popalezio and I went in the front door and ran up the stairs, hoping to make the bedroom and save the child even before the truckies could vent the place. I guess we were about halfway up the stairs when the whole house blew again and we found ourselves back at the bottom of the stairs.

Now the house was burning so fiercely that there was no way to get up the stairs again. I ran out, grabbed a 25-foot wooden ladder and put it up against the front of the house. That ladder weighed 150 pounds at least, but I don't even remember lifting it. I just slammed it against one of the upstairs windows and started to climb. I had an MSA mask with me, a filter type, not as good as a Scott but better than nothing if I could get into the house.

The window had both storm sash and screens on it and I didn't have time to mess with any of this, so I put my head down, let my helmet crash the glass, and dove into the upstairs front room headfirst.

I stayed low. The room was like an oven, with a weird glow everywhere which must have been caused by burning gas. For five seconds I thought to myself that I would have to go back out the window, the heat was so intense, but then I thought that the baby might be just as close to me in one direction as the window was in the other. I decided to move in. I could hear the Engine getting water on the fire down below now, but it wasn't helping me any.

I crawled around, raising my hands above my head to feel for things. All of a sudden I ran smack into a baby's crib. The sheets and the blanket were starting to burn between the side slats. I stood a little higher, felt around over the edge of the crib and found something. Was it a baby—or a doll? With my gloves on and almost no visibility, I wasn't sure. But there was no more time. I grabbed the small form, dropped to the floor and really crawled on my belly to get back. The fire was coming over my head and going out the window like a blowtorch. Downstairs I could hear the truckies going around the house breaking windows with their hooks. That was a mistake. It only made the fire worse by supplying oxygen at the base. If they had vented the upstairs windows it might have been a lot better. Too late now to offer advice, I thought.

Bill Malew had come up the ladder to help me but had been unable to enter the room. In fact, the fire coming out the window was so intense that he had to crouch a couple of rungs below the window to avoid the heat. When I got to the window, I handed my bundle over the sill and Bill took the baby—it *was* the baby—out in one arm. I saw him starting mouth-to-mouth resuscitation even before he started down.

I was just trying to figure out how I was going to make it through that fiery flue myself when a third gas explosion solved the problem for me. The concussion blew me halfway through the window, tangled my coat in the top of the ladder and left me hanging upside down. Somehow I slid down the ladder head first and landed in a hedge in front of the house. It must have looked like a Marx Brothers comedy to see a fireman come flying out of a building like that, but the civilians who had gathered across the street must have missed the humor. They were screaming. I felt like a fool, but at least I was a living fool. The heat inside the McKeon house was something I would remember all my life.

Little Brian McKeon was pretty badly burned. They took him and his mother to Doctors Hospital in a police car, but not even open heart massage could save the infant.

Mrs. McKeon said she wanted to talk with the fireman who had gone in for her son. The woman had first- and second-degree burns herself and she was heavily bandaged when I went into her room. I'd had a few burns of my own fixed up myself while I was waiting, but I was feeling okay by then. The depressing thing was knowing that we'd all done our best and it still wasn't enough.

"Are you the man who saved Brian?" she asked.

I didn't know what to say. Had they told her yet or not? "You can tell me the truth," she said. "You must know." I said I thought her doctor would know better.

She just shook her head then and said, "No, if my baby was alive I think you'd tell me."

I said I was sorry. We'd all done the best we could.

The awarding of Fire Department honors is obviously not an exact science. I don't really know how the men on the Honorable Board of Merit reach their decisions. All I know is that over a 24-year career they were certainly generous with me. I have seven medals and countless other honors. I have no complaints. But I do have an observation. It is that some of the rescues for which I received only modest recognition were worth a good deal more than the board believed—and a couple for which I received higher honors were probably not worth the value that was placed on them.

It's like in boxing. The judges often miss the short, punishing punches and are impressed by the more flashy swings.

In the case of Brian McKeon, although we didn't save the little lad's life, I will always believe my effort was deserving of higher recognition than the award I received. I repeat: This is not a gripe. The greatest events—and rewards—of my career were yet to come. I could not ask for more. But speaking as the man who went into the fire, I can honestly say that, whether the Honorable Board knew it or not, the short trip between that window and Brian's crib was a lot rougher than my walk in the subterranean cool of the Queens sewer tunnel while breathing pure air from a Scott bottle. But I got only a Class A for Brian and a much higher Class Two for the sewer.

I'm sure this is something that other firemen who have won honors would agree with. From fire to fire, year to year, there can be no absolute guarantee of uniformity. The Board of Merit weighs everything and does its best. Its criteria for awards go something like this:

Class One awards, of which there are only three or four a year (I would ultimately win two), are given for an act beyond the call of duty which involves "extreme personal risk." Class Two, which I received for Mrs. Graziano and also for the Queens sewer incident, is given for situations in which there is "great personal risk." Class Three (I would ultimately win four of these) is given for "unusual personal risk."

Below the numbered class awards, service ratings designated Class A and Class B are given when a fireman's work showed initiative and capacity and/or personal bravery in one degree or another. I won a lot of these, including the one for the McKeon fire.

Just to make the situation a little more confusing, the 30-odd medals the Fire Department awards each year do not always carry the same value. One year a certain medal will go to a Class Two winner. The next year it may go to a Class Three. Sometimes a Class Three recipient wins a medal; sometimes (if there aren't enough gold pieces to go around) he doesn't. Of the four Class Threes I was awarded, only one came with a medal.

Of course, there are cash awards to go with the honors, and extra points which help on examinations and promotions.

There is one final prize—if you want it. When you die, you may lie in a coffin in a great cathedral, and under the Gothic arches four firemen will stand solemn watch and your medals will gleam on your dress-blue uniform as never before.

Then it doesn't matter anymore how you got them.

DISHONORABLE MENTION

It's not something that a fireman likes to admit about other fire-
men, but it's nevertheless true: There are a few men in the department
who lie about what they do behind the curtain of fire.

We went to a fire with 56 Engine one time and before anyone got
upstairs with a hoseline, I went above the fire to search for people. I
found an old man in a bedroom. He wasn't in bad shape, just a little
confused. He'd been in bed, maybe asleep, and he didn't know where
he was at first. I got him up and took him out into the hall, then asked
him if he could find his way out of the building from there.

"Yeah," he said, "I know how to get out, but my wife's still back
there in the apartment."

"Don't worry about her," I told him. "You just take care of
yourself. Go down the stairs and right out to the street and you'll be
okay. I'll go back and look for your wife. And if she's pretty," I said,
"I'll run off with her!"

It was the kind of thing you say to take the edge off, to calm an
old fellow who was scared and needed a little encouragement.

"If you find her, you can have her!" he said with an attempt at
a smile. "I'll get me a new one!" Then he disappeared down the stairs.

By now there were a couple of other Rescue guys in the hall with
me, so we all went back into the apartment to look for the woman.
There was a good deal of smoke in the building, but the fire was on the
ground level in back and it didn't seem to be spreading. We were able
to take our time looking through the apartment, but we could find no
trace of the old man's wife.

It was one of those situations that could mean any one of several
things. The wife could have run into another apartment. She could have
run out of the building. She could have jumped into the rear yard. Or,
just possibly, the old man didn't have a wife. Of one thing I was sure:
She wasn't in the apartment.

We went back to the street and reported to the chief. I told him that I found an old man on the top floor, but we couldn't find the wife. The chief said not to worry about the wife, that she was the one who had pulled the alarm and she was okay. Then he added that one of the guys from 56 Engine had made a helluva rescue in saving an old man.

"What old man?" I said. "The one with the crew-cut white hair?"

"Yeah," said the chief, "that's him."

"And where's the guy who says he saved him?" I asked.

"Over there, leaning on the truck," said the chief.

I went over to the 56 Engine fireman and asked him where was the man he'd rescued. "Over there," he said, pointing to an old guy sitting wrapped in blankets.

"Hey, pop!" I called to the old man. "Come over here!" He came over. "You ever seen me before, pop?" I said.

He looked at me, still a little confused. "Were you the one who was going to take my wife if she was pretty?" he said.

"Yeah, pop, that was me," I said. "I was the one who told you to walk downstairs, too."

The other fireman just shuffled off around the end of the truck then and didn't say any more about his rescue.

Later the chief asked me, "Why did that fireman do that, lieutenant?"

"Oh, I guess he was just looking for an Academy Award," I said.

14

A COMMAND OF MY OWN —AT LAST!

I took the Fire Department exam to become a lieutenant in the fall of 1959. I had almost nine years in the FD then, approximately three in 17 Truck, two in Rescue 3, four in Rescue 4. I'd seen a lot and survived a lot. I'd served under good officers and bad. I'd seen great firemen and humpty-dumptys. Now it was time for me to put it all together and try to have a command of my own. I thought I was ready.

The exam is a tough one—100 multiple-choice questions and some essays. A bunch of us in Rescue 4 got together and took the usual tutoring courses at the Delahanty Institute, a school that specializes in helping people pass various civil service exams. But we also did a lot of cramming on our own

Eddie Brennan, a college man, was in charge of "school" at the firehouse.

Ginny was also a great help. She insisted on me cracking the books in my off hours at home. She knew I wasn't much for paper work and classroom stuff. I have a hard time retaining things I read. Give me a practical problem, an action problem, and I can usually solve it. But exams give me the willies.

The weekend before the test I was sitting around the house not doing much and Ginny asked me why I wasn't studying. I said it was the best advice of all the experts that the candidates just take it easy on the day before the test and not tire their minds. "Nonsense!" said Ginny. "Just go pick out one of your books and review it. You never know what it might mean."

She must have had ESP. I found the answers to three of the questions during that last-ditch effort. I probably would have missed them otherwise. Obscure things like "Why are the nozzles on fireboats designed the way they are?"

I was pretty sure I had passed the test when I was finished. At least I knew I'd handled the hundred multiple-choice questions okay. As for the essays, who knew? If I was really a writer, I wouldn't have needed the help of Charlie Barnard to do this book you're reading. Then the results were posted. Out of several thousand who took the exam, I had come in number 46.

I don't know whether they ever make a man a lieutenant posthumously in the Fire Department, but while I was waiting to get my grade on the exam I got involved in a scrape that almost made the results academic. I remember thinking at the time that it would be tragic enough to die, but it would be even more tragic to die and waste a passing grade on the lieutenant's test!

We had been called to a cave-in at an excavation site in Greenpoint, a section of Brooklyn that Rescue 4 covered. A very deep trench was being dug for a large sewer pipe. The place was so near the waterfront that at high tide the trench would fill up with water and muck, weakening the walls. We were told that when the walls gave way one of the workers had been trapped and buried at the bottom, but that he might still be alive if he was trapped in earth that was porous enough.

The first thing to do was start moving dirt. This was something I had always drilled on quite a lot because at certain seasons of the year, spring particularly, these cave-in accidents are quite common. If you go about the problem logically and efficiently, you can often save a life. If you just start digging everywhere and tossing dirt right and left, the chances of saving anyone are poor. So we made our plan: We would dig from one place, move the dirt to a second pile, follow a systematic approach.

We weren't working very long before there was a second cave-in. The walls of the trench were obviously pretty weak, so everybody ran. At this point, Rescue 2 was called in to give assistance. Now we had more manpower for the shoveling job.

I had just gone down into the trench for the second time to see where we stood when a big crane that was moving timbers for shoring swung its load out over the trench—and dropped a six-foot 12 × 12 on my head about 35 feet below! It had to be a glancing blow or I would have been killed right then and there, but even a glancing blow from a timber weighing several hundred pounds and dropped from high above was enough to knock me silly.

They say the regulation fire helmet, old-fashioned as it is and made of horsehide, can withstand a 200-pound smash and still protect the wearer. My helmet was demolished by the falling beam. The first thing I remember was crawling around in the muck on my hands and knees like some kind of wounded animal. The remains of the helmet were around my neck. I was cross-eyed with pain and a little incoherent. They lifted me out of the trench and took me to the hospital for observation.

Now I had another problem. There is a rule in the Fire Department that no man may be promoted in rank while he is in the hospital or on sick leave or anything like that. My greatest fear was that there would be something wrong with my head and I would be passed up for lieutenant because of that rule.

But things worked out. There wasn't anything wrong with

my skull, so they sent me home. One more reason for believing that I led some kind of charmed life. I really was beginning to believe that. I thought: If I were in an airplane crash and everybody was killed, I'd be the only survivor.

On Saturday morning, November 14, 1959, I was appointed lieutenant in the 38th Battalion. I had to leave Rescue 4 because there was no vacancy for a lieutenant there.

But first they sent me to officers' school where I learned a lot of administrative stuff. Becoming a lieutenant, I realized, was going to be my introduction to paper work, and I might as well face it and learn. After six weeks of school I was given some choices of duty. I went first to the Supervisory Engineers of the Fire Department for temporary duty. They are in charge of hydrants, standpipes on bridges, that sort of thing. Next, I did duty with engine companies, truck companies, anybody who needed a replacement lieutenant for a shift or a few days. It was good experience, it gave me a chance to make up my mind about a few things. I decided that I was still a rescueman at heart and I hoped that's where I'd end up when it came time for a permanent assignment.

One day after about four months of working around Brooklyn as a swing lieutenant, Chief Richard Denahan called me to his office and said there was an opening for a lieutenant on Rescue 2 on Carlton Avenue in Brooklyn. Would I be interested?

Would I! Two was the busiest rescue outfit of them all! That's what I had been hoping for. I didn't want to go back to Rescue 4, and I had no interest in Rescue 1, that fancy-pants outfit in Manhattan that took care of problems at the Shubert Theatre and Saks. Rescue 2 sounded great. I said I'd take it.

"Fine," said the chief. "I think they're expecting you."

They were. The word had gone ahead of me: Rescue 2 is going to get a hotshot lieutenant. The Fire Department may consist of almost 15,000 men, but it's really a small community, a sort of family. Reputations spread, and you can get to be known, one way or the other, pretty quick. Certain firemen are known from one end of the city to another, and guys with rescue outfits get known quicker than any others because they cover such a wide territory and work with so many other firemen in the course of normal duty.

The Rescue 2 firehouse on Carlton Avenue is a narrow three-story brick building built in 1912 for horsedrawn fire equipment. The street floor where the apparatus is parked has a very high ceiling that allowed all the harness for the horses to be suspended overhead. When an alarm came in in the old days, the harness was dropped onto the horses' backs, the cinches were tightened, and out the big doors they went with a clatter.

Rescue 2 doesn't have the firehouse to itself. It shares quarters with 210 Engine, so there are always two trucks on the floor, parked tandem. Sometimes Rescue's big red box is in front, sometimes the pumper. It doesn't matter; they respond to a lot of alarms together. The two companies are nevertheless separate. Each has its own captain, three lieutenants and 24 firemen, and there was a certain amount of rivalry between the two groups. When I got there Rescue 2 was commanded by Captain Martin J. Lawler, a former fireboat officer with a quiet nature and not too much experience with rescue operations.

The day of my arrival, Captain Lawler was having an inspection and the men were getting everything cleaned up. As I walked through the bunkroom on the second floor, I could feel their eyes on me. Much later Fireman Jack Kelly told me he didn't know what to expect on that first day. He said, "I'd heard so much about you before you came, I guess I expected to see John Wayne!"

Although I was anxious to start shaping the character of my own outfit, I took things slow at first. I wanted to see what kind of firemen I had inherited. Had they been well trained? Was the equipment maintained? Was the morale good? The answers were mostly positive. This wasn't a replay of my Rescue 4 experience. It might not be quite as sharp an outfit as 3 had been, but I thought I could make it that way before too long.

I saw one problem in the first week: There were a couple of guys in my group who mouthed off too much at fires. We'd roll up and they'd jump off the back with a lot of smart talk like, "Never fear, Two is here!" I knew enough about firemen to know that this probably didn't sit well with guys from truck and engine companies. Rescue is élite, sure, but that didn't mean we had to rub it in. There are some great firemen who don't happen to be in Rescue.

One day at a fire we took a line in for an exhausted engine outfit and we made a difficult job look easy! After we'd knocked the fire down and everybody was back in the street getting ready to take up, I heard one of my pop-offs saying to the Engine, "You guys couldna done that! But *we* did it!" I made a mental note and the next time we went out on an alarm I gave Mr. Big Mouth a special assignment.

"You stay here by the truck," I told him, "and when one of the men needs one of the tools, you go get it for him." My order seemed to stun him. He looked at me with anger, but he didn't say anything then. Later at the firehouse, he came over to talk with me.

"Nobody ever made me stay with the tools before, Loo," he said. "I always go into the fire like everybody else."

"Fine," I said. "I need all the help I can get in the fire. But I don't need your big mouth." Then I explained my philosophy. Let your tools do the talking, I told him. If you do a good job at a fire, other fire companies will see that and respect you for it. Later, I told everybody in my group the same thing. Don't ever ridicule other guys, I said. If there was an engine or a truck company at a fire before we were called, remember—conditions might have been a lot worse when they got there. Just because we can do things well it doesn't mean other firemen are slobs.

The message got through. The men quieted down, and were more professional for it. Within a couple of months I noticed they were even showing other firemen how some of our tools and equipment worked. The rivalry with 210 Engine in our own firehouse cooled down, too. I was glad to see this. I didn't want to be in burning buildings with people who didn't like me.

Some of the men I had in my first group at 2 were with me for a long time, some drifted off to other assignments, and one guy I put out of the company because he was a drinker. But I remember Tony Motti, a really great fireman. Jim McQuade was another one and a good storyteller. He could take the edge off. Ronnie Foote, Freddie Vanacore, Joe Keller. Good men, all of them. Plus Hank Zuercher. I'd had my eye on him for quite a while when he was at Ladder 108. When I had a vacancy in my group, I recruited him to join 2. He was the kind of guy who had a very humble personality, very quiet. But he knew tools. He trained well. He was strong. I'd seen him take some terrific beatings at fires and snap right back. I felt he was the kind of man we needed.

I didn't know when I brought him into the outfit that he'd be the first man to save my life in a fire.

15

I'll BE HOME FOR CHRISTMAS—MAYBE

My first year with Rescue 2 wasn't exactly uneventful—I was working the men hard on training programs and we were responding to the thousands of alarms which become routine—but it wasn't until December 16, 1960, that something really big happened. That was the day two airliners collided over Staten Island—a United DC-8 and a TWA Super Constellation, I think they were. One crashed on Staten Island; the other landed about eight blocks from our firehouse. By some grim coincidence, it crashed head-on into the Pillar of Fire church on Sterling Avenue, Brooklyn. It was a pillar of fire all right. Eighty-two dead.

I wasn't working when the crash came, but it was such a huge emergency that all off-duty rescuemen were called at

131

home to report at once. I jumped into my VW and took off. I went to the firehouse first to get my working clothes, and then went to the scene.

When I got there, almost all of Rescue 2 was working, all 28 men under Lieutenant Joe Galvin. There wasn't much skill involved in this job, you just had to have a strong back and a strong stomach. I'd never seen anything quite so gruesome. We dug through debris all that afternoon, and when darkness came we set up the big searchlights and went right on digging. There were parts of bodies everywhere. With the exception of one little boy who died later, not one of the victims so far as I can recall was intact. An arm here, a head there. Some were burned, some weren't. It was a nightmare of crushed aluminum, shredded upholstery, burst-open luggage, everything charred, waterlogged and mangled. After we found the flight recorder we took a break and they gave us hot coffee in the basement of another church nearby. When I finally got home it was long past dinnertime, but Ginny had a roast beef waiting in the oven. I took one look at the meat and knew I couldn't eat it.

The next day was my regular tour of duty and I returned to the crash scene. It looked like another day's work at least. We were all bent over, our attention directed to the mess underfoot, so we didn't notice the large column of smoke rising into the sky in the general direction of the Brooklyn Navy Yard. When we finally did see it, I thought it was probably coming from some large industrial stacks in that area—until the radio began to crackle, that is.

"Hey, Loo," my chauffeur, Bob Smith, said, "they're calling you!"

I started back toward the Rescue truck, thinking something was wrong at home. But the dispatcher said, "Take your company to the Brooklyn Navy Yard immediately, lieutenant. There's an aircraft carrier on fire." It was 11:30 A.M.

I'd seen some pretty big things burning in my life, including the aircraft carrier *Bunker Hill* during World War II, but by the time we got onto the pier next to the carrier *Constellation* I knew this was going to be the biggest fire of my life. The ship was the largest in the world at that time, several city blocks long and several stories high, a great gray giant that was still under construction. It was incredible to see smoke coming out of all parts of her like a smoldering bomb. The dock area was already a madhouse of activity with firemen, police, shipyard workers and ambulances everywhere. The temperature was below freezing and a light snow was beginning to fall.

I didn't have time to think about being tired. The one-two punch of two major catastrophes in 48 hours was too much to comprehend. I just knew that we were in for another rough assignment.

The first orders we received were to get handlines up onto the flight deck and start pumping water onto whatever was burning. I didn't think this was going to do much good. I had the advantage of knowing what a carrier was like inside, how it was built, and I knew from my experience aboard the *Midway* that this fire could be buried pretty deep within the many decks of the ship.

Along with a few hundred other firemen from many companies around Brooklyn, we clambered aboard, finally making our way to the huge flight deck. The smoke was getting heavier now. The fire seemed concentrated at a place near the center of the ship, but it was all down below. What had happened was that the driver of a small truck had run into a drum full of fuel on the flight deck, knocking the spigot off and letting the fuel run unnoticed through the plates until it came to a place where some welders were working. Then everything went *kabooom!*

The most serious problem with ship fires is that you can only come at them from the top. In a tenement fire, you can work up on it from underneath in relative safety, but a fire in a steel vessel is contained everywhere but at the top. You have to climb down the chimney to get at it, and that's what we did.

Workmen were coming up out of the ship by every available exit, stumbling out into the clear air and light snow like drunks. The fire had obviously gotten quite a head start before we got there. For almost an hour the contractors had tried to put it out by themselves. Now it was really roaring down below.

I knew that not all the workers in the ship were going to be able to make it out on their own power, so I signaled my group to follow me and we started down, pulling on our Scott airpacs as we went.

Under the flight deck of a carrier is a second, cavernous deck where airplanes are stored. This is called the hangar deck. Below this is a deck where there are storerooms, workshops and other small compartments. It was in one of these that we found a group of 15 or 20 workers all huddled together, afraid to come out. The smoke in the room wasn't particularly heavy, but the heat was building up and the men thought they had been cut off by the fire. When we told them there was a way out, they wouldn't believe us. They were on the edge of panic.

I didn't want to have to haul these men to safety when I was sure they could make it themselves. I knew there were going to be others who were worse off. "Look," I pleaded, *"we* got in here. *You* can get out. All you have to do is follow a leader. I'll send one man ahead with you. All of you join hands and follow single file. It's going to be smoky, it may get pretty bad, but you'll make it if you stay cool."

They finally agreed and the last I saw of them they were following one of my firemen out to safety.

That left me with Hank Zuercher and Tony Motti. We moved one deck lower into the ship, and at this level we began to find dead bodies. The fire must have hit some of these men with great suddenness. They were roasted to death right where they were working. Others were piled up against bulkheads they couldn't open. All the power was off on these lower decks by now, so we could only see with the help of our lanterns. When we found bodies, we hollered up to the firemen behind us and passed the dead back. It would have been easy enough to just put a corpse on your shoulder at this point and use it as your ticket out into the fresh air. I wouldn't blame any fireman who did that. But I knew we had a more important job. There might—just *might*—be somebody still alive in some of these compartments. It was Rescue's job to find out.

A foreman who was frantically running through the smoke

looking for some of his men came up to us and said, "I've got four friends in here, I think they're four decks down, right under the fire." I looked at Hank Zuercher and he looked at me. The deck we were on was pretty bad; we'd pulled a couple of dozen bodies out already. What would it be like one more deck down? The foreman was desperate. "If somebody doesn't go after my friends," he said, "I know they're going to be dead." I could have said that I thought the chances were pretty good that they were dead already, but that's never a fireman's answer. We said we'd see what we could do.

The foreman led us around until we found a ladder going down. I told Tony Motti to try and find a rope and a handline to back us up with. He said he thought we were crazy. I pretended I was calm. I said I was going to try and get under the fire. If you can, I said, send some water down where we're going and cool things off a little. Motti just shook his head.

The deck under our feet was slippery because the heat was melting the soles of our boots. In some places the plates were beginning to turn a dull red. I knew there must be a lot of fire below us—but there were also those four guys.

"We'll be coming back up in a while," I said to Motti. "Don't forget the water!" Then I started down the ladder, Zuercher after me.

Up to now we'd used about 6 of the 20 minutes of air in our Scott bottles. We also had one spare bottle for the two of us. From this point on, it was going to be hard to live without them.

The ladder went straight down. I could feel the heat of the steel rungs through my gloves. We climbed past bundles of electrical cables with the insulation melting off them, some of it still smoldering. Finally our feet touched bottom and we began to move along a steel corridor that seemed to radiate heat like the inside of an oven. The smoke choked the beam of my lantern so I could only see a few feet in front of me. I thought I could hear some water coming down behind us. Maybe Motti had found a handline. We moved ahead, looking through the eyepieces of the Scott masks, searching from side to side.

We had moved only a few yards from the foot of the ladder when I spotted the four men—the foreman's friends. They were all in a heap, moaning, but at least they were alive. They'd been lucky. If they'd been in much farther we might not have found them. They hadn't been burned, but the smoke and heat had brought them down and they were losing consciousness fast because there wasn't much oxygen left in these compartments.

The first thing to do was slap my mask on each of them for a minute or two to give them some oxygen. I pulled the facepiece off, held it over each man's mouth and nose and gave each a few good shoves in the stomach to get him breathing again. Of course, I couldn't hold my breath while this was going on, so I just inhaled whatever was available in that inky atmosphere. As things turned out, it must have been a pretty poisonous mixture—but I wouldn't know that till later.

I thought the men would probably live if we could just get them out of there in the next few minutes. Zuercher was back at the foot of the ladder now, and good old Motti had found a roof rope somehow and was lowering a line to us. We got the first man into a hitch, I gave him a couple of lungsful of air, and up he went. We repeated the process with the second man.

As I was feeding air to the third man, I realized that I had only a few more minutes in my Scott. I let the guy take it all, and while he was being hauled up I switched to the spare, which I'd probably have to share with Zuercher.

While I was getting a hitch around the fourth man, I began to sense trouble. I thought I could feel the carrier moving under me. Of course, it wasn't. When I tried to reach for the rope, my arms wouldn't obey. Although I knew the symptoms of carbon monoxide poisoning, I tried to ignore them—*had* to ignore them; there was still one man to save. With Zuercher's help, I got him roped up and hauled away.

Even with the fresh Scott bottle, my condition didn't improve. I'd taken in too much carbon monoxide during this operation and now no amount of air was going to help me. The stuff was in my blood. My mind was still working okay, but my body was turning to rubber. I took one last look around the compartment, saw a big open hole in the deck, crawled over and focused the beam of my lantern into the void below. I could see some machinery and other stuff, but no bodies. I figured we'd done all we could, so I said, "Okay, Hank, let's get out of here."

Zuercher nodded and started for the ladder. That was when I discovered that I couldn't make a move to help myself. I knew where I was, I knew what I had to do, but I couldn't move a muscle. It would only take a minute or two to climb back up the rungs of that vertical ladder, but I knew I couldn't do it. I didn't say anything to Hank, but he saw the problem at once and just said, "Look, Loo, you sit on my shoulders and we'll go up together."

I don't remember much after that. All the heat and the smoke seemed to disappear. I think I remember Tony Motti and others reaching down to pull me off Zuercher's back. Then they put me in a Stokes basket and I could feel the snow falling on my face like cold needles. They used a big crane on the pier to pick me up and swing me off the ship, but I only know that because there was a picture of it in the *Daily News* the next day. As for the ride to the hospital, it must have been a nightmare for the guys who rode with me, because I had lost consciousness altogether by then and all they could do was scream at the driver to hurry up because I was either dying or dead.

I came around a little in the emergency room. They had cut all my clothes off me, right down to my underwear, and I looked up into the lights while they stuck all kinds of tubes and wires into me. One of the firemen, I don't remember who it was, was looking down at me and he was crying. I said, "What are you crying for?" and he said, "I'm not going to tell you, Loo." Under the bright lights the skin on my arms and hands seemed to be turning purple. That's strange, I thought. Is he crying because I'm going to die?

The cop who called Ginny must have had the same information. He didn't waste any words, or soften them either. "You better get yourself over to Kings County Hospital, ma'am," he said, "because your husband is dying." As I've always said, compared to firemen, cops have no compassion.

Outside the emergency room though, New York was being blanketed by a heavy snowstorm. Ginny, desperate as she was, couldn't get from Wantagh to the hospital and had to wait until the next day when she took the kids out of school and another fireman drove them all in.

I woke up that next day in a big private room, the kind of place where hospital people always put firemen (at city expense) if there's space. All I could think of was the flight deck of the carrier. "What am I doing here?" I asked a nurse.

"Be quiet and lie still," she said. "Right now you're supposed to be only fifty-fifty to live, but you're looking better to me." She winked and that helped.

"Where's Fireman Zuercher?" I asked.

"He's okay. He's alive."

Then Father Fox came in. He was a sort of honorary Fire Department chaplain, a nice man. I'd known him a long time. He moved to the side of the bed and said, "Do you want to say anything to me, Dick?" His tone was very quiet and serious.

"Yes," I said. "I want to go home."

"No, no!" he said. "You certainly can't do that. But how would you feel if I gave you the last rites of the Church?"

"Last rites! Who needs last rites?" I said. "Anyway, I'm a Lutheran, not a Catholic."

"Well, I'll tell you," said Father Fox, "I already gave them to you once, on the deck of the carrier yesterday, but you didn't know it. Now that you're conscious, I'd like to do it again."

"It won't work, Father," I said. "I'm a black Protestant."

He just smiled. "I know, Dick," he said, "but every little bit helps." Then he started whatever it is they do and I saw a couple of the Catholic nurses in the room crossing themselves and I really began to believe something must be wrong with me.

When Ginny arrived she looked pretty grave, too. There was talk around the bed about transfusions and blood washes. What the hell was going on here? I was Dick Hamilton! Ten years a fireman! My body wasn't ever going to fail me. Besides, Christmas was only a few days off and I wanted to be home with my family. A fireman doesn't get to spend Christmas with his family very often.

They let me out on Christmas Eve, only after I promised the doctor to take it easy. I was still weak and sick, but I could walk. The first thing I did was hang Christmas lights. I stayed home until the middle of January. It was that bad. But still I was lucky. Fifty-two people died on the *Constellation* that day. It had been a mass roast.

While I was home, I began to hear talk about what Zuercher and I had done. They were saying it was the best rescue of the day, a sure bet to win a medal. I was beginning to have mixed feelings about these honors, but on June 6 the following year, Fireman Hank Zuercher and I both won Class One awards for our work on the carrier. It was the first time in the history of the Fire Department that two men had won Class Ones for the same event. Mayor Robert Wagner presented me with the Emily Trevor–Mary B. Warren medal. Then, for saving *my* life, Hank was awarded the William H. Todd Memorial medal, the same one I'd earned the year before for the Queens sewer job. We both went back to Rescue 2 full of pride.

And on June 7, we went back to the false alarms and the garbage fires.

THE CASE OF THE 500-POUND LADY

We always referred to her as the 500-pound lady, although whether she really weighed that much, no one will ever know. The Welfare Department called us to her assistance—to remove her from an apartment to a hospital. There wasn't anything unusual about the call. Rescue outfits were often asked to help move people who were sick, or caught in some unusual situation. The dispatcher gave us the address but no details, so we rolled into the block with no notion of what we were getting into.

There were people in the street who apparently knew we were coming, and when we innocently said we were there to help the lady on the fourth floor, they just laughed. "You ain't ever going to help her," *they said. "She's there to* stay, *man!" "Yeah, yeah, sure," we said, "but we're the Rescue. We know how." I took Tony Motti and a couple of the other guys and we went up to the fourth floor. We had the usual stuff with us for cases of this sort: canvas stretcher, first-aid kit, oxygen, etc. But when they let us into the apartment, we could see there was nothing usual about our problem.*

The woman sat in the middle of the living room like a huge Buddha. I'd never seen such a big human being before, not even in a circus. She was sitting on a sort of throne, a giant chair that had been built for her out of two-by-four lumber. This was supported by a foundation of cement blocks, just like a house. Inside the foundation, under the chair, there was a big pot which was the woman's toilet. It was obvious that she not only never left this apartment but never left the chair. She ate, slept and carried out all other physical functions right there. The place smelled like a latrine. Tony Motti looked at me as much as to say, What do we do now, *boss?*

Various members of the family were hanging around, obviously wondering too. The 500-pound woman was aware of us, but she was too sick to say anything. Her arms hung at her sides like two barrels. Her head was held semierect by a pillow wedged under her several chins. She was draped with a sheet. There wasn't a dress made that would cover her.

It was obvious that we weren't ever going to get this woman onto any stretcher, nor was there any way to get her down four flights of stairs. She would have to be lowered out the window and down to the sidewalk below with block and tackle, like a grand piano.

One of the men went to the roof and cut a hole big enough to fit a long timber that would act as a boom. We attached our roof ropes to this and lowered the blocks to the level of the fourth-floor window. Inside the apartment, we passed heavy slings under the framework of the chair and, lifting one corner at a time by brute force, we were able to kick the block foundation out from under it. The stench was overpowering.

Next we had to get the chair from the middle of the room to the window, where we could hook the roof ropes onto the slings. But the chair was impossible to slide on the floor. We found some cooking oil in the kitchen and spilled it around as a lubricant. Now the chair would slide. But when we got it over to the window, it was obvious that the window frame was too narrow for the operation we had in mind.

So out came the window, frame and all. Now we had a big opening in the side of the brick building. In came the block and tackle, up went the load over the height of the windowsill and down went the 500-pound lady into a waiting truck below.

We breathed a sigh of relief.

Later that day we got another call from the Welfare Department. We thought it was going to be some kind words about what a good job we did. No such luck. The 500-pound lady's family was complaining about the window. Would we please go back and repair the damage we caused?

16

A HOUSE IS
NOT A HOME —UNLESS
YOU MAKE IT ONE

The *Constellation* fire and the honors it brought were like hitting a home run early in the ball game; it gave me an edge on the pitcher, just what I needed to establish authority in the company. For one thing, I had demonstrated on the carrier that I wouldn't ask anything of the men that I wasn't prepared to do myself. Also, if there were some at Rescue 2 who had harbored some doubts about their new lieutenant's credentials, they were given some eyewitness confirmation. Hamilton wasn't all legend. I don't mean to boast, but Zuercher and I sure as hell had showed them what I thought being a fireman was all about. It had to be convincing; it had almost cost me my life.

This doesn't mean that from that moment everybody fell

automatically in line with my way of thinking and doing things. I still had personnel problems, and they were tougher to lick, in some ways, than a stubborn fire. I had learned how to deal with *that* old enemy, but people are more complex. I guess it's like the difference between multiple-choice questions and essays on an exam.

A fireman really has two homes—one where his wife and family live, and the other a house where big red trucks are parked in the living room. I was determined that we would keep our home-away-from home as clean and comfortable as we could. Years ago, back in the days when firemen were considered little better than bums who sat around and drank and played cards all day, the firehouse was a rowdy sort of place where housekeeping came after everything else. In this respect I soon realized that the old Rescue 2 quarters on Carlton Avenue could stand some improvements. I figured if I could raise morale at the fires and emergencies, I ought to be able to raise it in the firehouse, too.

The first thing I noticed was that there was no real place for the men to eat. The small kitchen where food was prepared was at the back of the building on the apparatus floor, but the men often ate standing up behind the trucks, sitting on the back step of the pumper or just on an empty box. I didn't see why we couldn't all get together and build a sitting room onto the back of the building, next to the kitchen. The land was there. We had a number of guys in the outfit with skills as carpenters, masons, electricians, etc. All we needed was a plan and some materials.

When I started talking this up, I was soon made aware that not everybody in the two companies who shared the firehouse was in favor of "the new lieutenant's improvements." Some of the old-timers laughed openly when a few of us in Rescue talked about the sitting room and what a nice place it would be to eat, read or watch TV. "We been eating here behind the engine for fifteen years, Loo," one of the veterans said. "We don't need no sitting room."

I said I didn't care about the past, I cared about now. But no matter what I said, there was muttering. I decided to ignore it.

The next and more serious obstacle was posed by Captain Lawler. When he got wind of our plan he said, Stop! It seemed we couldn't do anything like that without permission from the Building Department. *Groan.* If our idea ever got tangled up with bureaucracy, forget it! "Why don't you call the department and ask permission, Cap?" I urged. But he wasn't that enthusiastic about our idea. He stalled. He pointed out that the old firehouse had so many building-code violations on it now that it was unlikely we'd ever be allowed to make alterations. He also raised the question of expense. He didn't think the men should be asked to pay for it.

So I called the Building Department myself. And I found out the captain was right. The man I talked to said, "Not a chance in the world. That firehouse of yours is so old you'll never get permission."

"But we have to eat right next to the toilet!" I told him. "What if we go ahead and do it without permission? Who's going to know the difference?" I was upset. So was the guy at the Building Department.

"If you do that," he said, "don't say you called here!"

"We're going ahead!" I said.

"I don't remember you called," he said, and hung up.

But Captain Lawler still wouldn't let us begin. The guys were already figuring on what kind of furniture we would put in the sitting room, where the TV would go, all that, so it was a big disappointment. We went around for days in a blue mood. Our pet project had been shot down by the brass. I decided it was up to me to think of something. I was the new Loo, after all, and it was my idea.

One day when I was off duty I decided on a plan. I called the firehouse and asked for the captain of the engine company, who, as such, was nominally in command of the quarters. I said, "Captain, this is [so-and-so; I just made up a name] from the Building Department on Church Street."

"Yeah, what is it?" he asked.

"Well, it's about your request for a building permit, captain. . . ."

"Yeah, what about it?" He sounded vague. He hadn't heard much about our scheme.

"Well, it's been approved. You can go ahead." Then I hung up.

The next day when I came on duty everybody was excited. "Hey, Loo," the guys were saying, "somebody called from the Building Department and okayed the sitting room!"

"Really?"

"Yeah, really! We can begin!"

The next problem was where to scrounge the materials we needed so we wouldn't have to put out any cash for them. We knew better than to shake anybody down, and we made up our minds never to take something that no one knew about. This was going to be a highly ethical operation—but cheap. For example, at this time they happened to be building an addition to Brooklyn Hospital and there sure was a lot of building material lying around the site. There was also a contractor who seemed to like firemen. One day I told him what we were trying to do, and he said he'd like to help. "What do you need?" he said.

I told him we needed 18 sheets of plywood and so many two-by-fours, that sort of thing. "Sure, you can have it," he said. "The only trouble is, I don't have any way to get it over to you."

"Don't worry about that," I told him. "We've got a big truck."

It was the same with other stuff we needed. Cement. Roofing. Little by little we were accumulating our supplies and storing them in the yard behind the firehouse. Some of the old hairbags in the two outfits would see us coming in loaded down and they'd make cracks about our sitting room, but we didn't care. If they didn't want to share it with us, they could keep on eating on the back of the pumper.

We'd been getting ready for the actual construction for

almost a month when I came on one evening for a night tour and stuck my head out the back door to see if any new supplies had arrived during the day. What I saw instead was a shambles —all our lumber had been cut up into short pieces and tossed all over the back lot! I could feel the rage building up as I turned back into the quarters.

"What happened to the lumber?" I asked, tight-lipped.

Nobody answered, or nobody knew. A couple of the guys looked scared. I think I said something about there being some pretty stupid jerks in this outfit, and then I stomped out and up the stairs to catch Captain Lawler before he went off duty.

"What happened to our supplies, Cap?" I said.

"I'm not sure," he said, "but I think some of the men had a drill out there this morning. I heard the chain saws."

So that was it. The hairbags had gotten their revenge. And the captain didn't really care. I was heartsick. I went back down the stairs at half the speed I had gone up. When I got back to the kitchen there were two or three of the oldtimers standing around with coffee mugs in their hands. They weren't saying anything, but they were smiling.

"Okay," I said. "You guys sawed up six or seven hundred dollars' worth of our lumber today and I hope that makes you feel good inside. But let me tell you something. You're not going to break my chops! I'll go out and get more lumber and we're going to have our sitting room if I have to saw you punks up into small pieces first!"

But it was a setback and it would be quite a while before we could get up the enthusiasm to start again. Instead, we turned to a project in the basement; at least that didn't require many supplies. We built a Ping-Pong table and a big fish tank and some of the guys went to the aquarium to find out how to care for tropical fish. Hank Zuercher was a weight lifter, so he built a rack for weights and we put down some mattresses to work out on. Somebody else brought in an old pinball machine and a shuffleboard game. Pretty soon we had a very respectable recreation room in what had been a cellarful of old junk. Nobody interfered with us this time. The new Loo and his crowd were getting the upper hand on the hairbags by sheer output of energy.

It wasn't just in the area of fun and games that I wanted to make improvements, however. I also wanted to instill professional pride in our work. As I say, a lot of people used to regard firemen as near the bottom of the social order, drinkers and womanizers. But I felt very strongly that what we did was a daring and dangerous *profession,* and that meant having professional standards. And especially where the public was watching us. For example:

We were called to an accident on the elevated one day. A young Puerto Rican boy had been riding between the cars of the train and had fallen to the tracks and been all chewed to pieces by the wheels. It was a gory mess and it drew quite a crowd of rubbernecks in the street below. The power was shut off and my crew got in there and started recovering as many of the chunks as we could. The cops were down below and they were telling us to go ahead and shove the pieces of the body through the tracks and let them fall into the street. That seemed just too gruesome to me. I wouldn't let my guys do it. We got an aerial ladder in and brought the boy's remains down the ladder. The Spanish-speaking people in the neighborhood seemed to appreciate this. "Watch how the *barberos* do it!" they were saying. (*Barberos* is their name for firemen.) I think we gained their respect because we went about the job with some professional class.

We were often called to subway accidents like this, and they were invariably a mess. I always told my men: "Treat every bit and piece of a body as if it were your own mother or sister! None of this tossing a leg up on the platform like a piece of meat! Cops may operate that way, but not firemen." I wanted the public to understand that firemen have respect and compassion. We would always spread sawdust on pools of blood and we never left so much as a fingernail behind for the morbidly curious to gawk at. At automobile accidents we administered first aid as neatly as doctors; and if we had to do any cutting of flesh, we never made a big show of it; one man would always stand so as to block the public's view of what we had to do.

One time some people from Canada were involved in an auto accident on the Brooklyn-Queens Expressway and we were called to help with the injured. The car was pretty well demolished and it was raining, so we took a couple of uninjured children who had been passengers and put them into the back of our truck to keep them safe from the heavy expressway traffic. Then a couple of the Rescue guys took off their coats and held them over one of the injured who was lying in the roadway to shield him from the rain until the ambulance arrived. Many weeks later, a letter from the family, sent through Mayor Lindsay's office, arrived at our firehouse, thanking us for the professional way we had cared for these visitors from another country.

I'm not saying that the men of Rescue 2 were the only ones ever to do such things. I'm sure firemen in companies all over the city have demonstrated the same sort of compassion over and over again. As a new lieutenant, I just wanted to be sure that there would be no better example of professionalism than *my* outfit.

Too many times I had seen a fireman make a mad dash back to the truck to get a tourniquet out of a first-aid kit. I knew that seconds count when you're bleeding to death, so I ordered all my men to carry a length of rubber tourniquet in their pants pockets at all times—and I went down to Cumberland Hospital and got the hose and cut it up into lengths myself. Not long after, we were called to an explosion in a chemistry lab at Brooklyn Poly. A young student had been nearly blown apart, fingers were missing from both his hands and he was bleeding heavily. The tourniquets came out of the rescuemen's pockets even before the first-aid case was opened. The boy lived.

As our skills improved, so did our morale. Not only were we the busiest rescue company in the city, we were sure we were the best! Pride, they say, is a sin, but we had it. And speaking of sin, I didn't mind letting the men know how I felt about religion either. I'd tell them, "When they come around to your house and ask you to donate to the stained-glass window at the church—or maybe it's a pew they want you to buy—don't give because of any sense of guilt. A fireman gives to humanity every day of his life." That was my philosophy and that's what I told my men. "You don't have to buy your way into heaven, not any of you. You've saved people right here on earth. I mean, you've *really* saved 'em! People are walking the streets today because you saved 'em! So when they come around with their hand out for another donation, you can tell them you gave at the office!"

Morale or esprit or whatever you call it grows in many ways and many places, but we all knew that the most important place to have it was in the midst of danger, where every one of us was depending on the other fellow. Sometimes, when we were beat and discouraged and we'd tried for a quarter of an hour to gain a few feet against a building full of fire, I'd try to rally the guys against what I called the Red Devil—the fire, the enemy, the guy we had to lick. "Come on! Let's get that Red Devil!" I'd say. "Are you going to let that Red Devil drive us back?" And the guys would respond, "Okay, one more time, here we go against the Red Devil!"

Sounds silly doesn't it? Grown men acting like kids at a football game. Hit 'em again, hit 'em again, hit 'em again H A R D E R!

Kill the Red Devil!

You did it, Rescue 2! You can do it again!

17

A LEGEND BEGINS
TO GROW

No matter how anxious we were to prove ourselves, individually or as a rescue company, the opportunities didn't come every day. Food-on-the-stove fires never win medals. Street brawls are only a chance to get hurt. False alarms sometimes cause traffic accidents, but never headlines. I don't mean we were all sitting around just waiting for the moment when we could be heroic, but there was a certain rhythm to the alarms. Months would go by in which we would deal with routine incidents until that was all there seemed to be, but I sometimes felt the rhythm and I knew a big one was coming. That's the way it was almost from the beginning at Rescue 2.

First there was the *Constellation* at the end of 1960. Then began a series of annual events that seemed almost to have been planned. I remember them by the street names, usually, although of course there were people involved, too. Felix Street. Clymer Street. York Street. Grant Street. Pacific Street. Five disasters, each about a year apart, and all of them resulted in some kind of honor for me. It was exciting, but it was also troubling. My battle against the Red Devil was beginning to look like a personal vendetta.

I came to very close grips with him on March 29, 1962, on Felix Street in Brooklyn. It was one of the alarm boxes that Rescue 2 always ran on, so I knew from experience it was a bad area, full of highly flammable old buildings, all of them death-traps under the right circumstances.

When we got to the fire, Engine 56 was already there, but no truck company had yet arrived. The building was what we call a "20-by-40," a three-story tinderbox. No fire was showing at the front, but the block was full of smoke. People who had fled the building told us that the fire was on the second floor and that there was a whole family in the third-floor apartment trapped by the fire below. I sent two of my men to vent the roof and then I took Frankie Carino with me up the stairs as far as we could go.

When we got to the second-floor landing we found the men from Engine 56 lying low on the floor, waiting for water. Even if there were people upstairs, the Engine was just doing its proper job; it was Rescue's job to move up and search. I was just getting ready to climb over the enginemen and head for the stairs when the fire blew out of a door into the second-floor hall and started climbing the stairs I was going to use.

This changed the situation completely. I took a quick look at the way the flames were licking at the base of the stairs and I figured if I jumped up high on the banister and climbed fast enough, I could stay ahead of the fire and make the third floor anyway. I hollered at the Engine to hit the blown-out doorway as soon as they got water and try to push the fire back in. If it kept coming up those stairs, I knew I'd have serious trouble.

Then I took a big leap, grabbed the midpoint of the banister, hauled myself over ahead of the fire and scrambled up to the third-floor hall.

The hall went straight from the front of the building to the back, with several doors leading off it. A regular "old law" tenement layout. The smoke was thick and visibility was zero except near the floor, so I crawled, heading first to the front. I found a door and tried to force it in, but no go. It wouldn't give even when I put my back up against the opposite wall and pushed with my feet. By its location, I figured this had to be a bedroom, but I heard no sounds of people, so I moved back down the hall toward the rear. I hit the last door with my shoulder and it caved in.

The smoke in the room was 100 percent; I couldn't see a thing. I felt around and knew I was in a kitchen, but there were no bodies anywhere, so I moved on through the apartment, working my way toward the front again.

The first two rooms I came to after the kitchen were bedrooms. I found the beds, felt around, but there was nobody. Was the report of a family up here a mistake? It wouldn't be the first time, I thought. The heat was building pretty fast now. The fire in the apartment below was still going strong, and still no sound of the water. If worse came to worst, I was thinking, I could jump out the window at the front when I got there. I'd probably break a leg, but that would be better than what was going to happen to me in this apartment in a few minutes. I was sure there would be no way down the stairs by now, not without water on the fire. I wondered where my men were. Frankie Carino must still be on the second floor and worrying about me.

In the third bedroom, the front one that I couldn't get into from the hall, I found the bodies, a big pile of them, so many that I couldn't even be sure how many. They were all jammed up behind the door, one on top of another. No wonder I wasn't able to push it in, with hundreds of pounds of unconscious humans blocking the way. I started pulling them back, tumbling them off one another, operating more from touch than from sight. There were men and women, kids and grownups. Finally I pulled the last one back far enough to get at the door and open it. And there was Frankie Carino on the other side!

I pulled two of the people to the door for Frankie to haul away. They had water on the fire now and the smoke was beginning to lift a little along with the steam and the stink, but it was still thick in the bedrooms, and flames were coming up through the baseboards from below. I could see one more small room off this front bedroom, so while Frankie helped with the first batch of bodies, I searched some more. I found a girl unconscious on a bed, and a young man kneeling by the bed as if he were praying. I pulled them both back to the hall door, then down to the stairs. I guess my strength was about gone by then, because the next thing I knew I was falling down the stairs to the second floor with the guy on top of me.

When I got to the street, I counted the bodies—nine people all laid out with the resuscitators working on them. All nine ended up in the hospital, but they all lived. What could have been a mass roast turned out to be a mass rescue.

I took some oxygen from Fireman Bob Basti of Engine 210, gathered a little fresh strength and went back into the building. I wanted to take another look at that apartment. The fire was knocked down by now, and I always liked one more opportunity to see what we'd done right and what we'd done wrong. It was one of the best ways I knew to avoid making the same mistake twice.

When I got to the front room again, I made a sad discovery. Under the smashed, bent remains of a venetian blind I found the body of a baby, an infant girl. She wasn't burned, but she'd been crushed by something heavy. I looked around at where I was and where the body lay. I knew it was possible that I was responsible for this. While I was pulling the other bodies around, I might have kneeled on this baby without knowing it. The thought bothered me and lingers still. The only death in the fire. Had I caused it? Could I have prevented it? I had to study the question. I knew mistakes can be made in burning buildings. As a professional, you can understand almost any honest error that a fireman may make. But that didn't excuse them.

They awarded me a Class Three for Felix Street. Some people thought it should have been more. You're allowed to appeal if you think you've been slighted on one of these honors, but I never did in 24 years. Over the fire? Yes, it's the most dangerous place you can be. Nine lives saved? Yes, that was a lot of people. "You did it again, Dick!" They told me, and I heard them building the legend again. Okay, fine. It would be good for morale, anyway, good for Rescue 2—and we were going to be the best in the business.

MIDSUMMER NIGHT'S NIGHTMARE

The sliver of glass was seven inches long and it had gone through the palm of my right hand while I was searching under a bed for two children trapped in a fire. I didn't know what I had done until I tried to pass one of the kids to another fireman and felt the little boy's pajamas pinned to my red rubber gloves. Then I saw the spear.

It was the beginning of a crazy, mixed-up night.

I broke the glass off the palm and back of my hand so I could pull the glove off, and when I did, a lot of blood spilled out. Also, two of my fingers wouldn't move, so I knew it was time for a trip to Cumberland Hospital.

Dr. Adams, a police surgeon, happened to be in the emergency room. I was lucky; he was a good man. He put a couple of needles into the hand to kill the pain and then he probed around, took out all the glass, fixed two cut tendons, X-rayed everything and was just finishing with nine stitches in the palm, four between the fingers and three on the back when Johnny Hopkins, one of my men, came in from the truck to say there was a bad fire in Red Hook and a bunch of kids were trapped.

If I'd had any sense I'd have reported the injury to the dispatcher and gone home. But we had a tradition to preserve: Rescue is always ready to respond—even if we have to send two guys in a taxi! So I thanked Dr. Adams for fixing me up and took off for Red Hook. The hand didn't feel too bad.

When we got to the fire we found a Puerto Rican guy making trips in and out of the building, carrying his clothes out on wire hangers and putting them all in his car. We asked him if there were any kids upstairs and he said yes, there was one. "My keed on second floor," he said.

One of the firemen asked him if his clothes were more important than his keed.

"Keeds are easy to get," he said. "New clothes cost lot of money!"

One of the Rescue guys ran into the building and in a minute was back with the child from the second floor. He handed the little boy to a cop who was there. "Here," the fireman said, glaring at the father, "this is an abandoned child. Take care of it!"

"That's my keed!" said the father. "No abandonado!"

Then the fireman hit him right in the mouth.

"Arrest heem!" screamed the father, getting up from his pile of clothes.

"I didn't see nothing," said the cop.

There was so much excitement, I almost forgot about my hand. It was numb from the needle anyway, so I went up on the roof with some of the men and we chopped a hole and vented. The fire was getting worse, and more and more apparatus was arriving. When it finally went to four alarms, that automatically brought a Fire Department doctor to the scene.

By then I'd been working pretty hard and my hand was a mess again. The bandages were hanging off like dirty ribbons, the stitches had pulled out, and I was all bloody.

"What happened to your hand?" asked the FD doctor when he saw me.

"I cut it," I said.

The doctor was confused. He thought the injury had occurred at this fire. "Did you try to sew it up yourself?" he said.

I tried to explain about the other fire.

"You're going to get yourself in bad trouble with that story," said the doc. "You know what the rules are about reporting injuries!"

"Okay, doc," I said. "Would it be better if I said it happened here?"

"In that case, there's no problem," he said. "Get yourself to the hospital."

I went back to Cumberland. Dr. Adams was still there.

"Sorry, doc," I said.

18

FRIENDS AND NEIGHBORS

If a fireman has two homes, he also has two neighborhoods, two places in the world where he feels at home because he knows the people and the ground and the air. For me, this meant quite a contrast. Ginny and Richard Jr. and Sherree were in quiet, peaceful Wantagh. It might not be a famous or fashionable suburb, but it was white, middle-class and respectable.

Carlton Avenue, home of Rescue 2, was something else again. It was mostly black or Puerto Rican; it was also poor, dirty and dangerous. But it became just as much mine as Wantagh, and after a while, the color of the place faded and the dirt and danger weren't so noticeable either. I told my men: "We live here. These are our neighbors. Let's make the best of it." What may have seemed repugnant at first became, if not lov-

able, at least more understandable as my time in Brooklyn went
on. The black man who didn't want to remove his finger from
a bullet hole in his friend's chest was someone to be handled
with patience, not anger.

*Come on, man. We can't fix your buddy up 'less you get that
finger out.*

The difference between a commuting fireman and a commuting office worker is this: The fireman not only works in his
city neighborhood, he *lives* there. He cooks and eats there, buys
his food there, sleeps there, parks his car on the streets, sits in
his front door and watches the people go by. The bright, polite
kids who have been brought up right, the junkies and drunks,
the young mothers, the whores. And when there is a fire or an
emergency, the fireman goes into their houses. He knows how
his neighbors live, what they eat, where they wash, how they
make love, and how they kill. I knew more about my neighbors
on Carlton Avenue than I knew about my neighbors in Wantagh.

The world changed a lot between 1959, when I first came
to Rescue 2 as a new Loo, and 1973, when I left for the last time.
In the old days, if both fire companies were out responding to
an alarm, people used to look after the firehouse for us, close
the big doors to keep the heat in in winter, that sort of thing.
Not anymore. If everyone has to leave the firehouse today, we
lock everything behind us. Some of our neighbors would steal
us blind. And others would tell us later who did it.

One night a fireman, Brian Spitalle, caught a neighbor
stealing watches and wallets from our lockers on the third floor.
The thief ran, and the fireman went after him—barefoot. They
raced through the streets. This fireman had had training in
karate, so when he caught up with his man in the shrubbery
near one of the housing projects, he didn't have any trouble
subduing him. And just to be sure he didn't lose him, he pulled
the robber's clothes off, right down to his underwear.

"Then I began to worry," Spitalle said later. "Here was
this guy on the ground and me on top of him and he's hollering
his head off and black people are beginning to look out the

windows. Suddenly I realized that it looked very much like a white guy was mugging a black man. So I took his clothes and left him there for the police to deal with."

Not all our neighbors came to the firehouse to steal. Some only wanted to borrow. Late on a Sunday night, when the filling stations were all closed, we'd often be asked for a gallon of gas to get somebody home. Just be damn sure you bring the can back, I'd say. And usually they would.

Tools were also popular, and everybody knew our Rescue truck was loaded. Sometimes it was just a pipe wrench that was needed to fix some leaking plumbing. Sometimes it was a bolt cutter when the key to a chain lock was lost. Once the police returned a bolt cutter we had loaned.

"This looks like it might be yours," the cop said.

"Yeah, it's ours. Where'd you find it?"

"Couple of guys just used it to break into the TV store."

But just because we got taken once in a while, it didn't stop us from trying to be good neighbors. Later, the Fire Department had some sort of a fancy community-relations program. We had ours much earlier. When the man down the block came to us and said he'd locked himself out of his apartment, we had a ladder that was long enough to get him in the front window.

"You sure that's *your* apartment, now?"

"Yes, sir."

"You sure you live on the *second* floor?" (It paid to check.)

Most of our neighbors looked upon firemen as well paid, always with a few extra bucks in our pockets. As a result we were offered a variety of merchandise, always at bargain prices. One night it was an automobile battery. Five dollars is all the old man wanted for it, and it seemed to be in almost new condition.

"That's a damn good battery if anybody needs one," Bob Basti said. "It costs forty dollars new. I've got one just like it in my own car."

The next morning, of course, he found he didn't have any battery in his car. "Son of a bitch!" he said, "Why didn't I buy it?"

We weren't in the charity business, but we tried to help in small ways. Firemen brought sneakers and gloves and too-small sweaters from their own kids' closets at home, and these found new owners on our block. Sometimes, when I caught a big bluefish in Long Island Sound, I knew people in Brooklyn who would help me eat half of it. And there were certain kids in the area who were always glad to cash in firemen's soda bottles for a few dimes.

I suppose the way we helped most from day to day was with first aid. In summer it was sunburns, cut feet, knife wounds. In winter it was scalding water or hot fat from the stove. Sometimes it was a premature birth. And always the bruises and slashes of fights. We were a lot closer than the hospital, where you had to wait in the emergency room and then show your Welfare card.

We also took care of the dead. We didn't investigate—the police came along to do that later—but we were usually there first.

We found Willie lying facedown in the backyard of his tenement. Nobody seemed to know much about him until we asked the old woman drinking beer on the front stoop if she'd come back with us and take a look.

"I think that's Willie," she said.

"You know Willie?"

"Yeah, I know Willie. He's my common-law."

"You live with Willie?"

"Sometimes. He's my common-law."

"What happened to Willie?"

"I dunno. He hurt?"

"We think Willie's dead."

"You dead, Willie?"

No answer.

"Don't worry, Willie. I find me another man."

We picked Willie up and put him in the Stokes basket and carried him through the hall and out the front door to the stoop. A young man was standing there waiting for us.

"That Willie?" he said.

"It's Willie."

"Who's the chief here?"

I said I was.

"You do me a favor, chief? Jes let me go through Willie's pockets before you take him away?"

"What for?"

"He owe me a dolla! How'm I ever goin' to get ma dolla if you take Willie away?"

I don't know whether these people loved us, admired us, respected us—or maybe hated us. They saw what we could do with our heads and our hands and our tools. They knew we went into burning buildings like stepping into a hot shower. Some of them knew that the fella with the white hat, the lieutenant, had saved some people's lives. They must have understood that we did this for young and old, rich and poor, black and white, anybody. They knew because they used to stand around and watch. They lived on the streets where we practiced our profession.

On Clymer Street there was an old Civil War brick building, near the Navy Yard, and it had machine shops on each of its three floors. At some time they had installed a sprinkler system throughout the building and they had a big holding tank for water on the roof.

The alarm came to us on the telephone about noon. Three rings, which meant Rescue goes! Building collapse, someone said. We rolled. It was only about 12 blocks from the firehouse. When we arrived we didn't see any sign of collapse, but the air was full of dust, and the street was full of people. As we tumbled off the truck we grabbed axes, first-aid kits, Halligan tools, rope.

When we got inside we saw instantly what had happened. The water tank for the sprinkler system had crashed right through all three floors of the building. We looked up between the walls to the sky above. But in the middle was a huge mountain of timbers, masonry, machinery, columns, shafts, brick, iron castings—a whole factory turned into rubble.

The first thing to find out was how many people might be

under all those tons of debris. Since it was lunchtime, a lot of the workers had left the building just before the collapse. I scanned the "IN" side of the time-card racks (a search technique I had recorded in my little black book long ago), and they showed that only three people were still in. These three were probably somewhere under the pile. A foreman helped us figure out where they might be. One worked on the first floor—we found him in the basement with a broken arm but nothing else wrong. Another worked on the second floor—we found him sitting in the wreckage of the toilet where he had been when the roof fell in. No injuries, just surprise.

Where was the third man? Jack Barnett, a machine operator who worked on the third floor, always took his lunch right by his lathe, I was told. Find the lathe and we'd find Barnett. It wasn't going to be easy, and the chances didn't seem promising. This man had probably fallen two floors, and some of the stuff that fell with him weighed tons. Like his lathe.

We started digging and climbing. In the wreckage where the second floor had been we found the lathe with Mr. Barnett under it, pinned by some heavy timbers. He had a lot of broken bones and he was in some pain, but he was very much alive. The only problem was how to lift a 3000-pound piece of machinery off this man with not much but the blue sky above to hook onto. It was obviously a job to test our ingenuity and our best tools.

Fortunately, there were a lot of big timbers in the wreckage which we could use. I found a big 12-by-12 not far removed from the lathe and we pulled it into place like a bridge over the void where our victim and his machine were submerged in rubble. After we had manhandled this into place—no easy job in itself, because we couldn't find secure footing anywhere—we next brought two powerful Grip-Hoists from the truck. This tool has the same tremendous lifting power as a chainfall, but it's operated by pumping on a long handle. We rigged one of these to each end of our 12-by-12 and then attached the lifting hooks to each end of the lathe below. Each of the hoists had a 1 1/2-ton capacity, more than enough if we'd done everything right. Slowly we started jacking up the weight.

We had just managed to relieve some of the pressure on Barnett when I heard a commotion among the men standing above the hole. I looked up to see a captain from Rescue 4 hollering that all work should stop. I didn't even know 4 had been called in to assist on the job and I couldn't see who the man was at first. Then I recognized the voice.

Lieutenant—now Captain—Douglass!

"You can't do it that way," he was saying to the chief. "That's dangerous! I'll give the orders!"

Same old Douglass! Only now he wasn't in my outfit and he couldn't order my men around. I came up out of the hole to see what would happen next. Douglass saw me and started telling me that the hoists should be secured to some old iron columns still standing where the third floor had been.

"I think you want to pull the rest of the building down!" I said.

"Who's in charge here?" Douglass asked, turning to the chief.

I didn't wait for the answer. I said, "I'm in charge of my men and you're in charge of yours. Why don't you take 'em someplace and do something useful—captain?"

The chief picked up on this and told Douglass to take his group to the basement to search for more victims. Of course there were no more victims down there and we all knew it, but it was the best way to solve a problem. Then we got back to work on Mr. Barnett and finally lifted the lathe and all the timbers off him. He must have been in the hospital quite a while, but he came out of it all right and the following Thanksgiving he showed up at the firehouse to present us with a turkey dinner and all the fixins. Must have cost him fifty bucks, but that didn't matter as much as his gratitude.

We used to run into Captain Douglass every once in a while. Whenever we ended up on the same job, my men always worked four times as hard and fast just to show him up. There was just something about the man that turned people against him, but it wasn't altogether fair. He was a capable man and conscientious; he just totally lacked the ability to lead men.

Meantime, I was beginning to have just the opposite kind of problem. The way events were breaking for me was contributing to the myth that I had some special powers. At things like the Clymer Street collapse, firemen from other outfits would come up and start working with my men. "Mind if I work with you, Loo?" they'd say. I'd ask where their own company was working. "Oh, they don't need me right now," was the usual story. Then they'd say, "I thought I might learn something by working with you."

Flattering, yes, but also a little disconcerting. I wasn't a performer. I couldn't put on an act or a demonstration while I was absorbed in doing a job.

In the Bronx one time, a train went off the tracks and three men were trapped inside. Police Emergency was there trying to lift the whole impossible weight of the train with jacks. When we arrived I took one look and told my guys to start digging a tunnel down under the train to take the men out. The cops thought that was remarkable. What a genius idea!

I didn't think so. Rescue was *expected* to come up with solutions that the average cop or fireman wouldn't think of. That was our job.

19

SOMEONE ELSE'S TURN
TO BE A HERO

I didn't know whether or not I would ever win the James Gordon Bennett medal. When I was a probie, the Fire Department's highest honor seemed like something entirely out of reach, an Everest. But as the years went on and I succeeded in getting quite a number of honors in various categories, I guess the possibility of the Bennett didn't seem so remote. Then, when it was won by one of my own men in a fire where we were working together, I had a better idea of what kind of courage it would take.

I think most firemen would agree that you shouldn't go hunting for medals. Either you're in the right place at the right time or it isn't going to happen to you. There's no way to force the department's cherished honors. If you go hunting for them

—and, oh, yes, there are guys who do—you could get yourself killed.

Of course, you *could* also get yourself killed doing what Jim Bowler did.

At 8:30 A.M. on September 20, 1964, Rescue 2 was called to a fire in a high-rise apartment project on York Street. When we got there, everybody was looking up at only one thing: A woman was standing on a window ledge 11 stories up. Her back to the street, her head turned to the side to avoid the smoke pumping out the window of her apartment, she was holding onto the center pole of a casement window with both hands. It looked like a classic jump situation. Even though you who are reading this now say you'd never, *never* jump, every fireman knows there is a point in a fire where everyone will jump. The question is when. And the job is to keep it from happening. This woman looked pretty desperate.

There is no way to save someone who jumps 11 stories; no net or air bag yet invented can break such a fall, and there is no aerial ladder in any fire department in the world that can reach that high. To save this woman, somebody was going to have to go get her—and fast. While the chief kept hollering at her not to jump, I headed into the building with all my men. It was a situation in which a couple of our training techniques paid off right away.

In project fires it was our rule never to put on the heavy boots. You didn't really need them in these modern buildings and you could move a lot quicker without them, especially when you were climbing stairs. So we went in in our shoes.

The second rule was never to take the elevators. Even if 11 floors seems like a terrific height to climb and still have any wind left when you got there, I still preferred my feet. Elevators get stuck, and sometimes their doors may not open on the fire floor. *Then* where are you?

As we passed through the lobby of the building there were a lot of firemen standing around waiting for the elevator. We took off on foot up the fire stairs while they either looked or laughed. "There go those smart guys from Rescue!" I heard them say. But we got to the fire floor before they did.

I divided my men, sending Jim Bowler and George Lee to the twelfth floor with orders to lean out the apartment window just above the woman on eleven and try to talk her out of jumping. Sometimes, I knew, seeing a fireman that close will persuade a panicky fire victim that help is really on the way.

The rest of us found the door to the fire apartment on the eleventh floor quick enough; smoke was coming out all around the frame. We gave it a couple of good belts, but the door was locked, so two guys went to work on it with the Halligans and axes. Meantime, I took Paul Zydor into the adjoining apartment where I leaned out the window to tell the woman hanging outside that it would only take another minute or two to save her.

If we could only get the door open!

By now the hall was full of other firemen from the Engine and Truck who had arrived by elevator. They couldn't seem to get the door open either. There was a terrific crashing and banging that told me there was some unusual problem with the lock.

I knew what the apartment walls were like in these housing projects; usually they were built from terra-cotta blocks, easy enough to smash through if you have to. Zydor had an axe with him, so I told him to poke a hole through from the apartment we were in. I figured we might get in quicker through the wall than the men coming through the door. Zydor started swinging the axe. The lady whose apartment we were wrecking never said a word as the plaster flew.

When the hole was big enough to get your head and shoulders into, I asked Zydor to crawl in and take a look. He did, but pulled his head out almost at once and said, "There's nothing in there but a void!"

"A void? What do you mean?"

"There's nothing in there but black space," he said.

I had to take a look for myself. When I did, I could see that the "black" was smoke. I got my shoulders into the hole and crawled all the way in. But I might as well have been at the bottom of a coal mine. I dropped as low as I could to avoid the heat and look for light. I knew where the window must be where the woman was hanging and I headed in that direction until I could see some light coming through the smoke. I crawled past a bed, then I came to the wall, reached up, felt the windowsill, reached up farther and grabbed her two legs.

My grip must have startled her, coming out of the black smoke. She was screaming and almost hysterical. I tried to pull her toward me, but she didn't want to move in the direction of the fire. One thing I was sure of: She wasn't going to jump with me holding onto her; not unless she took me with her. I was just wishing she'd loosen her grip on that window frame.

Then two things happened almost at once. The men in the hall finally broke through the elaborate locking bar that was holding the door, and I could hear the water hitting the fire. In a few minutes that would help.

But in the meantime, we still had a problem with the woman. The smoke was lifting a little now that the door was open, and I could see out the window. In fact, I could see some very strange things out the window. I could see two feet and a pair of legs in blue pants dangling above the woman's head! They were swaying back and forth and she was looking up and I could hear a voice saying, "It's okay, lady, we'll have you out in no time."

Jim Bowler! Coming down the outside of the building like a human fly!

On his way to the apartment above the fire, Bowler had grabbed a length of linen hose that was hanging in a glass case in the hallway. We call these things "house lines." They are notoriously undependable because they are never used and seldom inspected. In the projects, the nozzles are usually stolen and sold for brass, and the hose itself is often rotten. Jim wasn't going to use it as a hose, however. He tied one end of it around his middle and told George Lee to secure the other end around something like a radiator so the line could be payed out. Then, instead of leaning out the twelfth-floor window, he *went* out.

Once that woman saw Jim coming down the outside wall, I guess she realized she wasn't going to have to jump, after all. I got her into the apartment and finally through the smoke and into the hall, where she passed out. After a little mouth-to-mouth she came around again, however—and then she told us that her two kids were still in the apartment.

In I went again. The Engine was still working on the fire, so I headed for the bedrooms. The beds seemed empty, but I'd been fooled by that before in fires. Kids will go anywhere when they're scared. I'd even found them curled up in bureau drawers. These two were between a bed and the wall, alive but unconscious. I brought them out into the hall, one in each arm. They were four and six and they looked as if they were only asleep.

Bowler had swung into the room from above while I was taking the woman out, but I couldn't take time to talk with him. By the time I found him in the hall, he and George Lee were laughing it up and feeling pretty good about what they'd done.

"I didn't know he was going all the way," George was saying. "I thought he was just trying to lean a little farther out and wanted to be safe with this hoseline around him. The next thing I know, I look up and he's gone!"

Jim didn't want to take much credit for what he'd done. "*You* saved her, Loo!" he said. "You got her out of the apartment." But I knew she might not have been around to save if Bowler hadn't come down to stop her from jumping. I also knew that he took a helluva chance using that old linen line. If the truck company hadn't been waiting around in the lobby for an elevator, there would have been a roof rope available. It would still have been risky, but much less so.

When we got back to quarters, everybody was chattering and slapping Bowler on the back. Our morale was higher than a kite. Rescue 2 shows them again! It was a terrific feeling. It was also a relief not to be the center of attention for a change.

Jim's was an unselfish act in the best tradition of the Fire Department and we wrote him up with full details and praise for what he had done. He was the father of six children then —13 now—and he needed not only any honors he could get but the money that usually goes with them.

The Honorable Board of Merit decided it was a Class One rescue and in June of 1965 they awarded Bowler the highest award he could get, the James Gordon Bennett. Somebody was also kind enough to give me a Class A for getting the woman and the kids out to the hall. There was a big difference between the awards. Just like there's a big difference between having two feet on the ground and swinging through thin air 11 stories up!

A WORKOUT FOR SHADRACH

In the Bible there is the story of Shadrach, Meshach and Abednego, who were cast into a fiery furnace, yet escaped alive. At Rescue 2 we used to cast an occasional nonbeliever into a fiery furnace of our own if he had anything uncomplimentary to say about us.

I remember one time we had a cocky young fireman detailed to our outfit for one tour of duty when one of our regulars was out sick. This guy was from a nearby truck company, and he wasn't sitting around our quarters long when we could see he was afflicted with an all too common idea. "You guys," he said, "are overrated. There isn't anything a rescue company can do that a good truck outfit can't do just as well."

"Okay," I said, "I'm always looking for new talent around here, so tonight, when we roll, you stick with me at the fires and I'll check you out."

"All you have to do is tap me on the back when you want me, Loo," he said, and I said, "No, that's not the way it's going to be. You tap me if you need anything, son, because I'll always be in front of you."

The first fire of the night was in a tenement, and it was Rescue's job to go in, vent the roof and then search. I took my bigmouth friend with me and we headed for the floor above the fire, the riskiest spot you can be in.

"Why are we going above the fire?" the guy asked.

"Because you're coming with me," I said, "and I'm going above the fire."

So up we went to the fourth floor and into a room that was pretty bad with heat and smoke. "Look under those beds for kids," I told my man. "Feel under 'em with your hands, don't just stick your head down and holler 'Are you there?' " I stayed in that room longer than necessary, but I wanted to teach this guy a lesson about rescuemen. When we finally backed out, he was wheezing and gagging.

"*What's the matter with* him?" *somebody asked, and I said,* "*I don't know. Must be asthma or something. Couldn't have been the smoke.*"

The second good fire of the night, we were called to relieve a couple of companies who were dead beat from hard work. They couldn't make the top floor of a building, so we were assigned a hoseline and told to push in. I decided it was a good spot for the nonbeliever, so I put him on the nozzle and up we went to where it was really hot.

"You really going to let him handle the nob, Loo?" one of my guys asked, and I said yes, I was going to give him a good roast.

We knocked the fire down in the fourth-floor hall, and then I said, "Come on, let's move into the apartment itself."

"I can't take any more of it," said our friend. "I gotta get out of here."

So I put John Drahosky up on the nozzle, but we kept our guest with us. In fact, I think I kneeled on him so he couldn't run away. "I'm dying from the heat," he said, and I said, "Yeah, that water's pretty hot when it flows back on you, isn't it?" Finally, he wriggled free and retreated down the hoseline to the hall.

After we knocked the fire down, a couple of the Rescue guys had to give the newcomer a lift to the street. His legs were rubbery, his eyes were red, he looked lost.

"What's wrong with that man?" the chief asked, and I said, "I don't know, chief. I don't even know what outfit he's with."

"I'm with the Rescue!" said our friend, looking around as if he were about to be abandoned.

"No you're not," I said, "you're not with Rescue. Maybe you came to the fire with us, but when you backed out of that room up there, you weren't one of us anymore."

We called him Shadrach after that. He wasn't a bad guy, really, and he took back all he'd said about rescuemen. "I just didn't know what I was talking about," he said one day, and I said, "That's okay, Shadrach. Just remember, though, that's *how we pull people out of burning buildings while a lot of other firemen are complaining about the heat.*"

20

LUNCH AT NATHAN'S

Our dream of having a sitting room never really died; it was just postponed. One day there was a ship fire in the Red Hook section and we noticed that some big lumber was being unloaded at the same pier where we answered the alarm. One of the guys said, "Hey, Loo! We could use some of that to build the room, couldn't we?" I was way ahead of him. I'd already had the same idea. And *this* time, I said to myself, nobody was going to saw up our lumber. There had been changes made in personnel by now. Some of the troublemakers had moved out of the outfit and a lot of others had changed their minds about the lieutenant.

I went over to a man who seemed to be supervising the unloading of the lumber and I had a talk with him about what

173

we were looking for. It was just a friendly chat about whether they ever had more timber than they needed or whether there was ever any left over when the counting was finished.

The guy was very friendly and he seemed to understand our situation. "How much stuff do you need?" he asked.

I said we needed so many of those big 4-by-10 beams if he could spare them.

"Okay," he said, "You can have 'em, just give me five minutes to walk away."

The timbers were just what we needed, better in fact. The only trouble was, they were 24 feet long! When we loaded them into the back of the Rescue truck, they stuck out more than 12 feet in back. To keep them from tipping out on the way back to quarters, four of the firemen stood on one end of the pile; and to keep from being a hazard in traffic, Ronnie Foote sat on the end of the pile that was sticking out and waved a big red flag.

When we came home with this load, everybody's enthusiasm for the sitting-room project picked up again. We divided ourselves up into groups: carpenters, cement workers, roofers, etc. For some reason, I was appointed chief procurer of supplies. It was amazing how much good stuff was actually forced on us as the project went along. I told one supplier that all we needed was some half-inch plywood for the roof, but he wouldn't hear of it! "Take that good one-inch stuff," he said. "It's been treated against rot." It was the same with other materials. One construction foreman wrote down a list of our needs just as if I were placing an order: Sheetrock, nails, tape, paste . . . Delivered it all, too.

When the room was finished, we dipped into some surplus money we had accumulated in our commissary fund and bought a new TV. Engine 210 acquired some tables and chairs from a church, and we were in business. The room gave us a terrific lift in morale; we spent more time there than in any other part of the firehouse.

That took care of the downstairs. Next I turned my attention to the upstairs. In our bunkroom the beds were pretty poor and the mattresses worse. I remembered that one time when we were having a drill down at Kings County Hospital I'd seen a lot of unused beds in a storeroom. So one day I went over and asked one of the administrators what they were going to do with all those old, *useless* beds. This nice lady said, "You're welcome to them if you can use them." I said I thought I could—if only they had mattresses. So she told me how to go about getting some mattresses, and blankets, too.

What I was finding out was that the community was willing to do a lot for firemen—all we had to do was ask.

Next we put a big fan in the bunkroom and that cooled things off on hot summer nights and got rid of the mosquitos too. We even put an air conditioner in the officers' room, but that got us in a little trouble with a deputy chief who pointed out that it was against regulations. But I knew a place that rebuilt air conditioners and I was able to pick one up for free. We went over and installed it in the deputy's office one hot summer afternoon—and heard no more objections from him about air conditioners.

The way I looked at it, morale was a tool. I not only wanted to be the best fireman in the department, I wanted my outfit to be the best, too. And one way to do this was to keep the men happy and enthusiastic about their work. Of course, this consisted of more than letting them watch TV in comfort.

I knew that drills could be a bore to firemen unless the man leading the drills made them interesting. I did this by always thinking of new ways to use our tools. For example, one time we figured out a way to hang a jackhammer so it could be used horizontally to breach a wall. We all experimented with this until we had it pretty well perfected. Then other outfits heard about it and we'd get calls to come and demonstrate what we'd developed.

I was also always interested in new tools. I read all the magazines in which new things were described and if I saw something that I thought we could use on the truck, I'd write to the manufacturer and we'd "borrow" a sample for testing. I think I was one of the first people in the Fire Department to see the usefulness of circular-bladed "Partner" saws. They were made originally by a Swiss outfit. I acquired one for tests with Rescue 2 and we soon saw that it could do things that no other tool could do. Before long, these saws became almost standard equipment throughout the department. Now they're carried by all truck companies.

To make our drills more realistic, we often used vacant buildings where we could practice the fastest ways of venting a roof or doing rope work. We got a little flak about being away from quarters, but my answer was always that no matter where we were, we had our radio on and we were ready to respond to any alarm. Chief of Department O'Hagan supported me in this.

One Sunday a crisis of morale came up in our kitchen. Dinner was being prepared, but for some reason the meal was turning into a disaster. Whatever the dish was, nobody liked it much anyway. When things started to go wrong there was general grumbling, and not altogether good-natured at that. One of the men stomped out of our new sitting room and said, half joking, half serious, "Come on, Loo! Why don't you take us out to lunch?"

"Okay," I said, "where would you like to go?"

It sounded like a gag, so the fireman went along. "Why don't we all go to Nathan's in Coney Island?" he said, laughing.

"Okay," I said, "let's go to Nathan's."

Now some of the other guys were gathering around and they didn't know whether to take me seriously or not.

"You want to go to Nathan's," I said, "let's get in the truck and go!"

There was a moment of general disbelief, but when the men saw I was serious there were whoops and shrieks. "Hey! We're goin' to Nathan's for lunch!"

I notified the dispatcher that we were leaving quarters for a drill. I said we might be over around Coney Island, which is quite a distance from our firehouse, but they had gotten used to our travels by now so this caused no comment. Our radio would be on; we could respond to an alarm no matter where we were. And anyway, I remembered that there was a special high-pressure hydrant near Nathan's that delivered 120 pounds of water pressure. Maybe we ought to look at that, I rationalized. Or maybe we ought to take another look at the roller coaster in case somebody got stuck in it someday. No doubt about it, there were many things in the vicinity of Nathan's that really ought to have the periodic attention of a rescue company!

When we got to Nathan's we pulled the apparatus into a parking lot behind a couple of buildings because I didn't think it would be too nice for the public to see that some of their firemen were going out to lunch, and with the truck, too! There was a cop on the corner who asked us what we were doing there and I said, "Oh, we're just out to lunch." He said, "Yeah, but you're from the Navy Yard area aren't you?" (smart cop) and I said, "Yes, we are, but the men are hungry for some of Nathan's hot dogs and seafood." The cop did a sort of double take, but I didn't pay any attention. In fact, I asked him to please watch the truck and listen for our radio calls while we went to eat. He said he would, but he was shaking his head a little at the same time.

We had a feast of lobster sandwiches, french fries, milk shakes, the works. We happened to have a fireman detailed to my group from another company that day, and of course he'd never seen anything quite like this. "You guys do this often?" he wanted to know. "Oh sure," said Jim Bowler. "Whenever we get a hankering for some Nathan's food, we just run over."

On the way back to quarters we went by a place where another company was out having a drill. We decided to stop and see what they were doing. They had a ladder up against an old building, and a chief was directing them. When he saw me, this chief said, "Afternoon, lieutenant, are you supposed to be drilling with us today?"

"No," I said, "we're not drilling today. We just came out to have a little lunch at Nathan's." Of course, he thought I was kidding. He laughed, then asked again: "Seriously, aren't you supposed to be drilling with us?"

"No," I said. "We checked some alternate routes in this area to see which was the quickest way back and forth from

Nathan's, but we really just came out to have lunch."

We all stood around watching the drill for a few minutes. Then I heard the chief asking one of my men: "Didn't you really come out here to drill with us?"

"No, sir," my fireman said. "The good lieutenant just took us to lunch at Nathan's."

By now the chief was convinced. He said to his aide, "If you need me, I'll be upstairs in the building. I don't want anything more to do with this!"

When we got back to quarters, the night shift was coming on. They looked around the firehouse, saw a bunch of Nathan's cartons and paper cups here and there and wanted to know what happened—was there a fire at Nathan's?

The word got around pretty fast about this happy-go-lucky outfit that took its Sunday lunches at Nathan's in the summer. Of course, we only did it when I happened to have Sunday duty, and even then it wasn't exactly a regular thing; sometimes instead of going to Nathan's we went to the aquarium. (After all, we had to know what to do in case one of those big fish tanks burst.)

I never thought of a fireman's job as an eight-hour shift anyway. I knew that when we had to we could work harder in one hour than the average man does in eight. Anything an officer could do to grab a little recreation for his men without jeopardizing the public's safety was only right, I thought. After all, sometimes we had to work 12 hours straight and the only rest we got was switching from one kind of tool to another.

The emergency at Grant Street was a good example. It took all night and there were no milk shakes for anybody. A man's life was slowly being squeezed out of him in a mass of tangled metal and it was up to us to get him out, dead or alive.

The alarm came in at 8:20 P.M., Grant Street and Pitkin Avenue. It was a June night in 1965, and in the streets it was hot. But we were headed underground to a big subway yard where hundreds of trains are stored at the end of the line to await the next morning's rush hour. A motorman had somehow lost control of one of the trains and crashed it. That's all we knew until we got there.

There was a big crowd at the scene. Police Emergency had arrived first, but there were also crews of workmen from the Transit Authority. They showed us where to go down through a grate in the street. We took a few tools each and headed down, climbing three levels below the street before we came to the tracks. A lot of lights had already been rigged and they were all aimed at one of the biggest masses of crushed steel we'd ever had to deal with. It made the ordinary automobile accident look like child's play.

Over all the noise and confusion, we could hear a man screaming. The man's name was Martin Patterson, and for the next 12 hours he was going to be my personal responsibility. I wasn't exactly sure what this was going to mean, but I had an idea. Years before, when I was in Rescue 3, I'd helped get a subway motorman out of a similar jam after four hours' work. That time I ended up cutting his right foot off to save his life. This time it looked worse.

The train had run into the bumper at the end of the line with such force that it had driven itself and the bumper into a concrete foundation wall. The first 12 feet of the motorman's car—everything in front of the first set of passenger doors—had telescoped down to about two feet. But the force of the collision had also jackknifed the car up into the air so there was a big hump in the middle. The front truck, with four wheels on it, was hanging several feet above the tracks.

The first thing I had to do was find our man. His cries seemed to be coming from under the train, in the area of the hump. I lowered myself into the debris and worked my way around through what spaces I could find until I could see where he was. The only part of him that was visible was the top of his head. The rest of him was compressed into a space which we later measured—ten inches by ten inches! When he cried out, the whole mangled subway car seemed to cry. Martin Patterson had become an integral part of the train now, as if he had been fitted to it, like an astronaut in his couch, only more so.

I came back up and reported what I'd found and what I thought we could do. I had the new Partner saw in mind for a lot of the cutting that was going to have to be done. When fitted with a carborundum silicon blade, this saw can slash through heavy metal pretty fast. We weren't going to be able to make a direct approach, however. First, it seemed to me, we would have to enter the rear of the car, cut a hole in the floor that would admit us to the hollow hump area underneath, then cut another hole going forward. We were going to use a lot of saw blades!

A doctor at the scene asked me to take a syringe of morphine down and try to stick it into the motorman anywhere I could reach. While the men were getting the saws ready, I went back to the victim and cleared away enough metal with hand tools so I could reach his neck right below his left ear. I gave him the morphine (as I would five or six more times between then and eight o'clock the next morning) and I also stuck a plasma needle into a vein in his neck and secured it in place with a piece of adhesive tape. I'd never done this before, but I'd seen it done often enough in emergency rooms. I knew if you got the needle in the wrong place a little football bulge would develop under the skin. I got it in right the first time.

We went to work with the saws. They're powered by gasoline engines and it takes a good deal of strength just to hold them while you're cutting. When one man's arms got tired, another would take over. The shriek of the blades in the heavy steel of the subway car filled the tunnel with a frightening sound. Exhaust from the engines began to drift up into the searchlights. Showers of sparks made grotesque shadows on the walls. The motorman was drugged into an uncertain silence. Once in a while he talked, to no one in particular. Between turns on the saw, I would go forward and check to see if he was still alive. There was no sign of bleeding, but I knew a great many of his bones must be broken.

When we finally got under the train we found a new obstacle. The huge steel kingpin on which the wheel truck pivoted was right in our way and it was too heavy for the Partner saws.

It would have to be cut away with acetylene, but it was going to take a long time to burn. Maybe an hour. But time seemed suspended. We lost track of hours. We just measured our progress in terms of feet and inches. Above us, on the subway platform, a crowd of willing hands waited without much to do. There was only space for two or three men at a time under the subway car.

After we cleared the kingpin we were within a few feet of the motorman's compartment, or what was left of it. A heavy sheet of aluminum formed its rear wall, and when we got some light on this we knew we were in the right place because there was a perfect outline of Patterson's head and shoulders stamped into the metal.

We were so close to our man now that we couldn't use saws or cutting torches for fear of injuring him further. Until we could see all of him, we'd have to use hand tools—Grip-Hoists, Port-O-Power jacks, anything that might loosen the terrible grip of the steel on what was left of the motorman. To make his breathing easier and protect him from the fumes of the saws and torches, I slipped a Scott mask over his face and we supplied him with uncontaminated air.

As we moved the metal jaws from Patterson's body and more of him became visible, I couldn't understand why he wasn't dead. His splintered bones, especially in his legs, had come through his skin in many places. The control handles with which he had operated the train up to the instant of disaster were piercing his stomach. At one point the doctor gave us only another hour to work. "Then we'll just have to cut his legs off and take him out of there," the doctor said.

We didn't want that. It had become a matter of pride to Rescue 2 to get this man out in one piece. We had to risk the use of power tools again.

It was a subway worker who cut the last piece of steel to release the motorman. We poured water on the metal to keep it cool while an electric saw broke the last grip of the wreckage. Then they lowered a Stokes basket and we put Mr. Patterson into it, being careful to leave him in approximately the same crippled posture that he'd been in for the last 12 hours. After what he'd been through, nobody had the heart to bend him straight.

When we came up into the street, it was a beautiful June morning, even for that part of Brooklyn. People were going to work, hurrying down the subway entrances, most of them not knowing that anything had happened, that about 35 men had worked the night through to try and save a fellow man's life.

The exhaustion that hits you after a job of this sort is like a blow from a padded club. There's no sharp pain in your lungs as there is in a fire. It's your brain that aches—from what it has seen and done—and part of you continues the battle under that crushed subway car, as if the job would never really be done.

It didn't help any when we learned, a week later, that Martin Patterson had died in the hospital. Of pneumonia.

At least, I thought, he went with his legs on.

21

BLACK WASN'T
ALWAYS BEAUTIFUL

The year 1967 was like *the long hot summer* in New York. It was a year when firemen had their patience and their patriotism and their dedication very badly shaken, no doubt about it. The race riots and senseless destruction that took place in areas like ours in Brooklyn were hard to understand. A lot of the men were bitter. We were running to fires that were totally unnecessary. And when we got there, our friends and neighbors of many years threw rocks and garbage at us, attacked the equipment that had been used to protect their lives, even shot at us. Why? Just because we were white?

I couldn't control how my men felt, but I didn't want to see their effectiveness as firemen damaged by anger and outrage either. I tried to keep them cool. "We still get our paychecks every two weeks," I told them. "We're still professionals. Let's try and act it."

This period was even tough on meals. We were responding to so many alarms that there wasn't time to eat. That's the way it was on the night of September 6, 1967. We'd been into Brownsville on two multiple-alarm fires since the beginning of our tour at 6 P.M. Now it was 2 A.M. and we were hoping to get back to the firehouse to catch a bite. We were making our way through the tense streets, listening to the police sirens, hoping our radio would keep silent for a while, when the dispatcher caught up with us. A chief was short of help at a fire. All he had was one Engine. He needed a truck company, but none was available at the moment. Could we help? In a case like that, there's only one answer. We put our plans for food in the back of our minds and headed for Pacific Street to assist some of our *white* brothers! I hated to think that way, but at the time it was natural.

I didn't know when we turned the truck around that this was going to be another of those occasions when I would be in the right place at the right time. There was a young black man waiting for me in a burning building. And the following June there would be a gold medal from the Steuben Association waiting for me, too.

When we got to the fire, Chief Phillip M. Hermann was out in the street with only five working firemen from the original engine company, plus five from a truck company that had just arrived. I could see he was going to need our manpower. The fire seemed to have total possession of a two-story frame house. The Engine didn't have any hoselines charged yet and the truckies were being driven back from a front second-story window where they had placed a ladder. It was a sad sight. These men were dead beat. They had probably answered as many alarms as we had already tonight. The fire had gotten ahead of them. There was a good chance it was arson anyway, and now maybe somebody was going to get hurt trying to put it out. I've never heard a fireman utter the words, but I just

knew what some of my men were thinking now: Let the sonofa-
bitch burn!

But that was before we knew there was a man trapped on
the second floor. The black people in the street said he was still
up there. They were milling around the trucks, menacing us
with their very numbers. Some were drunk. Some were belliger-
ent. Some were saying we'd better hurry up and save their black
brother or there was going to be trouble. Our three trucks were
parked close together. There wasn't a cop in sight. Smoke swept
down in giant spirals of heat.

I thought about what I'd been taught when I was a probie.
I remembered the things I'd told many a young fireman myself:
"You've got to be ready and willing to go into a fire to save
anybody, black or white, young or old, winos, criminals, skels
[our term for derelicts]. In that moment when you go in after
a citizen, you're both equal. You may both live or you may die
together. But you've got to try because that's your job. That's
what you're paid to do."

I told Ludger Brooks to follow me up the ladder to the
second-floor window. Then I told the chief I was going in.

"You won't make it, Ham," he said. "Hundred eleven
Truck couldn't make it through that window five minutes ago
and it's hotter now."

"I haven't tried it yet, chief," I said, "so here goes."
Ludger and I headed for the fire. The truckies said no, don't try
it, but we just went past and up the ladder. I didn't have an
airpac; I didn't want one. I knew from what I could see above
that I wasn't going to be in there long—if I could get in at all.
I flipped down the eyeshield under the visor of my helmet as
I came up on the window. It really looked like we were too late.

The window frame was burning all around. The curtains
were dropping like lumps of fire. The Engine still hadn't been
able to push in with a line on the first floor. Whatever was going
to happen was going to happen quick.

I dropped over the windowsill, staying as low as I could,
and started crawling around the front room. I heard Ludger

come in after me and I told him to take the next two bedrooms while I made my way to the back. We were both moving very quickly, racing the fire, racing the tempers in the street, racing to get ourselves out alive. I could tell how hot things were getting by the stuff that was popping. The TV tube went first; that was a familiar sound. Then the food jars. Then the aerosol cans. They sounded like gunfire in various parts of the house. They also carried a message: Not much time left.

Suddenly I thought I heard some human sound from the rear of the building. It wasn't a scream, it was more like someone moaning in his sleep. The heat was coming up through the floor in the hall so fast that I knew the whole place was going to blow in a couple of minutes if they didn't get water on the fire below. It reminded me of the fire I'd been in with Packy Radican when I wanted to push ahead and save the young man who was screaming in the back bedroom. I remembered what Packy had said later that night when he pulled the bottle out of his desk drawer and we talked about my first roast: "We're only expected to do so much," he'd said. "We're not supposed to kill ourselves in hopeless causes." Was this a hopeless cause? Should I back out now?

There was a doorway ahead of me. It had to be the last room at the back. The moans had stopped for a moment. Was there still a life to save? I crawled into the room, which seemed to be a kitchen. Flames were coming up the walls from below now, eating through the house behind the plaster, probably spreading out, unseen, over the ceiling.

I felt around on the floor where I heard some breathing and snorting. Under the kitchen table, lying on his back, was a young black man in his twenties. He held one arm over his eyes, but he couldn't help himself much. He seemed to be drunk. I got him up by the shoulders and started to pull him out, dragging him along on the floor. I didn't know whether I was going to have to go all the way to the front of the building and out that burning window again or whether there might be another way out. If the Engine would only get some water on the fire below, I might find the stairs. . . .

The solid stream of water ripping through the building sounded like a runaway train. It pounded on doors and turned them into drums before they blew in. It went through plaster like a fist through a paper carton. It turned fire to steam and pushed smoke ahead of it like a strong wind. From the hall I could see three helmets with the engine company frontpiece on them coming up the stairs behind the nozzle. The water hit the ceiling and came back down on us like a hot bath. The man I was dragging had passed out—or was he dead?

Ludger came down the hall and together we got the unconscious man around the firemen on the stairs and down to the street. We laid him on the sidewalk and started giving him oxygen. I was aware of the crowd closing in around us, leaning over Ludger and me and the man we'd brought out. It was like a football huddle, only instead of one man calling the signals, there seemed to be several.

"How come it took so long to find our brother?" one voice said.

"This the best the Fire Department's got?"

"How come only three fire engines?"

The young man didn't seem to be coming around. Ludger looked at me and there was a question in his eyes: What should we do next? Call a doctor for this guy or call the police for us? The resuscitator kept up its steady rhythm. We didn't look up. The voices sounded meaner.

"He dead."

"They let him die."

We knew an ambulance was on the way, but if this guy looked dead when they took him away, I was afraid we were going to have trouble with this crowd. It was after three in the morning. Why weren't they all in bed instead of giving us a hard time?

Then the young man on the sidewalk stirred, pushed at the resuscitator with his hands and took a couple of deep breaths of his own. He was okay! If he hadn't been drinking, he might not have passed out. We made him as comfortable as we could, kneeling by him on the sidewalk every minute until the ambulance arrived.

The crowd was still in a bad mood. We heard curses about the all-white Fire Department. Some of the young men seemed disappointed when the rescued man came around instead of lying dead still. They'd been itching for a fight, but now they'd lost their excuse. Their brother was alive and it was a white man who had saved him.

"Thank God you did," said Chief Hermann. "There would have been trouble here."

It isn't true, of course, that the Fire Department is all white. Even at that time, in 1967, there were black men throughout the organization. The fire commissioner himself, Robert O. Lowery, was black. For some reason, however, there had never been a black man in a rescue company. Some people might say that was a form of élitism, but I don't think so. There are never more than about 100 firemen in the four rescue outfits in the city and openings didn't come along every day. Maybe there weren't all that many black firemen who *wanted* to be in Rescue.

Whatever the reasons, though, the Fire Department decided in 1967 that Rescue should not be all white, and we were told to take on one black fireman. So I said to myself, I'm going to recommend the best black fireman I can and bring him to Rescue 2. The news went around fast: They're going to put the first black man into a rescue company. But which black fireman would it be, and which company would he go to?

I was pretty sure it wouldn't be to Rescue 1 in Manhattan. They were the New York Yankees, the pinstripers, the showcase outfit. We were the Dodgers, so we got Dave Floyd from 108 Truck. I couldn't have been more pleased.

Floyd had worked in Brooklyn companies for about eight years before he came to us. We often used to run into fires with 108 Truck so we all knew Dave and we liked him. He was a superfireman, a big strong guy, quiet and capable. If any fireman I knew could make it in rescue work, it was Dave Floyd.

I had asked Captain Lawler to assign him to my command and he did. Then I had a talk with my men. I told them that as far as I was concerned all firemen were the same color in a smoke-filled room.

The day Dave reported for duty, I was on day tour and I made it a point to get there early so I could give him a proper greeting.

"Welcome aboard," I said. "I'm glad to have you."

"I hope so," he said, and we shook hands.

"Go get yourself a cup of coffee," I suggested. "Then come up to the office and we'll have a talk."

"Okay," he said, "but first I'd like to say something. I'd like to thank you for asking for me to be in your group."

"I did that for a reason," I told him. "You see, I'm a southern boy from West Virginia and I'm planning to break your butt!"

He laughed a little shyly and I laughed with him and things felt okay.

Some of my group took him into the kitchen and started to show him around. Freddie Frank. George Lee. Johnny Hopkins. They began explaining the truck and the stuff that was on it. Then, after a while, they sent him upstairs to see me, the Old Gray Fox. "He's mean as hell," they warned him. "He's going to rip your skin off and try and make a white man out of you!"

"Personally, I don't care what color you are," I told him. "I'm a lieutenant, so I'm not going to be your brother. And I'm not going to try to be your father, either. Maybe I'll be your uncle. . . ."

"I hope not my Uncle Tom!" Dave said, and we both laughed.

"You're going to get needled," I continued. "You're going to hear all kinds of remarks about niggers and this nigger neighborhood we work in. But you know and I know that there are white neighborhoods that are just as bad. So you're going to have to keep your cool. Just like Jackie Robinson did on the Dodgers years ago."

Dave said he understood, and things went along fine for

several weeks. There was no test, but I was sure one would come. There were about 65 men in the two companies that lived in our firehouse. Half of them weren't even rescuemen. But we all lived together, slept together, slid the poles together and ate together. I'd had fights with other firemen when I was younger. I knew how we could flare up. Firemen aren't diplomats. If we were, we'd be lousy firemen.

We had one man in the house who was always popping off about niggers. "Keep them boogies away from me!" Yancy would say when his friends were listening. I worried about what might happen someday between Yancy and Floyd. I knew Dave could take care of himself if it came to a fight, but could he take care of himself *short* of a fight?

The test finally came one morning in the sitting room. Several of the men were around the table in the middle of the room having coffee. Dave was one of them. He'd just drained his cup and put it down on the table in front of him when Yancy came along, picked it up and tossed it in a big trash can in the corner.

Dave watched the flight of the cup, heard it crash, looked slowly around the table at the other men, then got up. Yancy had been sitting on the couch. His coffee mug was still on the floor where he had left it. Dave went over, scooped the cup up in one big, black hand and sent it crashing it into the trash can.

"What'd you do that for?" said Yancy, somewhat sobered by the restrained anger Floyd was showing.

"If you won't drink out of my cup," Dave said, "I sure as hell am not going to drink out of yours!" And he walked out.

"Guess he can't take a joke," said Yancy, looking around the table at the other men. But they didn't answer him. Dave Floyd had passed his first test.

Of course Dave, being the last man aboard, was automatically the company Johnny. This meant he was asked to do all the menial things that all Johnnies have to put up with. I told him I couldn't spare him this experience, had, in fact, endured it myself. He said he understood, and I never heard him gripe.

In fires, I put him into the toughest spots so he could

demonstrate to the other men that he had all the skills they had, if not more. And whenever we had a situation like we did that night on Pacific Street, it was always Dave who would speak up to his fellow blacks and take the heat off the rest of us.

Dave and his wife lived in Humboldt Housing in Brooklyn, and one night when we were coming back from a fire near his apartment he said, "Why don't you all come up to my place for a cup of coffee and some cake?"

"You kidding?" came a voice from the back of the truck. "We don't eat none of that soul food!" Everybody laughed, including Dave. Actually, we were wet and cold and the idea of some coffee and cake sounded great. I accepted the invitation for all of us.

When we got to the apartment house there were black people in the lobby and on the elevators obviously curious about this sudden invasion of wet, dirty firemen. Dave didn't explain, he just said hello to a few people, led us up to his apartment and waved us all in saying, "These are my friends and they need some coffee!"

Then Jim Bowler said, "We'd like some *soul* cake, too!" and the ice was broken forever.

PALLBEARERS FOR A GOOD LOO

We'd been called into Manhattan to help with an emergency at a fire in the tenement district around 4th Street and Avenue D. Rescue 1 was uptown on another alarm, so Rescue 2 from Brooklyn would cover. We didn't know what the problem was when the dispatcher first called us out, but I inquired via radio on the way over the East River and was told that a fireman from Engine 23 had collapsed on the fourth floor of a burning building. Help was needed to get him out.

Something about this call didn't sound routine. It isn't unusual for a fireman to collapse in a burning building. It's usually up to the men of his own company to get him out—or any other firemen at the scene. To call a rescue company from one borough to another sounded like something more than smoke poisoning.

We wailed over the bridge with the siren wide open, pressing hard because it was one of the brothers who needed us. When we got to the fire, the Engine had made the top floor with a line and they were knocking down the fire. We had no trouble getting to where we were needed. Four of us bounded up the stairs with all our gear. In the hall, on the top floor, a lieutenant was stretched out unconscious with several of his men crouched around him. They had done all the right things as far as first aid went, but when we took one look at the man we knew it was serious. Probably a heart attack. Probably dead.

I looked up at the guys from Engine 23 and I could see that the fire they'd just put out was forgotten; all they cared about now was whether their Loo was going to make it. You could read their estimation of their officer in the concern on their blackened faces. He must have been a good man.

Rescueman Ludger Brooks went to work on him instantly, mouth to mouth, while we hooked up the resuscitator. Even with the machine, we got no response. The doctor came. The hall was getting crowded. I told the firemen from 23 it might be better if they waited in a room down the hall. They shuffled away, pulling gloves off their hands and cursing fate. Big, tough men disgusted by life's bad luck.

The doctor took a scalpel from his bag and opened the lieutenant's chest with a long incision, big enough to get a hand into. Brooks broke the ribs away so there would be room for the doctor to reach in for the heart. Another of our guys was holding the officer's limp wrist, waiting for a pulse if it ever came. The doctor squeezed and released, squeezed and released. It caused a pulse, but it didn't mean life. The lieutenant was dead. Brooks put a big compress on the wound over the heart, and somebody else brought the Stokes basket to carry him out.

I went down to the end of the hall where the men from 23 were standing. They knew from what they'd seen that their man was gone. "It's a tough way to lose your boss," I said. "I'm sorry." One of them spit at the wall of the tenement. Another just swore, quietly. A thief had come to rob them—not the old enemy fire that they all fought together but another kind of thief that had come unseen and done the unexpected.

Rescue had the body in the Stokes now and my men were getting ready to take the lieutenant out of his last fire building. Brooks led the way down the stairs and the men from 23 followed us down.

When we got to the street floor I told Brooks to hold it. Give the basket to the Engine, I said. Let them be the ones to carry their officer out.

Twenty-three's stained faces looked at us without expression at first. "Go on," I said, "take him out yourselves. Easy now, carry him head first. It's the last time you'll be able to give him a hand at a fire."

Then Rescue stepped aside and let them pass.

22

OCTOBER 16, 1970

When 1970 arrived, I began to think about retiring from the Fire Department. I would have my 20 years in on November 1, I could get out with a pretty respectable pension and I'd only be 46 years old. My second son, Gregg, would be five years old in March and my second house, in St. James on Long Island, would be five years old in the fall. I thought both my son and my home probably deserved a little more of the old man's attention. Ginny certainly did. She'd put up with all the problems of being a fireman's wife for two decades. She'd known all the terrors that go with every newscast, every telephone call. She'd often been told I was a hero, to be sure, but she'd also been told I was dead. I don't think one made up for the other.

As far as I was concerned, it had been a good career. I'd

had a lot of luck and a lot of rewards. I was alive, relatively unharmed by the experience and I'd been given honors far beyond my expectations. The James Gordon Bennett had eluded me, but then I hadn't become fire commissioner either! I had five gold medals to hang on my jacket (if I ever felt like dressing up for an old-timer's parade) and so many other awards that I couldn't keep them all straight in my mind.

Of course, you don't *have* to quit the Fire Department until you're 65. If I wanted to go on and make captain and end up in an administrative post, I knew I could probably do that too. But after 20 years in the arms of the Red Devil, I was sure I could never stand some sort of fireproof job.

Ginny and I talked about it, but we didn't make any final decisions. One thing we had to admit: for a little while longer a full paycheck was better than a half of one, especially since I still felt full of strength and ability.

There was another thing. I enjoyed being recognized for my work. I'll admit I was proud when people told me I was Chief O'Hagan's model for other officers in the department. I was flattered when they asked me to talk to classes of new young firemen. And if I was useful to the department as inspiration, would I be letting others down if I quit while still in my prime?

Sometimes I worried about the legend in another way. I could hear those voices over the years. *You did it, Dick! You can do it again, Dick!* I had to admit that it urged me on. I was never a showboat fireman—I knew that that was a sure way to get hurt or get killed—but when I knew people were watching with great expectations, did I perhaps take just an extra foot or an extra ten seconds of risk because I knew that's what the cheering section wanted? When DiMaggio came to bat with men on, he didn't have to be told what his teammates were hoping for. He knew. And I knew.

One of my favorite magazines in those days was called *True,* "the man's magazine," and I remember reading a story in it one time about a famous Spanish bullfighter who did something just a little more daring every time he went into the ring because he knew that's what his fans expected. If he was only as good as the last time, they booed. But if he moved another inch closer this time to the bull's charging horns, they cheered. Eventually, of course, the bull killed him.

The story of that bullfighter worried me. All my training, all my common sense and all my instincts said I wasn't doing what the bullfighter did, yet there were "fans" in *my* life, too, and I wasn't sure what they were doing to me.

These were not thoughts that I ever had all at once, the way you're reading them now. They came to me in bits and pieces, in little moments of introspection. It wasn't enough to make me quit. But I was starting to think. Now, if we had a fire in a vacant building, I'd back off. In my younger days I would have gone after a fire in a chicken coop. I knew better than that now. But if a life was at stake, I still felt as I did that day with Packy almost 20 years ago. I had to try to save that life.

Jim Geraghty was a lieutenant in 235 Engine, a nearby company. We often went to the same fires and we got to know each other pretty well. Jim was a very honest, straight-forward man. He never left you in doubt as to his meaning. He was about 40 years old, married, a big man, over 200 pounds. He and Jim Bowler were good friends, too. He was godfather to one of Jim's dozen kids. Whenever the three of us got together we shared a few jokes and enjoyed each other's company.

I remember one time they wanted an air conditioner at Jim's firehouse, but they couldn't cut it into the brick wall. We went over with all our tools, made the hole for them and helped install the machine. Then they invited us to stay for dinner.

There were a couple of good men in Jim's company who wanted to join the Rescue. Jim was the kind of officer who wouldn't stand in the way of a man's ambition even if he hated to lose him. He'd send these fellows over to us on detail every once in a while so I could see them work and get to know them better.

In other words, Jim Geraghty was the kind of man you wished there were more of.

The date his life story and mine crossed was October 16, 1970. It was the night that 219 Engine, about 12 blocks south of us, was having its annual company party. They had hired a hall and everybody had the night off. Officers and firemen from nearby companies had been called in to work tours so the guys from 219 could forget fires for one night. Jim Geraghty volunteered to cover for the 219 Loo, and other firemen filled out a six-man team to work the tour. This meant that on this night 219 would be entirely made up of strangers, but this was no problem. If they were a minute or two late getting to an unfamiliar box, 210 Engine would probably be there early anyway.

Around 7:30, an alarm came in from Carlton Avenue and Fulton Street. Knowing this box, which was only six blocks from our firehouse, we didn't always expect a real fire. It was an intersection where there was a liquor store on one corner, an old run-down social club on another, a vacant grocery store on the third and a plumbing-supply business on the fourth. Drunks coming out of the liquor store often pulled this box just for the hell of it—or prostitutes hanging around the social club would sometimes turn in an alarm if some john hustled them out of their money. It was that kind of a neighborhood. When we rolled up, the drunks would be gone, but the whores would stand on the corner and scream bloody murder and expect us to do something for them.

But though it seemed unlikely that we were going to have a fire, that didn't mean we loafed. There were some real bad tenements further up the block and we always prayed that it wouldn't be one of them.

Carlton Avenue crests before you get to Fulton. As we came down the incline, I started observing what was ahead. Sometimes you can tell from the color or the smell of the smoke what kind of situation you're getting into. Sometimes you see a suspicious character running away, or someone standing alone on a rooftop. I always kept a sharp lookout ahead; it was a habit. This night I didn't see any heavy smoke, but there was an unusual haze in the air; you could see it in the headlight beams. I hollered back to the men that it looked like a real one.

I could hear them bracing up then, grabbing the tools and cutting the chatter.

As we got into the block, I saw 105 Truck coming in from the other direction. Captain Jim Duffy said he hadn't seen any fire on the way in to the box. Neither had we, but I thought I could smell wood burning. I decided to go around the block. We made a left turn, went up a block, made a right onto Adelphi Street, and now the smoke was heavier. It also smelled of rubber. I knew we were in the right place because smoke was coming up through cracks in the sidewalk and around the foundation of a one-story building. We called the dispatcher to correct the address so other companies would come to the right place, and 256 Engine and 105 Truck rolled in right behind us.

The building had two big overhead doors at the front, both locked. It was apparently occupied by a business that sold automobile tires. From the smell, that's what was burning; and from the way the smoke was coming up, the fire was in the basement. It wasn't a promising combination.

We were working on getting the big front doors open when 219 Engine came along with Lieutenant Jim Geraghty. We were going to need his help.

When we finally forced the doors open and hauled them up by their chains, smoke came out of the building in tremendous volume and so black we could see it against the night sky. Most of this smoke was rising from the basement through what looked like a big hole in the main floor, a four-foot-square opening through which tires were apparently moved upstairs and down. Someone told me later that the company kept all its more expensive tires in the basement to protect them against snatch-and-grabbers in the neighborhood. The stock was hoisted up and down on a pulley; there was no ladder or stairs. Additional access to the basement was by a stairway at the back of the street floor. There was also an outside door leading to the basement at the rear of the building.

The chief told me that 256 would try to get at the fire through this rear door. He told me to take a couple of men and go help the Engine push a hoseline in. A couple of my other men went to the roof to help vent. Before we went off to our assignments, I heard the chief telling Geraghty to take a couple of men on a reconnaissance of the main floor to see whether fire had come through from below yet.

When I got to the rear door, 256 had it open about a foot, enough to see that the inside of the basement looked like the inside of a furnace when you look through the peephole. The flames were a deep orange, mixed with black smoke. It was going to take a lot of water to bring this under control. With this kind of heat we could lose the whole building and the tires would still be burning. Still, we had to try and push in.

I was just about to relieve one of the 256 boys on the nozzle when I heard the chief on my walkie-talkie. Lieutenant Hamilton! Lieutenant Hamilton! Report to the front of the building at once. Two men have fallen into the fire!"

In all a fireman's experience, there can be no more dreaded report than that some of your men have dropped into the flames. It's the sort of thing nightmares are made of—falling . . . falling . . . and at the bottom, the inferno that you've been fighting to escape all your life.

I ran to the front, having several disconnected thoughts as I went. First, I was glad I hadn't used any of my Scott bottle so far on this fire, because now I was probably going to need it. Second, I thought it was probably that damn four-foot hole in the floor. Why hadn't we covered it with something? Third: *Who fell in?*

When I got to the front, Jim Duffy filled me in quickly. Jim Geraghty and a fireman named Orokes had fallen into the hole when they got lost in the smoke. The third man who was with them almost fell in too, but he stopped in his tracks when he heard his two buddies yell as they tumbled into the void. He explained they'd all three become disoriented, didn't know which way they were going until they saw some flashes of red from the Mars light on top of one of the trucks out in the street. But two of them had fallen through anyway.

There was no sound from below but the deep rumblings of the fire. Somebody had already tilted a 20-foot ladder down into the hole, but almost 10 feet of it was still sticking out and the angle was so bad I could see no one would get down that way. My chauffeur, George Lee, had come down from the roof and saw the problem. He pulled the long ladder out and put a shorter one in the hole at a better angle. It wasn't easy even to put a ladder in the right place. Smoke was belching from the hole like it used to come out of the steam locomotives along Buffalo Creek.

A lot of the firemen from several companies were gathered around the hole now, standing helplessly. The word had flashed fast: Two guys have gone in. It would have been better if everybody had just stuck to his assignment, but it was natural for them to want to be here. I asked the fireman who had been with Geraghty and Orokes if they'd said anything or made any sound after they landed in the basement. He knew me; he was with 210 Engine, the company that shares the firehouse with Rescue 2.

"I didn't hear anything, Lieutenant Ham," he said.

"Did they have their Scotts on?" I asked.

"Yeah, Loo," he said. "You couldn't have been in here without 'em."

I took off my helmet, pulled the facepiece of my airpac on, then replaced the helmet and started for the ladder and the hole. I knew everybody was watching me, the men, Captain Duffy, the chief. I didn't need any orders. I knew what I had to do. I knew that on the front of my helmet there was a word I had to live up to: Rescue.

Duffy came over to the edge of the hole. "You going to try to make it down there?" he said.

"I'll make it all right," I said. Then I started down the ladder. The heat that was coming up was terrific, like a scorching wind. It pushed so hard against me that it got under my canvas coat and started to lift it up around my body like a girl's skirt in the funhouse.

When my head was level with the floor, I took a last look around through the eyepiece. I could see firemen's boots all in a row. Then I saw John Mills and Paul Green, two more guys from 210. They had a hoseline and they were getting ready to play water into the hole. They thought better of it when they saw what I was going to do.

John said, "Here, Loo, for God's sake, take the line with you!" He was leaning down with a pleading look on his face. I didn't know whether I should take the line or not. It's almost impossible for one man to hold a 2 1/2-inch line alone because of the force with which it can whip around. But then I thought, I've never gone down into anything quite like this. Maybe I ought to take the water. I nodded to Mills and took the nozzle over the edge. I could feel the guys from 210 feeding me line as I went down the ladder.

People have asked me why I didn't ask somebody else from Rescue 2 to come with me. It just never occurred to me. But even if it had, it wasn't the kind of place you could order anybody to go. It would have to be on a volunteer basis. I guess I figured if somebody wanted to come help me, all they had to do was come down the ladder after me. I certainly wasn't trying to hog the show. I didn't even know whether I was going to make it or not. I only knew I was going to try.

It was like the overflow pipe in the carbide-company dam. I wasn't afraid of the hole just because I didn't know what was inside. I figured the only way to find out was to go. Besides, the men down there were friends of mine.

When I got to the bottom of the ladder, I tried to look around with my lantern, but it was useless; the beam went nowhere. I had to look down at the lens to be sure the light hadn't gone out. I dropped the light so I could have both hands free for the hoseline. I couldn't see any fire, but I thought if I could get some water bouncing down off the ceiling it might help Geraghty and Orokes wherever they were.

I opened up the line, holding the nozzle as tightly as I could, but the force of the back pressure slammed me backward. I fell against the ladder I had just descended, and the water went everywhere, wildly. I knew this wasn't going to do any good. If I hit either of the two men with the full force of the stream, I might injure them or knock something down on top of them.

I decided to move around in a circle below the hole, feeling around as I crawled. After a while I concluded that if both men had dropped straight down and landed unconscious, I would have found them by now. They must have crawled after they hit—but in which direction? Did they stay together, or did they go separate ways? I tried to remember everything I ever knew about search. My gloved hands pawed through the debris.

Then, from somewhere ahead, I heard a voice, someone talking. I tugged the hoseline with me and crawled faster. I don't know how far I moved before I found the man huddled on the floor. Fifteen feet. Maybe twenty.

It was Orokes. There was too much smoke to see him but I could feel that his helmet was off. He still had his Scott mask on, but whether he was still getting air, I couldn't know. His voice was muffled under the mask. "God save me," he was saying. "God save me." His body rocked back and forth. I touched him on the shoulder and said, "Look, you can get out. You can get yourself out. Feel this hoseline," I said, trying to find his hands. "Just follow it and move fast. It'll take you to a ladder."

Orokes wasn't incoherent, but he wasn't making much sense either. I figured he had just enough strength left to make it on his own. I still had to find Geraghty. I listened to Orokes crawling off behind me. Way ahead of me the rumbling of the fire was getting louder and I could see curls of red flame wrapped in the black smoke, but the fire wasn't giving enough light to help me find Geraghty. I opened the hoseline and let a blast of water hit the ceiling and fall back on me. It didn't do much good. Then I aimed the stream at the far corner of the basement where the tires were burning. All it did was make them go *whoom!*

Somewhere over all the racket in the basement, I now heard a new sound. It was musical, like distant chimes, and it faded when the fire roared; then, in quiet moments, I'd hear it again. *Ding. Ding.* Like the last few notes from a run-down alarm clock. Alarm clock! That was it! The alarm on a Scott airpac, the bell that warns that the air is running out. It had to be Geraghty, somewhere just ahead. I strained for the last dying bells and crawled on as true a course as my ears would lead me, pulling the hoseline with me.

He was in a heap, unconscious. The Scott bottle had emptied, the bells had stopped. I ripped the hose from the regulator so he wouldn't suffocate. Better to breathe a little smoke than strangle in a vacuum.

Now there was a choice: Give up the protection of the hoseline, or radio for help. I knew I couldn't handle big Jim Geraghty's dead weight and still lug the nozzle. But if I radioed, help might arrive too late. I was about to drop the line and start pulling my friend back through the darkness, hoping to find the foot of that ladder, when then I felt something move behind me.

Orokes? Still lost in the cellar?

"It's me, Lou Polera," a voice said. "Let me give you a hand." Polera was a relatively new man in Rescue 2 and I hadn't worked with him much; he was in Captain Lawler's group. I realized that he'd probably come down on his own. It took a lot of guts.

"We need a rope," he said, and I radioed for one. Then, suddenly, the strain of what I'd been doing loaded all my muscles with fatigue. I hung onto the hoseline while Polera tied a rope around Geraghty's body under the armpits. I knew if I ever lost my grip on that hose while the nozzle was open, we'd all have trouble. A 2 1/2-inch line waving wildly under pressure can whip around and split a man's skull like a melon. It could also knock the ladder down and cut off our escape. So it was hold onto the line or else. I had no idea how much effort I was exerting in those minutes. Later, however, I would know and I would have the torn ligaments to prove it. For life.

We worked our way back toward the ladder. The fire, which had now gone to a second alarm, was advancing from the rear of the cellar, eating its way into ceiling-high piles of tires, toppling them in great liquid splashes of dirty red flames.

Geraghty was limp and silent. When we finally got him to the foot of the ladder, Polera suggested we lay him up against the bottom rungs, with his arms draped through, and secure him that way so they could pull him up, ladder and all.

We tried it. When we had him on the ladder we hollered, *"Pull! Pull!"* and I guess the guys up top pulled all right—they pulled the ladder right out from under Geraghty and he fell in a heap again. Then we knew we'd have to do it with the rope.

Geraghty went up like a sack of grain, twisting around as he rose while the men heaved on the rope.

Now Polera and I were alone in the cellar. There was no ladder, no rope. Only the radio. And the fire. It was advancing along the ceiling, sending out long peninsulas of flame, licking at anything that would burn. It was looking for a way out. A chimney. The chimney was a four-foot hole over our heads. Jim Geraghty was in it.

The bells on our airpacs started ringing almost at the same instant. We'd each been in the cellar 20 minutes. We disconnected the air hoses from the bottles and tucked the open ends inside our coats to filter out some of the smoke. From now until we got out, we'd breathe whatever was inside our clothes.

They were having trouble getting Geraghty through the hole. We couldn't see this clearly from below, but the problem was that the rope was being pulled up in a corner of the square opening. When the lieutenant's unconscious body was raised to the level of the floor, he wedged there. The men pulling on the rope were out in the street; they couldn't see what they were doing but were guided by directions from other firemen who had crawled to the edge of the hole. So much fire and smoke was coming through that space now that no one could stand near it. Unfortunately for Geraghty, he was suspended in the chimney, turning slowly at the end of the rope like meat on a rotisserie.

We could hear the commotion above. At certain moments the draft changed and we could see through the smoke. I spotted a fireman leaning over the hole, reaching for Geraghty's body with the end of a hook. He caught the hook in the lieutenant's coat and pulled him free at the same moment the rope haulers gave a heave. The body disappeared over the edge. They seemed to have him. I thought, If he's alive, he's lucky, but I doubt it.

We hollered again for a ladder. We didn't want to be forgotten. I might be the legendary Lieutenant Hamilton, but I'll be damned if I could fly up through that hole.

They lowered an aluminum ladder, and I told Polera to go up first; I'd give the fire one final belt with the hoseline to try and reduce the heat as we went up.

We only had 10 feet to go, and after 20 years as a fireman, if you had asked me, I would have said I could stand the flames of hell for 10 feet if I had to. Oh, I had respect enough for fire, no doubt of that, but any healthy human who's ever climbed a ladder more than once in his life can surely scramble through ten feet of hot air and come out the other side! We'd come *down* through the hole, hadn't we? Why couldn't we go the other way?

Polera disappeared ahead of me, and I started to climb. One rung, two rungs, three . . . Then the hot wind caught me again. I remembered a temperature chart I'd studied for my lieutenant's exam. One hundred fifty degrees on the floor can mean 700 degrees at the ceiling. Four, five, six . . . only three steps left. I was wearing red plastic gloves. They were melting and sticking to the rungs of the metal ladder. I couldn't tell if it was gloves or skin, but it was painful. I buried my head as deep as I could into the collar of my coat, praying that the Scott mask would protect my eyes, nose and mouth. It was like walking into the exhaust of a jet engine, but up close, not at 50 feet like I remembered on the deck of the *Midway*. That was a mere warm breeze, faintly scented with kerosene, compared to this blowtorch, scented with death. I could smell my own hair burning.

I climbed until hands reached down, grabbed me under the armpits and lifted me, lighter than air, glowing, shimmering, laughing—but actually none of these things except in delirium. —They laid me on my back in the street and tried to remove my smoldering canvas coat. The steel buckles that secured it down the front were too hot to handle without leather gloves.

Then they gave me oxygen and put me in an ambulance with Polera and off we went to the same hospital where they had taken Jim Geraghty.

I don't remember anything about the ambulance ride. I guess I started to come to in the emergency room at Brooklyn Hospital. The first thing I knew was that I couldn't open my hands. They were all tightened up like claws. My arms seemed to feel the same way. I was lying on a table, looking up at the ceiling lights. How did I get here? Where had I been? The aircraft carrier? No, that was years ago. But all fires seemed to leave the same taste in your mouth, the same pain in your skull.

I wanted to see what was going on in the room. There seemed to be a lot of activity north of my head. I turned to one side and saw doctors and nurses working over the naked body of a big man on another table. They had a lot of tubes and wires attached to him and an aspirator in his throat. I could hear him gurgling unevenly. His face was black and burned. One of his arms was hanging down off the table and I saw that the fingers had pieces of burned skin hanging from them. I wasn't sure, but I figured it was Geraghty.

On the other side of me, Lou Polera was also getting treatment, but I couldn't see what they were doing to him. A doctor came over to me and saw that I'd come around. I told him I couldn't move my hands or arms. He said that was because my muscles had been starved for oxygen; they'd get better soon.

Geraghty was still unconscious. They were giving him chest massage. Then, all of a sudden, they disconnected a lot of the apparatus and wheeled him very swiftly out of the emergency room.

"Did he die?" I asked the doctor.

"No, we're just taking him to another room. He's pretty bad," the doc said. I knew he had to be. He'd hung in that flue full of fire and smoke for over five minutes.

I felt pretty good again in less than half an hour. They took an electrocardiogram and I passed it okay, and my hands and arms were getting back to normal. I told the doctor I didn't want to stay in the hospital, so they released me. It wasn't even ten o'clock yet, but it seemed much longer since that first alarm came in for Fulton and Carlton. I decided to go back and see what was happening at the fire. There was a chief's car at the hospital and I got a ride.

When I got to the scene again, the whole picture had changed. The fire had gone to a fourth alarm by now and the street was packed with apparatus and firemen. There were even men from 219 Engine who had left their company party when they heard about a bad fire where two firemen had fallen in. There were wild reports that one man was dead. Some said it was me.

All my men were still working the fire, and I was ready to go back to work, too, but a Chief Whelan said, "Are you kidding, Hamilton? Get outa here!" I left, but not for home. I went back to the firehouse, typed out a three-page report and finished my tour. The next morning John Scott drove me home. It had been a long night.

The next day I felt my age. Forty-six might not sound like an old man, but I was ready to admit that it wasn't the same as twenty-six. The news that Geraghty had come around and was now out of danger did a lot for my morale, but my body was still beat. It brought up the whole discussion of retirement again. Ginny was getting tired of hearing that I'd been killed.

I stayed home almost two weeks, taking it easy and getting my strength back. My 20th anniversary in the Fire Department fell during this medical leave. It seemed almost as if somebody had timed this last rescue as a signal that I should get out. I'll admit I thought about it as long as I was around home with Ginny. But when I went back to duty, the idea of quitting didn't seem so attractive. The department offered me a couple of months of light duty somewhere, but I knew I'd feel like a fish out of water if I was anywhere but at Rescue.

Another thing that kept me going was all the talk about how I'd saved Geraghty. The talk wasn't just in the battalion or in Brooklyn, it was all through the department according to what friends said. Some people were even calling it the finest rescue in history, but there was always a lot of that kind of talk after somebody had done a good job. I figured it would probably mean another medal—number six. What kind of medal was up to other people to say. As far as I was concerned, I'd only done my job. Twenty minutes work in a hot cellar.

23

SECOND THOUGHTS ABOUT IMMORTALITY

It was that winter, after Geraghty. I'd gone back to duty and everything was the same. My hands hurt a little, I had lost a little more hair and I still had an occasional headache, but once again I had "temporarily" put aside the idea of retirement. I needed full pay, for one thing. For another, I hated to admit that I was slowing down, that I wasn't indestructible.

There was a Captain John Dunne I used to kid around with about this. "I'll go to your funeral," I'd say, "but you'll never go to mine!" Dunne was a nice guy. He was with 107 Truck, pretty far from my outfit in Brooklyn, but we'd sometimes join up on three-alarms. I knew him first when he was a lieutenant. We'd end up at the bigger fires together and when it was time to take the edge off, we'd kid around that way.

The truth was, I knew Dunne had an excellent reputation as a fireman. I didn't really expect to go to his funeral. I'd seen how he operated at fires. He did the same things I would have done. He wasn't the type to do anything stupid. He was aggressive, but smart about it. He pushed in when he had to, but you could see that he was always thinking ahead. I respected him. That's why our little game was possible.

Another thing I liked about Dunne was that he didn't take this reputation of mine too seriously. He was a good enough fireman to understand what I did and how I did it. He knew there was no such thing as miracles in fires. He knew he couldn't walk on water and he knew Dick Hamilton couldn't either. That's why it was easy to be around him. That's why I couldn't take it wrong when he'd hop up on the running board of his truck and holler across the street at me.

"I'll go to your funeral, Ham!"

"No way, captain!"

Dunne had a brother, Don, who was with 219 Engine—the outfit that was having the party the night Geraghty fell into the hole. I guess Don told his brother all about that rescue, because the next time I saw Dunne he said something flattering to me about it. Something like, "I hear you're playing the hero again!"

Dunne was the kind of guy who made you feel that all was right with the world—or at least with the Fire Department—as long as he was around. That's why, when he was killed in a fire, I felt as if I'd been killed myself.

Ginny and I were having breakfast one morning after I'd been on a night tour and we were listening to the radio news on WCBS. My ears always picked up the fire items fast, no matter what other conversation might be going on. ". . . Fireman killed in Brooklyn," the radio said. "People trapped . . . a fire captain . . ." What was the name—please!

Captain Dunne.

Still, I knew there was more than one Captain Dunne in the department. I went for the phone and called Johnny Hopkins at Rescue. Who was it? I asked. Which Dunne?

John Dunne. With 107. I hung up. I was sick. I had a funeral to go to.

The first thing I had to do when I came on duty the next day was find out how Dunne had died. What had happened? Did something fall on him? Did a wall collapse? A floor give way?

The fire had been a multiple-alarm in a tenement. Captain Lawler had been on duty at Rescue 2. He was there. Somebody at the scene had reported that there were kids trapped in a back bedroom. Dunne had put on an airpac and was last seen alive going up a rear fire escape, but nobody was sure which floor he had been headed for. Reports about people being trapped in fires are often unreliable. Somebody says fourth floor and means fifth. Somebody says front and he means back. Sometimes there's nobody in the fire after all. I knew how Dunne felt. He felt like I would have felt. If there was even a *rumor* that kids were in that building, he'd go take a look.

The next thing they heard from Dunne was a radio message from his walkie-talkie. "I'm in trouble," he said, but he didn't say how, why—or where. He didn't answer his radio anymore either. Captain Lawler passed the word to the chief, and a search was begun.

They didn't find Dunne for five minutes. By then the fire was knocked down and you could search the building easily. He was in the back bedroom on the top floor. He'd apparently made a search, found nobody and was on his way out. The fire was hot and dangerous. Every second would count. Dunne would know how to gauge that; he'd know how much time he had to search and how much time to get out. Just like I would. It's a sense you get, a clock ticking in your head. Ten more seconds . . . Five . . .

But if something takes your time margin away, you've had it. Dunne stepped into the wiry trap of an old bedspring and a bicycle in that back bedroom. He put his boots into the tangle, probably fell, became snared with more springs and spokes. The window and the fire escape were not far away, but neither were the flames. Ten seconds . . . five . . . zero. Dunne burned to death.

I went back to the building four days later when they were conducting an investigation. Department Chief O'Hagan was there. We all climbed through the blackened, charred, foul-smelling interior of the building. We went to the room where Dunne died. I kicked the bedspring which was lying there like an animal trap. I could see he'd had no way out. And I doubted that anybody else could have saved him either.

I'll go to your funeral, captain!

Dunne's death shook me severely. For 20 years in this job, I had always prided myself on the fact that I could dismiss the horror of death and dying. I cut it out of my life, surgically; shut my mind; blinded my brain to the realities. Now I couldn't do it anymore. Driving to work on the expressway, I thought about Dunne almost every morning. What had he gone through? What had he *really* gone through? Come on now, you're a fireman, I'd say to myself. You *know*. You've been burned. You *know*. Those burns on the neck and the arms and the face, the little ones, that's the way it begins, isn't it? I'd smelled my own hair burning. A little of it, around my ears, outside the protection of the facepiece. That's the way your hair goes when it *all* goes, isn't it? It stinks.

Nobody can examine the details of burning to death like a fireman can. To the public it's just an unknown horror. To me it was an intimate horror. I hoped it hadn't lasted too long for Dunne. Unconsciousness comes quickly for some people, slowly for others. He must have prayed for it, slumped in that room, caught by barbs of wire that wouldn't let him go.

I thought about this for weeks. At home. At the firehouse. But mostly when I was alone. And especially in the car. I had to work it all out. I had to make it all happen again in my mind and have it over with. I knew too much about the agony of death in a fire to just dismiss it as rotten luck. I'd heard people scream until the flames went down their throats and sealed their voice boxes.

I knew Dunne must have screamed.

Finally, I came out on the other side. There were a million reasons why this death shouldn't have happened, but it had. I looked at it professionally. If a lousy spring mattress in a lousy tenement fire could kill John Dunne, it could kill Dick Hamilton.

When June came, there was a department medal for John Dunne's widow on Medal Day. And for me, on the same day, from the hand of John Lindsay came the greatest honor of them all.

They gave me the James Gordon Bennett for saving Geraghty.

And they gave Lou Polera the prestigious Brooklyn Citizen's medal for helping.

It was a big day for all of us, triumphant but sad. Jim Geraghty was out of the Fire Department now on a three-quarters-disability retirement. His hands were burned and he was ashamed of them. He thought he was going blind. He couldn't seem to understand why it had to be *him*. I'd tried to talk with him, tried to take the edge off.

"Quit feeling sorry for yourself, Jim," I'd said. "If you don't, the next time you fall into a cellar I'm going to leave you there!"

Then there was Mrs. Dunne. She talked with Ginny that day and said, "For God's sake, get your man to quit the Fire Department!"

Ginny told her we were talking about it.

Mrs. Dunne also said she was sure if I'd been there I'd have saved her husband, just like I saved Geraghty. I told Mrs. Dunne that I couldn't have saved him. It wasn't the same as Geraghty.

Medal Day had always been a great time, a combination of Fourth of July and Memorial Day. I remembered my first one on the steps of City Hall when they gave me two medals for rescuing Mrs. Graziano. The sun was bright that day and I was happy. Now it was all different. Medal Day was held in a gymnasium at Pace College. There was no sun, and when the bugler played taps there was no place for the notes to float away.

Ginny and I went home that day with the greatest prize of my life, but there was something very heavy about it.

A BIG PSYCH JOB

One day we were on our way back from a smoky fire in the Mount Loretta orphanage on Staten Island. Just as we were coming over the bridge the dispatcher came on the radio and asked if we could take in a supermarket fire in Coney Island. Of course we could! I told him. But I knew that inside that old red box of ours I had six tired firemen. If we were getting ourselves into something tough, it was going to take quite a pep talk to get morale up again so soon.

When we got to the store, there were firemen lying all over the place trying to recover. The fire was in the basement and it had given a beating to everyone who tried to put it out. A chief came over and said he sure was glad to see us because his men were dead tired, all out of Scott bottles and ready to take a blow—our term for a rest.

"That's okay," I said, "we'll put the fire out for you."

"All I want you to do is try," said the chief. "I don't expect you can do it all by yourselves."

A lieutenant from one of the engine companies said we'd never make it into the basement. He said they'd all tried and been pushed back.

"Well," I said, "that may be, but I haven't been down there yet myself so I don't know. Just get a couple of lines ready for us and we'll see."

Then I got my guys into a huddle behind the truck and I talked to them like Knute Rockne at half time. I told them we were in a spot where everybody was going to be watching us—other firemen, cops, civilians. "Let's show them all something," I said. "Let's go in the back door of that cellar and come right out the front!"

The men pulled the Scott masks down over their faces and charged in. We had one hoseline with a solid-stream nozzle and one with a big fog nozzle. We split into two teams, three men each, and we started pushing the fire ahead of us.

It was hot, no doubt about it, and stuff was exploding all around us. But the big fog nozzle was doing a great job of cooling things and the solid stream was knocking over big piles of burning merchandise like they were kids' toys. In fact, pretty soon the men were beginning to enjoy the game. They were pulling each other's hoselines back and generally horsing around in a race to see who could move ahead fastest. Ten minutes before, these guys had been exhausted and looking forward to a hot shower and a cup of coffee. Now they had jumped into a new battle and forgotten the old one. All they were interested in was who was going out through the front of that basement first!

The chief came on the walkie-talkie and asked how we were doing. He sounded worried. I told him we were already 50 feet in. Then I heard him exclaim, "Hey! Water's coming out the front already!"

"Yeah," I said. "We'll be out in a minute."

We had the fire pretty well knocked down now and it was a close race to see which three guys would be able to hump their line ahead fast enough to get out the front door first. I decided we'd call it a tie and I'd go out ahead of them. It had been a terrific display of spirit by a bunch of guys who didn't know they had anything left, but who, when they got to the street, were all walking eight feet tall. I knew they must be really beat after working two fires in quick succession, but they weren't showing it. Nobody went for a drink of water and there was no leaning up against the truck and gasping out complaints. They just picked up their gear and climbed aboard.

On the way home the truck was filled with the babble of happy voices. "Did you see the look on those truckies' faces? And that chief! He couldn't believe it when the Loo climbs out and says the fire's dead!"

"Hot in there, wasn't it?"

"Hotter'n hell."

"My ears are burning off!"

"My throat's on fire!"

"Who's got some water?"

"I didn't want any of them to think we was thirsty."

24

I don't think most firemen's families ever get to know much about what their husbands and fathers actually do in the everyday course of their jobs. I've known a few firemen who talked a good deal at home about what they saw and did when they were out on alarms, but most of us don't. First of all, it usually doesn't make the best dinner-table conversation. Second, none of us wants to alarm our loved ones. Some of the things that a fireman does in the course of a routine day sound pretty dangerous, but the man doing them often knows the risk isn't as high as it seems.

Besides, much of what a fireman does gets pretty repetitious. Who wants to hear the same stories over and over? Tenement fire. Food on the stove. Garbage. It can be pretty boring

217

—to do and to listen to. I never bothered Ginny with much of
it, and she didn't ask many questions. She knew the work was
dangerous, but other firemen's wives told her more horror stories than I ever did. I didn't see any point in giving her more
to worry about.

My oldest son, Richard Jr., was another matter, however.
He had celebrated his seventeenth birthday the week before I
pulled Geraghty out of that basement and he'd been paying
visits to the firehouse during his summer vacations and on other
occasions for quite a few years. Like any other kid, he enjoyed
these trips to daddy's "office." It isn't unusual for firemen's sons
to make these visits; a firehouse can be a wonderfully fascinat-
ing place for any young boy—and especially if he gets to see his
father pull on that classic helmet and jump on the big red truck
to answer an alarm!

Of course, Fire Department regulations don't permit kids
to ride on the truck or participate in any way, but we all know
that these rules are sometimes winked at with a chief's blessing.
By the time he was 17, Richie had been to a lot of fires and had
gotten to know a lot of chiefs. I think he may even have been
seen wearing a helmet, coat and boots once he got old enough
to fit into man-size clothes. The biggest treat, of course, was
when he got big enough to stay overnight at the firehouse.

But even though Richie was a frequent visitor, for many
years he never saw the real inside, close-up work that I did. In
fact, although he was full of curiosity, he really saw very little
more at fires than the public does from the street. He didn't go
into any burning buildings and he didn't assist at any amputa-
tions. He saw the bright red lights and he heard the sirens and
he got to know the other firemen—all the fun things—but we
all shielded him from death or anything that was ugly.

As Richie grew older, of course, he wanted to see more and
more, get closer to the real action. I used to promise him that
someday we'd go in together on a New Year's Eve. That can
often be the wildest, most action-packed night of the year for
big-city firemen. But before that "someday" came, he learned
that most of the time his father answered a hundred alarms for

every one that turned out to be memorable. That was okay with me. I wasn't trying to provide him with entertainment, I just wanted to spend time with him as he grew up. A fireman's hours aren't the best for being around his kids, so every opportunity meant something to me. Sometimes, on a slow day, all Rich would do around the firehouse was help Louis DeFina, our cook. Louis was real good and he used to enjoy showing Rich how to fix certain dishes. In return, Rich would help by peeling potatoes. They had a great relationship, those two. Louis had a couple of daughters at home and he always wanted them to meet my boy. A regular matchmaker!

I think Rich learned some important things about being a man as a result of his exposure to Rescue 2 and its firemen. For one thing, he soon saw that in emergency situations we didn't go running around in a panic. This taught him calm, which isn't a bad thing for a young man to learn. Sometimes, of course, he'd want to come home and—calmly—tell his mother all about some of the exciting things he'd seen happen during his visit—and there went my hopes of shielding Ginny from anxiety!

One time, when Rich was about eight or nine, we had a fire on Lafayette Street and he came along to watch. It was one of those situations where we were told there was an old lady trapped on the top floor of this tenement. Actually, the old lady had gone out to the store before the fire started, but we didn't know that. When we got there, I just figured I was going to have to go in and get her.

I went up ahead of the hoseline and got into the upper hall. I had a filter-type MSA mask on, and as I busted in the door to the apartment I remember thinking it was just as well I was wearing this because it wasn't unheard of for a fireman to get a can of lye tossed in his face—or a pot of urine—when he kicked in a door where a woman lived alone. Well, anyway, nothing got thrown at me, but when I got in the room it was a lot hotter than I had expected. I broke a window to try and vent the place, but that only made things worse. I was groping around, not able to see much, but over the years I'd learned where to look for bodies—under beds, in closets. After checking all the usual places people go to hide when they're frightened, I was pretty sure there was no one in this apartment. But by the time I was ready to leave and looked out into the hall, I saw that the stairs was fully on fire now and there was no way out unless or until the Engine got up there with some water.

I tried to recall what the building's exterior looked like and I thought I remembered seeing a sort of ledge outside the top-floor windows. I worked my way back to the front window, stuck my head out, and, sure enough, there was a ledge just wide enough for me to get out on. It wasn't the safest place in the world, four stories up, but it was a lot more comfortable than the interior of the apartment just then. I crawled out.

I found I could lie down on the ledge and my head would be protected below the windowsill. I turned to look down into the street. I was hoping to see someone raising a ladder to get me out of this fix. I saw a lot of firemen and apparatus—and I saw Richie sitting on the fender of the Rescue truck. He was waving happily at me. "Hi, daddy!"

Some firemen were looking up at me. One of them hollered, "You all right, Dick?"

"I'll tell you one thing," I hollered back: "If you don't get a ladder up here pretty soon, my pants are going to burn off!"

They never did raise a ladder, but eventually a couple of the men reached down from the roof and hauled me up. I realized, of course, that I wasn't in any immediate danger, but it was a reasonably close call.

When I got back down to the street, Richie was all excited. "I saw you up there, daddy!" he said. "I saw you!"

"Yeah, Rich," I said, "it was getting pretty bad up there" —which was something I should never have admitted. Because when he got home that night, Rich told the whole story to his mother—with exaggerations. It had all been a great lark to him.

One especially good thing about Richie's firehouse visits was the chance it gave him to see how some other, less fortunate people in the world have to live. Since he'd lived only in suburbs like Wantagh and St. James, I thought it would be good for him to get to know the kids on Carlton Avenue. When I saw him getting along with these little black boys, I used to call it to the attention of the guys in the firehouse. "See?" I'd say. "Kids don't even *see* color."

The time finally came for me to keep my promise about a New Year's Eve visit. It was December 31, 1971. Rich was 17. He had long since come to understand that being a fireman wasn't what he'd thought it was when he was a little boy—a chance to ride around with a siren going and have people give you free ice cream—but he still hadn't seen anything really grim. What happened that night at 103 Sanford Street would change all that; it would even change the relationship between me and my son.

Even though it was bound to be a busy night, with fires, automobile accidents, drunks and what have you, we still tried to make something a little special out of New Year's Eve around the firehouse. My tour began at six, and things were fairly quiet for the first couple of hours. Louis DeFina even had time to prepare a spread of cold cuts, a little buffet supper for midnight—if we were lucky enough not to be out on an alarm when Guy Lombardo came on the TV.

At about nine o'clock, two separate alarms came in in quick succession. Bedford and Myrtle, then Franklin and Park. Instinct told me this was something real; it was a double box, but not in a false-alarm pattern. Apparently it was a fire that could be seen by a lot of people at once and that explained the two separate alarms. When we got to the scene we found a tenement that was really blazing and it was obviously going to be a full-assignment situation—that is, two Trucks, three Engines, Rescue and a battalion chief. What we call "all hands."

At the time we arrived, 102 Truck was putting an aerial ladder up to the front windows on the top floor. There were reports of a baby being there. The chief told me to see if I could get up to the rear of the top-floor apartment via the roof of an adjoining building. I said I'd try. I didn't have my regular team with me; many of the guys had worked out mutuals (which meant swapping holidays) so they could have the night off to be with their families. But I had Ray Downing with me and we went up together and came over onto the roof of the fire building. It wasn't vented yet, so I knew there had to be a terrific buildup of heat underneath. Sure enough, when Downing lifted the cover of a scuttle (a roof hatch) with a hook, smoke poured out like it was being pumped. I didn't have a mask with me, but I could see this was going to be the only way to get down into the burning building. I pulled the collar of my coat up as far as I could and started for the steel ladder that went down inside the scuttle.

Downing looked at me like I must be either immortal or crazy. "You're not going down in there!" he said in disbelief.

"I guess I have to," I said, "because there's people down there." And I started down.

It was pretty hot for the first few feet, but nothing to frighten anyone who had come up through that four-foot hole after Geraghty. By the time I reached the floor level inside the building, it wasn't bad at all. I dropped as low as I could get and hollered up to Downing that he could probably make it too. He started down after me.

The engine company hadn't gotten into the building with the water yet, so things were really going on this top floor. I could hear everything popping and crackling and I knew there wasn't going to be much time to find anyone alive. I figured the guys on the aerial ladder would take care of the rooms at the front of the building and I'd search the back. I kicked in the first door I came to and went into a bedroom that was all in flames. It looked hopeless. The fire had gotten quite a head start. I moved around quickly, looking in all the places where someone might hide. There was a lot of smoke and I couldn't see very well, but over in a corner I felt the shape of a small child's body. I scooped it up and started crawling out of the room as fast as I could.

When I got back to the hall, Downing was waiting for me. "I got the baby," I said. "Now let's get out of here."

The Engine was coming up the stairs, hitting everything with 240 gallons a minute, dumping plaster and hot water all over us. I told the enginemen I had the baby, and Downing and I pushed past them down the stairs.

When we got to the floor below, I stopped to see what shape the child was in. In the better light and clear air, I could see that all I had rescued was a corpse—a pathetic little charred body that was pretty shocking to look at. I found a bedroom door broken open, so Downing and I laid the baby inside on a bed, covered it with a sheet and went on down to the street. Now it was up to the coroner.

A death of this sort always made me think what I might have done to prevent it: Where could I have been five minutes quicker? Where did I lose time? Were we a minute slow getting out of the firehouse? Was there traffic delay in the streets?

I was leaning against the chief's car getting my breath and worrying about the dead baby when Richie came over. He was wearing fire clothes. For a minute I'd forgotten about him being with me. He wanted to know if he could go into the fire building.

By now they had the flames pretty well knocked down and Richie told me that a fireman named Steve DeRosa from 102 Truck had made a terrific rescue of an old man and a child down the aerial ladder (for which he would win the James Gordon Bennett medal). I didn't know whether the chief wanted Rich going into the building, however, so I said I'd have to ask permission.

Chief Tortoriello said sure, he could go in there, and Jim Drake volunteered to take him in—and as soon as they were out of sight I grabbed for some oxygen. I'd only been in the fire a few minutes, but I could sure feel it. Old Superman Hamilton wasn't so super anymore, that was for sure, but I didn't want Rich to see that. The chief suggested that I go back to quarters and rest for an hour or so, but I didn't want to do that either.

Pretty soon I saw Richie coming out of the building again with Drake. He was all wet and dirty from climbing around in there where the truckies were overhauling. And he had a funny look on his face. I knew right away that somebody had shown him the dead baby. He walked straight over to me and he did a very unusual thing—he put his arms around me and said, "Gee, dad, I'm proud of you. All these years, I didn't know it was like *that* inside a fire."

You have to know Richie to know what this meant. He was a very cool teen-ager, not one to show much emotion. But he'd just been face-to-face with a scene which he suddenly realized must be commonplace for his father. Including the roasted baby.

When we returned to quarters, I had to go up to the office and start making out my report. Pretty soon Rich came up too and sat down quietly on the bunk in the officers' room. I could see he wanted to talk. He was full of questions—like "How can you put something like that out of your mind, dad?"

I told him we had to shut our feelings off because we were professionals and because in the next ten minutes another alarm might come in and we'd have to be ready to do our best for the public again.

"I don't see how any of you can live for five seconds inside one of those buildings," Rich said, and I said it wasn't as bad as it looked really. I still didn't want him worrying—or bringing fears home to Ginny. But there was no shutting off what he had seen. Something fundamental had changed between us. Not only was my son looking at me in a new way now, but he had put another set of two and two together. There were tears running down his cheeks.

"I guess I've taken something for granted all my life, dad," he said. "I always figured you'd be around, that you'd come home from work like all the other fathers. Now I know better."

He looked straight at me then and he said, "Now I know that someday you're not coming home ever again."

25

A COUPLE OF
CLOSE CALLS

The Geraghty rescue and the James Gordon Bennett medal brought me a lot of attention. The story about how hot the buckles were on my coat got told and retold, and maybe exaggerated a little, too. As for the aluminum ladder that Polera and I had climbed out on—it was turned blue by the heat, they said, and was so warped that it had to be thrown away. Estimates of the temperature in the flue went around. Somebody *said* that the ladder manufacturer *said* that it would have taken 1000 degrees Fahrenheit to melt that ladder.

I heard all this, of course, and I was flattered, but there was something else on my mind now. Retiring. In the midst of the highest praise, I was getting other messages. Chief O'Hagan was beginning to say, "Take it easy, Dick." Nobody had ever told me to take it easy before. And when the chief offered to give me a transfer to any easy-duty fire company in the city, I was almost insulted. But I knew what he was trying to say.

I was also still thinking about Dunne—and remembering what Richie had said about not coming home someday. I was getting signals from my own body, signals I didn't like but couldn't ignore. My hair had started getting white after the *Constellation* fire more than ten years ago. Now it was silver and getting thin on top. My hands hurt from injuries, and the tendons in my left arm had been torn and knotted ever since I'd tried to pull Geraghty and the 2 1/2-inch line at the same time. I also had severe headaches at night.

Then one day in Williamsburg I got trapped over a fire. It was the kind of thing that had never happened to me in my whole career before—the kind of thing I never *let* happen. I always said good firemen don't get trapped; they know in advance where the dangers are and how to avoid them. This was what I'd told every Johnny I'd ever trained. This was what I said when they invited me to speak at probie school. Good firemen don't let themselves get trapped. Ha!

It was a second alarm in a three-story tenement on Broadway. When we got there the chief said they hadn't been able to search the top floor of this building yet, but not to worry too much about it because the fire wasn't actually in the building but on the outside at the rear. This turned out to be an inaccurate report which the chief had received, but we didn't know it at the time.

I took three guys with me—Jack Levy, Bobby Higgins and Bill Moore—and we headed for the third floor. On the second-floor landing I met Fireman Louis Piccone from 108 Truck as he was coming down from the direction of the third floor. "Where do you think you're going?" he said.

"I'm going up to search three." "You'll never make it," he said. "*I* couldn't."

Piccone had a Scott on, and even so he said it was unbearable when you got up higher in the building. I said, "Well, we were told to search, so I guess we better try anyway," and we went past Piccone. The last thing I heard him say was *"You'll probably make it!"*

When we got onto three, there was no fire but terrific smoke and heat. We went to the front of the building and worked back, kicking in doors and searching rooms. Bobby Higgins came with me and the other two split off. Higgins said something like "If the good Lord isn't ever going to kill Hamilton, then he won't kill me if I'm with him!" Bobby was a big joker, lot of fun. He always had a lot of faith in me, I guess, but this time he was in for a letdown.

As we worked our way down the hall to the rear, the heat kept building up. Something wasn't right. I raised my hand above my head and found I could barely stand the heat at that level. The fire had to be inside the building somewhere, not just outside. But where?

We soon found out. The fire burst out of the walls at us —it must have been mushrooming inside the frame at the rear —and started racing across the ceiling. In no time at all, the flames were two feet thick at the ceiling and had forced us right down on our knees. We could hear the heat breaking the windows at the back of the building. Higgins and I started back for the front room. When we got there we vented the two front windows by smashing the glass with our helmets. This let some smoke out, but it increased the heat.

Levy and Moore made it to the front room right after we did. They looked worried. "Look, men," I said, trying to sound calm, "I think we're in a jam, but don't worry because I've got my radio and we'll call for help."

Nobody said anything. The fire was making all the noise. Everybody was watching me. The four of us crouched low near the front windows as I got on the walkie-talkie and raised the chief. "We've searched the whole apartment, and there isn't anybody up here, I told him, "but now we're cut off ourselves." As I was saying these words, it occurred to me that I had never had to say them before. Cut off! It's an ugly phrase. And it's often followed by posthumous medals awarded to widows on a June morning.

The chief wanted more information about our situation. I told him we couldn't come out the way we came in because the fire was between us and the stairs now. I requested that an aerial ladder be put up to the windows, third floor front. What I didn't know was that there was no way to get an aerial ladder up to us because there was an elevated subway track in front of the building and they couldn't bring the truck into position. The chief didn't say anything except "Hang on."

I saw Jack Levy starting a slow crawl toward one of the windows. With the fire and smoke pouring out over his head, he looked like he was getting ready to do something desperate —like jump into the street. I said, "Hold it, Jack! We're caught, but we're going to get out! What the hell do you think you're going to do?"

"I think I might have to jump," said Levy.

I knew the fire was bad and the situation wasn't getting any better. If Levy had asked me for an honest opinion, I would have told him I thought we had two more minutes. That old clock was ticking in my head. Like it must have been in John Dunne's.

But Levy didn't ask, and since I'd never had one of my men jump out a window before and didn't want to see it happen now, I lied.

"Jump?" I said. "Are you crazy? We're on the sixth floor! If you jump, you're dead."

I didn't know whether or not I could confuse him enough with the lie to stop him. He couldn't see the street because of the smoke. Maybe he'd be rattled enough not to remember that we'd only come up three floors. Whatever the reason, he stopped at the windowsill.

I opened a door into the hall again, but the whole area was in flames now and the build up of heat and gasses was so strong that I could feel the pressure against the door when I closed it again. Apparently the roof hadn't been vented yet. Unless somebody got some water into that hall in the next minute or two, we were in real trouble.

I asked Higgins what he wanted to do. He said, "I'll stay with you, Loo." The tone of his voice was changed now. No more kidding around or jokes about God. He was just calm. "I'll stay here," he said. We huddled together, the four of us.

Meanwhile, in the street, 111 Truck had managed to get a portable ladder up to a window on the second floor, and when they heard our call for help, one of their men had grabbed a scaling ladder and was going to climb up and hook it into our window. It was a sort of desperate way to go out, but when we saw the hook of the scaling ladder come over the windowsill, it sure looked better than jumping!

I told Levy to go first since he seemed to be in the biggest hurry. Then Moore. Then Higgins. Out they went, hands and feet holding the small rungs of the ladder until they reached the bigger ladder one floor below.

I was going to go last, but when I found myself alone in the room, a lot of my worries disappeared. At least my men were safe. I never worried as much about myself. I decided maybe I wouldn't have to go out on that scaling ladder anyway. I never liked climbing on those things and now I was a little afraid of my hands. Could I hold on? I decided to take one more look into the hall.

When I opened the hall door again I could hear water! I looked down the stairs and saw two helmets with Rescue 2 frontpieces on them. George Lee and Ray Downing had grabbed a line from an engine company and were pushing in to come after me. I crawled down the hall toward them and then tumbled headfirst down the stairs to the second floor.

"Hell," said Ray, "the least you coulda done was wait for us to come save you! For a change!"

Down below I could hear the chief hollering, "Push that line! Hamilton's still up there!"

"No I'm not, chief," I said as I came out of the smoke. "I *was* up there, but I'm not anymore."

"Why didn't you come down the ladder with the others?"

the chief asked. "We thought you'd had it when you didn't come out."

"I'll tell you," I said, "as long as these buildings have stairs in them, I'd rather walk down." It was a cocky thing to say, I suppose, but I had to cover my true feelings somehow. The thing I really couldn't get out of my mind was the fact that Dick Hamilton had had to call for assistance for the first time in his life.

Time was running out. That was pretty plain now. When the winter of 1972–73 came I felt the cold—and my left hand and arm were always colder than my right. When I came home from shifts I was always tired and I didn't snap back like I used to. I even started taking naps in the afternoon. Ginny was worried. Other firemen's wives were telling her stories about me now. "Take good care of Ham," they'd say. "Make him quit."

If the Staten Island tank collapse had happened a few years earlier I would have seen it as a terrific training ground for the men in my company, a gigantic drill in the recovery of dead bodies. As it was, however, I was too tired to get any big thrill out of it. In terms of the number of dead (40) and the number of rescue workers involved (hundreds) it was one of the biggest operations I'd ever been involved in. But it happened in February, the weather was cold, it was a long drive back and forth across the Verrazano Bridge every day—and, perhaps most important, there were no lives to be saved, only corpses to be pieced together.

The tank was built for storage of liquefied petroleum gas and it was half buried in the ground and covered with a huge concrete dome. Some maintenance work was being done inside the tank when it was empty, and a fire started. There was an explosion and the whole roof came crashing down. The workers inside were squashed under thousands of tons of concrete.

When my tour got there, which was five hours after the explosion, I could see that the job was going to take many days. The tank looked as big as the Houston Astrodome, and when you climbed down into it you seemed to leave this world. The wreckage of the concrete roof was strewn around like some crazy moonscape and there was just no telling where a body might be found. All four of New York's rescue companies had men on the job. Rescue 2 alternated shifts with Rescue 3. About the only thing we had going to take the edge off was a sort of competition to see who would find the most bodies. Ultimately, Rescue 2 found 28, far more than any other company did, but before we would find the last body—nine days after the crash —we would work harder than I had ever seen. Using heavy tools like jackhammers, it was an exhausting, miserable, dirty, round-the-clock task, burning steel rods, smashing concrete, directing bulldozers and trying to identify half-frozen, half-cremated bodies.

One morning as our night tour was ending, I was climbing out of the tank on an iron ladder, hauling myself up one rung at a time, dog-tired. Jack Kelly was climbing up behind me and he was kidding around, saying, "Come on, old man, let's get the lead out," I knew I was being slow, but my hands hurt and I was trying to make sure of every hold I took on the rungs. It was a long way down if I fell—long enough to kill me.

Then, about halfway up, it happened. Just as I feared, I lost my grip with my left hand, lurched backward momentarily, lost my footing and tumbled down onto the men who were following me. Kelly, Bobby Mosier and the others grabbed me and steadied me until I could hold on again and continue my slow climb. There was no kidding now though.

When we got back into the Rescue truck for the trip back to quarters, I held my hands in front of the heater, to try and warm them. Johnny Hopkins leaned over from the driver's side and said, "That was pretty close, wasn't it, Loo?"

"Naw," I said. "Not close. I just slipped a little."

"Yeah, it was close," Johnny said. "You have trouble with your hands, don't you?"

"Nah."

"Yes you do, Ham."

Jack Kelly drove me home in his VW. He talked about it too.

"You lost your grip today, didn't you?" he said.

"I never lose my grip, Jack, you know that," I said, trying to make a joke out of it.

He didn't laugh.

Somehow I had never imagined things ending this way for me. I figured I'd leave the department when I was ready, not because I had to, not because I was any different than the first day I came in. Hadn't I always said that experience was the secret ingredient that enabled older men to do a better job than younger men? So what if my hands weren't as strong as they used to be? Couldn't I make up for that in other ways?

These things that were happening, they were just a series of bad breaks, I thought. It was merely coincidence that I should get trapped over a fire one month and almost fall to my death the next. Right?

One time in the kitchen—I think it was probably in March—I told some of the guys I was thinking of retiring on April 1. It was the first time I'd ever put a date on it, and I think I was just trying to see what they'd say. I wanted to hear them protest: Don't do it, Loo! How can we get along without you? But they didn't. Somebody even said it was probably a good decision, a "wise" decision I think he said.

I didn't say any more. I was afraid I'd already talked too much. April 1 was too soon. I wasn't ready yet.

When Richie graduated from high school in June, I took a day off to attend the ceremonies. When I came back to the firehouse the next day, I walked into the kitchen like I always did and there were a lot of my team of firemen already there and talking about a fire they'd had the day before.

"Thank God you weren't here yesterday, Loo," one of the men said. "If you'd been here, we might *all* be dead!"

It had been a double roast in a tenement, two dead in a fierce, fast fire. The flames had gained control of the building so quickly that there was no time to get in with a hoseline. Then the roof collapsed.

"You'd have pushed us into that building, Loo!" another man said. But there was no good-natured laughter after he made the remark like there usually was when somebody was getting needled. There was just a sort of quiet agreement around the room.

I couldn't understand it. I'd never killed anybody in a fire, not even myself.

Then somebody added, "Yeah, Loo. If you'da been here, we would have had that roof fall on us, sure as hell!"

"Baloney!" I said, trying not to take it seriously. "You know what would have happened if I was there? I'll tell you what would have happened! We would have knocked that fire down so fast that the roof wouldn't have collapsed, that's what!"

But I was troubled. Later I got Bobby Higgins alone and asked him, "What do you think, Bobby? Do you really believe what they're saying?"

"I guess not, Loo," said Bobby. "We were just having a big argument in the kitchen before you came and one of the guys had this idea that you'da killed us all."

"Who had that idea?" I was furious but trying not to show it.

"Homer."

"Homer! Well, he's a coward anyway!" I said. I'd never called one of my men that in all these years, but the word was out. I didn't like this discussion at all. I didn't like anything about it. I'd never had to ask one of my own firemen for his opinion of me. What the hell was going on here?

I thought about it for a week. Like I'd thought about Dunne. Were they right? *Would* I have pushed into that building? I knew the answer was probably yes. And maybe that would have been the end of me, too. Because I always went in first.

I thought about Ginny and the many talks we'd had. I thought about how stupid she would think me if I went and got myself killed just because I couldn't admit the time had come to quit. I thought about Rich when he said I wouldn't come home some night. Had his graduation saved my life? Shouldn't

I read all this handwriting on the wall? I was in my twenty-third year now. The odds weren't getting any better. Sooner or later the Red Devil was going to get me, wasn't he? He didn't care if he had to wait another year or two. Next year? The year after? Wouldn't it be one helluva note if that devil won the battle after all?

A PLACE TO COOP

Cops all like firehouses. A firehouse is usually a hospitable place to go to the toilet, make a phone call, get warm on a winter day, have a beer or take a nap. We had a lot of cops as houseguests. The first one I remember in Brooklyn was named Fusco and he was around all the time, always talking about cars. He'd make himself comfortable in the sitting room and read car magazines for hours. Then he'd have a cup of coffee or call a couple of girl friends. Finally, he'd get back on the beat. He was a sort of a sloppy, funny guy and we all put up with him. Even when a cop was a pest, you hesitated to toss him out. You never knew. . . .

When Fusco got transferred to another precinct, he must have told his replacement about what a nice place our firehouse was and how friendly the men were. Anyway, the new cop moved in on us right away. His name was Richie. He was, without a doubt, the worst cop I've ever known. We tried to tell him this in a variety of ways, but Richie had a thick skin.

When Richie made himself at home in the sitting room, he really, really got comfortable. He'd take off his belt and gun and all the hardware and just sit around in his shirt and pants. Sometimes a police car would cruise by and the cops would ask us if we'd seen Richie. We'd say no, haven't seen him, then go tell Richie they were looking for him. In a few minutes he'd put his gun back on and leave.

We were always playing tricks on Richie. I think the guys were hoping he'd get sore and leave, but no luck. One time when he left his walkie-talkie in the kitchen, George Lee, who knew a lot about radios, very carefully took all the insides out and replaced them with a bunch of old junk parts he happened to have. Then he brought the thing into the sitting room and asked Richie if it was okay to turn it on. Sure, said Richie, and just then George dropped the radio on the floor and all the planted parts came flying out like an exploding bomb.

"My God!" cried Richie. "What am I going to do? Those things are worth nine hundred dollars!"

I happened to be in the sitting room at the time, so I told him I'd be glad to write a note to his captain explaining that the radio fell out of bed while he was sleeping in our bunkroom.

Another time, someone took his gun and removed all the bullets. Then we pretended we were going to shoot holes in the ceiling. "Don't shoot it! Don't shoot it!" said Richie, but we didn't pay any attention. One of the guys aimed the gun straight up and pulled the trigger: click, click, click. I thought Richie was going to faint.

"Hey," we said, "what kind of a cop are you with no bullets in your gun?"

Finally Richie got moved to scooter patrol. He'd come in around eight o'clock in the evening, park his scooter behind one of the fire trucks and go upstairs to bed. He had an incredible nerve. He also had a love life that kept him constantly exhausted. But by now we were getting pretty fed up with the guy. He wasn't returning any favors. He wouldn't fix a parking ticket if we got one on our own car in front of the firehouse, and we couldn't even trust him to look out for thieves when we were out on alarms.

One night, after Richie was asleep, some of the guys carried his scooter upstairs to the bunkroom and parked it at the foot of the bed. Later, when both companies were out on an alarm, Richie got a call on his radio (which he always kept by his pillow). He jumped out of bed, pushed his feet into his shoes, grabbed for his gun—then saw the scooter. He knew he'd had it this time because there was no way he could get it downstairs alone.

The last straw came one night when there was a disturbance in the street right in front of quarters. Some of the firemen came running back to the sitting room and said, "Hey, Richie! There's trouble in the street! You better get out there!"

But Richie was in the middle of a TV show and apparently he didn't want to be disturbed.

"Call for a police car," he said. "They'll take care of it."

26

THE LAST HURRAH

There would be one more Medal Day for me, the last. I would get up that morning and put on my blue dress uniform and pin on my array of six glittering awards and go get number seven. It was June 7, 1972, and they had decided to give me the Dr. Harry M. Archer medal for having made the best rescue of the last three years. Again, it was for Geraghty.

The Archer medal can only go to someone who has already won the Bennett. It's an exclusive award restricted to members of an already exclusive club. In the last 24 years it had only been given 8 times. If I had been in the Fire Department's hall of fame before, I was in heaven now!

We went to the gymnasium at Pace College and everybody was there in the now-familiar scene: Mayor Lindsay, Fire Commissioner Lowery, Chief of Department John T. O'Hagan, the rabbis and the priests to say the prayers, the Emerald Society Bagpipe Band, the bugler to blow taps again, the color guard.

There was also Fireman Steve DeRosa who was getting the James Gordon Bennett for that New Year's Eve fire Richie had witnessed. And my old friend Tony Motti, now a lieutenant and about to be decorated for saving six lives.

The TV people were there, and the honored firemen and their wives—and all the new widows. Mrs. John T. Dunne, who had attended last year as a widow, was here again today to be given her late husband's Brooklyn Citizen's medal in return for the last five minutes of his life which he spent in what the program called that "three-story, NFP [nonfireproof] old-law tenement" on Halsey Street.

I looked over at my Ginny where she was sitting and I was glad she wasn't a widow this day. Now I knew she never would be. I'd made up my mind to get out, but to do it as quietly as I could. I didn't want any big celebrations or tearful goodbyes. I would just put my retirement papers in as a routine thing and that would be that.

I'd figured out a way we could get along on my half pay plus the income from a small business I was going to start. We'd make out somehow.

My mind was leaping ahead into the future instead of paying much attention to the Medal Day program. It may not be a nice thing to say, but I was getting used to these affairs by now. In fact, I didn't even like them anymore. I didn't like sitting there with all that gold pinned on my chest either because it took attention away from the younger firemen who had done heroic things and were getting their first honors. The TV guys always took one look at me and came over with their cameras. Mr. Fire Department, they called me.

After the invocation, a fireman sang the national anthem and then the mayor made a speech and then there was a prayer and then, finally, they got around to passing out the honors. DeRosa. Dunne. O'Connor. Gudelis. Rickert. An all-American roll call. Irish, Italian, Czech, Swede, Jew. I looked at them all now as if they were my sons. Even if I didn't know these men, I *knew* them. I knew what they'd been through to get here today. I knew how they felt if this was their first honor. I knew how their families would feel when they got their men home tonight for their own celebrations of the great day.

"Hamilton."

I'd almost forgotten I was getting one too! And then they read off the facts about Geraghty again, the bare facts, the old story being told again—" . . . the fire had encompassed the entire rear of the cellar. . . . In order to raise the unconscious Lieutenant, who weighed over two hundred pounds, the ladder that was in position had to be moved. . . ." They didn't have it quite right, but what difference? The mayor and the commissioner were standing there, waiting for me to take the two steps forward.

I wanted it all to be over.

Getting out of the fire department, I realized, wasn't going to be as easy as I had hoped. The legend was still alive. John Wayne wasn't going to be allowed to just ride off into the sunset. What right did I have to try and sneak out? What right did I have to accept a taxable, half-salary pension when I might apply for a tax-free three-quarters-salary disability pension?

It had never occurred to me. I'd had a few injuries, sure, but I was all in one piece. A few scars, a couple of fingers that didn't work quite right, some torn tendons, a few headaches. So what?

But the Fire Department wouldn't let me take a so-what attitude. Commissioner Lowery ordered me before a medical review board and the doctors found a lot of things wrong—more than enough for a three-quarters disability. They stopped my retirement papers and ordered me onto light duty while I thought about accepting a bigger pension.

That may sound funny considering how worried Ginny and I had been about getting along on half salary. But I really didn't think I deserved any special treatment. I knew guys who had really been maimed for life in this job. They were the ones who deserved disability benefits.

"Yeah," said somebody at headquarters, "but we got some bursitis cases who are collecting disability too!"

I hated the idea of light duty at first. They sent me over to Welfare Island, in the East River, and gave me three days to just wander around and pick out something I'd like to do. Okay, I said, I'll be good. From now on I had a department car assigned to me with a driver and I'd wear my dress uniform every day and I'd play the role of an officer and a gentleman.

As things turned out, it wasn't such a bad experience after all. They put me into a department that evaluates new techniques and equipment, and I learned a lot of things I never knew before. I also got to go to a fire once in a while, just to see how some of these new, experimental things worked. I liked that, and I must admit I was also flattered by all the attention I got wherever I went. Young firemen, probies, Johnnies, they all came to shake my hand.

"I'll never be the fireman you were, lieutenant," they'd say, and I'd say, "Oh, yes, you will. Just wait and see. You never know what you can do until the moment arrives."

"Yes, sir," they'd say. That made me feel old.

Finally, it was time to go. After a year of light duty, going around with a clean face and my shoes shined, the department and I agreed that I'd get out on May 1, 1974, with three-quarters disability and a much more handsome retirement pay than I had expected a year earlier.

The last week was hectic. The TV people wanted me for shows and interviews. When I showed up without the medals they were upset. "I'm no Mexican general," I told them. It seemed like every hour of my life was being taken up with something. Work had ceased. It was all ceremony now. I couldn't quite relax and enjoy it, however.

When the day came, Ginny and I with Sherree and Gregg drove in to lower Manhattan to meet the commissioner—now my old friend John T. O'Hagan—at his office on Church Street at 10 A.M. I didn't know what was going to happen. I'd never retired before!

The commissioner's aide, Sandy Sanservero, met us before

we went in. He told us that something altogether unprecedented was about to be done: They were going to retire my badge number—51—so no one would ever have that number again in the future of the Fire Department.

In a few minutes O'Hagan showed me Department Order 82 which made it official. The paper ended with the words, "This is the first time in the history of the department that a badge has been retired from service."

I felt like Babe Ruth. No New York Yankee will ever wear his number 3 again either.

It was a beautiful spring morning in Lower Manhattan as the six of us, Commissioner O'Hagan and his aide and the four proud Hamiltons walked along Park Row toward City Hall. We were going to see Mayor Abraham Beame.

Like all typical City Hall ceremonies it was brief and a little superficial. Someone told the mayor who I was and why I was there and he picked up his cues like the practiced politician he is.

"You look pretty good to me," the mayor said. "What are you retiring for?"

Laughter. Flashbulbs.

Then they gave him my badge in a little black leather case and he handed it back to me. Commissioner O'Hagan explained that, henceforth and forever, my name would always appear on the rolls next to Badge 51.

"If your son ever becomes a fireman," Commissioner O'Hagan added "and if we think he deserves it, we might consider giving him your number. But he's going to have to be quite a man to earn it."

Richie is quite a man already. Even if he never becomes a fireman, someday he'll have my badge.

Ginny will get the medals.

27

EPILOGUE

It had only been a week since my retirement became official and I hadn't yet become accustomed to not working the shifts. I was hanging around the house, getting in Ginny's way, feeling a little bit like a newlywed. The fact that it was all over hadn't sunk in yet. I was still a fireman, I'd always be a fireman. Someday there would be a big fire and they'd call me, wouldn't they? Or if a guy was pinned in a subway crash, the phone would ring and it would be Rescue 2 asking me to come on down and lend a hand.

When the phone did ring, it was Fireman John Klopp from the fireman's union. "Loo," he said, "there's a guy you know who's in the hospital and he's feeling pretty low because he's burned bad."

It wasn't the emergency summons for help I had imagined in my retirement fantasy, but I said of course I'd go see the man. I figured that's the kind of duty they expect of those of us who are no longer pulling on the boots and airpacs. "Who is it?" I asked.

"It's Louie Piccone, you remember him, with 108 Truck."

I remembered him. He was a terrific fireman. Their firehouse was not far from Rescue 2 in Bedford-Stuyvesant and we rolled to many a fire together. Piccone was always full of fun, full of pranks. He'd squirt water at me for fun at fires and I could hear this voice now. "Ooops, sorry, Loo, the hose got loose!" And I'd holler at him, "You dummy, you're not even dressed for fighting fires, put your gloves on!" He never wore gloves.

"What happened to him?" I asked John over the phone.

"They were on the top floor of an abandoned building and they were making a search for any old bums who might be sleeping up there. The fire wasn't too bad until someone opened one of the boarded-up windows and the whole place lit up and Piccone was caught. He got burned around the face and then he had some nylon pants on and they burned and got him between the legs and all around his rear."

It was hard to think of Piccone hurt. He was always laughing, never crying. I decided to try and make him laugh again. I went and found one of those cans that Italian tomatoes come in, Progresso or something like that, and then I dug up a nice big dandelion from the yard and planted it in the pot and fixed it all up pretty with aluminum foil.

When I got to the hospital they told me Piccone was in Intensive Care. It was serious. His spirits were low. He probably knew that he'd never be a fireman again. But he didn't need to die.

I held the potted dandelion in front of me as I came into the room. Piccone was propped up in bed, sheets covering most of him, face all bandaged. I couldn't tell if he was smiling, but his voice sounded like it.

"Hey, Loo," he said, "You shouldn't have done it!"

I told him I thought he deserved the best as I put the dandelion down with a lot of other pretty flowers in the room. He loved it. He ordered the nurse to put it front and center and it became his showpiece. Then we talked a while and he said something I'd heard before and never liked to hear. He said, "You know, Lieutenant Ham, if you'd been with me at that fire, I wouldn't have been burned."

The old legend was still there, the idea that I was some kind of a good luck charm, a guarantee. I told him no, it could happen to anybody if they went into enough fires; there are no guarantees. Then he said he sure was glad to see me and thanked me for coming and said there was only one thing he didn't like about the visit. I didn't know what he meant, but I saw him drawing his hands out from under the sheets on his chest. They were all bandaged.

"I just knew if you saw these, Loo, you'd give me hell for not having my gloves on."

Even though I've been out of the Fire Department for a number of months now, people still keep asking me what retirement is like for an old firehorse like me. They wonder if I jump every time I hear a siren, or if I feel lost without a firehouse to go to or a pole to slide down every time a bell rings.

Well, after the first few weeks, it didn't work out that way at all. Those stories about old firemen don't seem to be true in my case. After 24 years of service, I look back on it all and I know I gave two dollars' worth of value for every dollar I was paid—and I'm glad it's over. Never mind the sentiment. I know there are some people walking around alive today who would be in their graves if it weren't for me. I hope they use their lives well—but I know some of them won't. Some of them were drunks and wife beaters and cowards and thieves. They probably still are. I don't have any illusions that they were improved any just because I pulled them out of a fire—or a river—or from under the subway tracks.

I don't know yet whether my oldest son, Richie, is going to become a fireman or not. He's in the U.S. Marine Corps now and he chose duty with an air-crash rescue outfit in Hawaii. Not long ago he pulled seven men out of a burning helicopter, so maybe he learned something from all those visits to the firehouse on Carlton Avenue; maybe he learned something from his old man about keeping a cool head when everything starts popping. I hope so. He's got a few more years of service ahead of him, and then we'll see.

As for Rescue 2 and the old firehouse where I spent 13 years of my life, I don't go back very often. Some of the same guys are still there, but some have moved on already. The big grouper is still swimming around alone in the fish tank in the basement, but the Ping-Pong table is gone now and Zuercher's barbells are getting a little rusty in the corner. Louis DeFina is still doing the cooking, and the men still eat in the sitting room we built so long ago.

Who did they find to take my place? I'm glad you asked. Remember Dave Floyd, the first black fireman to join a rescue company? Dave went on to make lieutenant, worked at 123 Truck for a while, then, when I retired, they gave him my job.

I'm busy with all kinds of projects now, most of them purely recreational, I must admit. Ginny and I talk about traveling now, seeing something of the world.

The headaches and the nightmares have stopped. Ginny doesn't have to tell me in the morning that I was fighting the Red Devil all night in my sleep.

I have more time to think now, too. Oh, I don't sit around reviewing my life or anything like that, but it's funny how fragments of memory come back at odd moments. It's almost as if so much happened in that quarter-century that there was never time to fully absorb the drama, the humor, the tragedy of it all. Now there is, and it comes back in perfect pictures, like color slides flashing on a screen. . . .

I remember the "grenade" that a sanitation worker found in his truck. It brought the Rescue and the cops and closed off the street. It turned out to be a plastic toy which I fished out of all the garbage and then tossed like a hot grounder up the street just to see all the Police Emergency guys scatter!

I remember the old man who had a stroke and defecated all over the floor of his apartment before he died, and my guys from Rescue 2 cleaning up the mess because they didn't want his widow to have to do it.

I remember rowing around on a partially frozen lake in Bronx Park with Howie Wanser, trying to figure out which way the current went so we could find a little boy who had fallen through the ice.

I remember the construction worker who fell 35 feet and landed on some unfinished concrete so three reinforcing rods passed through his body from back to front, coming out like spears. "Just keep cuttin', boys," he said quietly as we worked with the hacksaws to free him.

I remember the woman who was burned out of her apartment in Brooklyn and had no money to get to her sister's place in the Bronx. The firemen took up a collection and raised eight dollars—and then the cab driver refused it because he said it wouldn't be enough to cover the fare and his tip.

I remember the fire in Brownsville when I heard the timbers of the old building cracking under us and told the men to back out slowly without wanting to tell them why.

I remember using a whole quart of liquid soap to lubricate a little kid's head which was stuck between the iron railings of a fence. His mother said she couldn't watch!

I remember when Footsie Curry slid down the chute in the mattress factory and we thought the fire had got him until we found him buried comfortably in a stack of mattresses on the floor below.

I remember the fire in an old movie house in the Bronx that had been converted into a furniture store. The theater marquee was still hanging on the false front of the building and when it fell onto the sidewalk it killed five firemen without an instant's warning.

I remember the odor-of-smoke alarm we had one night in the Catholic orphanage and how we went through the dormitories without turning on the lights because we didn't want to wake the kids. But they were awake anyway and some of us gave them our flashlights and one little boy asked me for a goodnight kiss.

I remember a suicide by hanging that we were called to. After we'd sliced the rope and dropped the dead man, we found out he was a fireman. He was Irish Catholic. His black girl friend said he had been very depressed.

I remember the workman who was fixing loose bricks around the top edge of a 200-foot-high smokestack in the Bronx. He got too much carbon monoxide and passed out, and two of us had to climb up and bring him down the iron rungs on the outside of the chimney.

I remember Chico who got his head stuck in a grate while committing a robbery. After the police took him away, I followed up his case and later invited him to the beach with me and the family. He'd never seen waves before.

I remember the first baby I'd ever seen born. It was in an apartment right under the Third Avenue el. The fireman who delivered the child was Tom Ryan, and the black mother promptly named her new son Thomas Ryan Jackson.

I remember jumping onto a burning tugboat in the Harlem River and keeping it from drifting into a bunch of oil barges nearby when other firemen threw me a line. I was still a probie hoping to be the best fireman in the world.

I remember the guy who was threatening to kill himself by jumping from the high cables of the George Washington Bridge. I thought he was a faker, so I hollered to him, "If you don't jump, I'm going to push you!" Whereupon he threw himself into the arms of a priest and screamed, "Don't let him kill me!"

I remember the berserk citizen who was holding a street-corner crowd terrified with a butcher knife as we happened to come by on our way back from an alarm. We stopped the truck and I grabbed a fire axe and asked the man if he wanted to fight fair. He dropped the knife.

I remember the truck driver with a load of steel reinforcing rods who was cut off by another car as he entered the Brooklyn-Queens Expressway. He slammed his air brakes, and the load slid forward through the cab of the truck and tore his head off. We took his skull off the ends of the rods in front of the radiator.

I remember a guard in a housing project who let his attack dog loose on my firemen who were rushing through the yard in answer to an alarm. One of the men had to knock the dog senseless with the flat of his axe. Afterward the security company complained that the dog was no longer fit for guard duty.

I remember the big Italian lady who was desperate to climb out of her burning third-floor apartment onto a Fire Department ladder. I was at the top of the ladder and I knew she didn't have to bail out because in another minute the engine company would have water on the fire. I asked her if she wanted to leave without her pocketbook, and she went back to look for it. She left by the stairs.

I remember the woman who jumped from her apartment window and impaled herself on an iron fence. At the hospital, her boy friend asked me, "She's dead, ain't she?" Then he added, "I don't care, you understand. It's what she wanted."

I remember climbing more than 100 feet up an electric utility pole in Queens to help John Dougal take a young boy off the live wires. John didn't want them to switch off the 6000 volts because sometimes it's only the electric current that keeps the victim from falling.

I remember the morning over in Red Hook when we were out on a drill near Long Pier and one of the guys said, "Hey, Loo! Lookit! There's a submarine!" So we went and "inspected" the sub and got ourselves invited to lunch with the crew.

I remember the guy who got sore at his girl friend for going to a Brooklyn dance hall with another man, so he bought a bucket of gasoline and tossed it up the dance-hall stairs and then threw a match after it. The only person killed was an innocent woman who was pregnant. We could see her baby where her stomach burst open.

I remember the nitric-acid leak in Brooklyn when we put on our Scotts and our rubber exposure suits and went down into a cellar to repair a ruptured pipe at the top of a big tank. They were covering us with spray from fog nozzles while we worked when a hoseline burst with a big bang and I was sure the tank had blown up under me.

I remember the little old lady who came to the firehouse to tell us there was a cat up a tree in Ft. Greene Park and it had been there for four days and wouldn't come down to get the food she was leaving for it. We scheduled a "drill" at the park and Ronnie Foote roped his way up to the cat and brought it down. A few weeks later we got a nice letter from Mayor Wagner. The little old lady was a friend of his.

I remember the jumper who was hanging onto a ledge on the 17th floor of an old hotel. "Women are no damn good," he was saying, and we were all agreeing with him. "If you'll just come in," I told him, "we'll find a real *good* woman for you— but if you jump you'll never see this dame we've got picked out for you!" He came in—and went to Bellevue.

And finally, I remember the last alarm I ever responded to. It was my last tour of duty at Rescue 2, the last few hours —a one-story factory building where they couldn't get the fire out because a gas leak kept reigniting the flames. I told the chief we'd have to go in and find the gas main and shut it down or the fire would burn all night.

"Yes," said the chief, "I know that's what has to be done, but I don't want you doing it, lieutenant. This is your very last chance to get killed and I'd like to see you miss it!"

"Yeah," said Johnny Hopkins, "let us do something on our own for once!" So they went in, Johnny and Jack Kelly and Jackie Farrell and Jack Williams, and they found the main and shut off the gas and came back out of the fire while I just stood in the street and watched. It was the strangest feeling—like my ship was sailing away and I wasn't on it.

But I'm all over that now. The bells have stopped ringing in my head.

All that is left is a deep satisfaction that I did something for my fellow man.

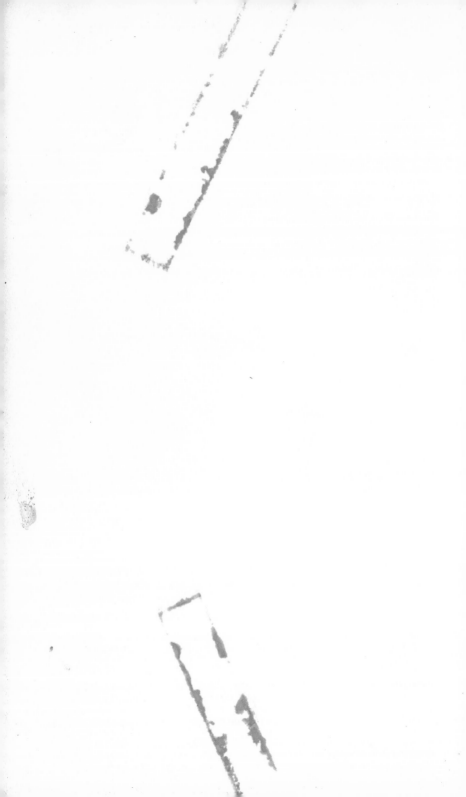